FURTHER PRAISE FOR

AMERICAN FIRE

OFFICIALLY WITHDRAWN

"*American Fire* . . . has all the elements of a lively crime procedural: courtroom drama, forensic trivia, toothsome gossip, vexed sex. It also happens to be a very good portrait of a region in economic decline. . . . One of the most elusive skills in narrative nonfiction, and Hesse has it, is knowing the proper order to arrange your facts. She also superbly conveys the folkways of the Eastern Shore and the disruptive, confusing effect the fires had on its community."

—Jennifer Senior, *New York Times*

"The propulsive pleasure of *American Fire* rests in author Monica Hesse's decision not to force a thing. . . . Hesse gathers the pieces but leaves connections to the reader. When they snap together, the feeling is a bit like gazing upon a blaze you've just lit."

—Karl Vick, *Time*

"A vivid depiction of a community that is struggling economically in present-day America, but is rich in its human connections."

—Ilana Masad, NPR.org

"Mesmerizing. . . . Hesse recounts the fires and their investigation and the subsequent trials with cinematic immediacy."

—Jonathan Miles, *Garden & Gun*

"Hesse forgoes paint-by-numbers suspense, revealing the culprits early on before backing up into their hard-knock love story, their eventual arrest, and perceptive snapshots of an unusually vivid corner of drug-racked Red America." —Boris Kachka, *Vulture*

"I had never heard of *American Fire*. I read it on the basis of a glowing review in the *New York Times*. I didn't possibly think it could be that good. But I was wrong. I devoured Monica Hesse's book. It is marvelously reported, written with a breezy style, a black comedy that is funny as hell and yet painful. I wish I had written it, which no author ever likes to admit."

—Buzz Bissinger, author of *Friday Night Lights*

"[Hesse] tells the story of the fires and of the Eastern Shore and the people she got to know there with an earned familiarity that, at the same time, speaks of the unknowability of a vast, rapidly changing nation." —*Booklist*, starred review

"*American Fire* is a wonderful book of page-turning, true-crime reportage, exquisitely reported with both humanity and humor. Books like this remind us, in an uncertain time, of what journalism is supposed to look like." —Nick Reding, author of *Methland*

"Monica Hesse has created a near-masterpiece in *American Fire*. . . . It's well-written and eye-opening, and I couldn't put it down." —Annie Butterworth Jones, *Tallahassee Democrat*

"A rare combination of reportorial know-how and literary flair, *American Fire* is a page-turner. Crimes and chaos, detectives and firefighters, headlines and red herrings, and it all boils down to a Gothic love story gone wrong. . . . People who think they don't like nonfiction will devour this book. People who love nonfiction will love it, too." —Melissa Fay Greene, author of *Praying for Sheetrock* and *The Underdogs*

"*Washington Post* reporter Hesse leads readers on an extended tour of a bizarre five-month crime spree in rural Accomack County, VA: a series of over 80 arsons, of predominantly abandoned buildings, committed by a local couple. . . . A page-turning story of love gone off the rails."
—*Publishers Weekly*

"A captivating narrative about arson, persistent law enforcers, an unlikely romantic relationship, and a courtroom drama. . . . Throughout, the author offers a nuanced portrait of a way of life unknown to most. . . . A true-crime saga that works in every respect."
—*Kirkus Reviews,* starred review

"America in decline, a love gone berserk, and fire . . . lots and lots of it. If you pick up this book and open it to the first page, I double-dog dare you to put it down."
—Dennis Covington, author of *Salvation on Sand Mountain*

"On its surface, *American Fire* is a riveting thriller about a rural Virginia coastal community ravaged by a serial arsonist. But *Washington Post* reporter Monica Hesse elevates to national levels the strange story of the man who confessed to committing the crimes with his girlfriend, and how the progressive decline of agricultural wealth in a once-prosperous area influenced them both."
—Anthony Schneck, *Thrillist*

ALSO BY MONICA HESSE

The Girl in the Blue Coat

AMERICAN FIRE

LOVE, ARSON, AND LIFE IN A VANISHING LAND

MONICA HESSE

LIVERIGHT PUBLISHING CORPORATION

A Division of W. W. Norton & Company

Independent Publishers Since 1923

New York | *London*

For firefighters and lovers everywhere,
but especially the ones in Tasley.

For information about permission to reproduce selections from this book,
write to Permissions, Liveright Publishing Corporation, a division of
W. W. Norton & Company, Inc., 500 Fifth Avenue, New York, NY 10110

For information about special discounts for bulk purchases, please contact
W. W. Norton Special Sales at specialsales@wwnorton.com or 800-233-4830

Manufacturing by LSC Communications, Harrisonburg
Book design by Marysarah Quinn
Production manager: Anna Oler

Library of Congress Cataloging-in-Publication Data

Names: Hesse, Monica, author.
Title: American fire : love, arson, and life in a vanishing land / Monica Hesse.
Description: First Edition. | New York : Liveright Publishing Corporation, [2017]
| Includes bibliographical references.
Identifiers: LCCN 2017014161 | ISBN 9781631490514 (hardcover)
Subjects: LCSH: Smith, Charlie (Arsonist) | Bundick, Tonya (Arsonist) | Arson—
Virginia—Accomack County.
Classification: LCC HV6638.5.V57 .H47 2017 | DDC 364.16/42092275516—dc23
LC record available at https://lccn.loc.gov/2017014161

ISBN 978-1-63149-451-2 pbk.

Liveright Publishing Corporation
500 Fifth Avenue, New York, N.Y. 10110
www.wwnorton.com

W. W. Norton & Company Ltd.
15 Carlisle Street, London W1D 3BS

1 2 3 4 5 6 7 8 9 0

CONTENTS

PREFACE

I FIRST DROVE DOWN to Accomack County, Virginia, on Halloween weekend of 2013. There had been a bunch of fires there, two people had been arrested for setting them, and one of those people was now scheduled to submit his plea. At the time I was in the cruddiest place a journalist can be—between stories and out of ideas—and I'd asked my editor to send me to Accomack mostly because I was looking for an assignment that would get me out of the office for a day. Inside the courthouse, a red brick building that looked like a movie-set courthouse on a movie-set town square, the defendant in question admitted he was guilty, but didn't say why he'd done it.

I spent the next two years trying to understand why he did it. The answer, inasmuch as there is an answer for these things, involved hope, poverty, pride, Walmart, erectile dysfunction, Steak-umms (the chopped meat sold in the frozen foods aisle), intrigue, and America. America: the way it's disappointing sometimes, the way it's never what it used to be.

But it also involved love. The kind of love that is vaguely crazy and then completely crazy and then collapses in on itself in a way that leaves the participants bewildered and telling very different stories about what actually happened. In this instance, the stories shared only one essential truth: When this string of fires began, the defendants were in love. By the time they finished, they weren't.

AMERICAN FIRE

CHAPTER I

"CHARGE THAT LINE!"

IT WAS COLD AND DRY, and Deborah Clark found herself wondering, briefly, whether the dryness was important. Fire had to come from somewhere, and if the dry ground had caused an electrostatic spark, then that would explain why, less than a hundred yards from her back steps, there were giant orange flames licking the night sky. A friend had seen them first; he'd pulled out of Deborah's dirt drive after dinner and then frantically banged on her door a few minutes later, yelling, "Hey—the house across the field is on fire." The field was small and rough and it had corn sometimes, with stalks that shook like paper, but it didn't have corn this time of year. On the night of November 12, 2012, it had nothing but brown grass, the burning house, and the flames rolling in Clark's direction.

Clark's niece lived next door, in a place that looked the same as Clark's and most of the other homes on that stretch of Virginia road: a pastel double-wide, well maintained but sinking, each plunked along a tight squeeze of a two-lane route. Now Clark ran to warn her niece about the burning house, which had been different from the others: it was fancy, two stories, white paint, hardwoods, generations of the same family living and dying and moving in and out, until finally somebody moved out and nobody moved in. Clark couldn't remember the last time anyone had lived in that house. She knew it didn't have working power.

Clark ran back to her own house and picked up the telephone. By the time the 911 dispatcher answered at 10:41 p.m., Clark had determined that electrostatic anomalies aside, there was really only one likely possibility for what had happened:

"I'm just calling," she began, flustered and out of breath. "Somebody done set the house on fire on Dennis Drive!"

"Okay," said the dispatcher at the Eastern Shore 911 Center, seven miles away. "What's the address, ma'am?"

"I'm on Dennis Drive—I don't know the address."

"Is it your house?"

"No—it's a big house, an empty house."

"Nobody's in the house, ma'am?"

"No," Clark said.

"Is anybody around the house?"

"*No*," she said.

Now the fire had lit the night like a flashbulb, causing the air around it to go bright and blurry and sending waves of heat onto her property line.

"It's blazing," she begged the dispatcher. "It's getting in the field. It's about to get everywhere."

"We'll go ahead and get the fire department on the way."

Before the call even ended, the dispatcher had already plugged Clark's location into his dispatch system, which immediately began calculating the fire stations that were in the jurisdiction of the call. The current policy was to summon four stations in order to make sure enough bodies and enough pressurized water showed up at the scene. All of the fire stations in Accomack County were operated by volunteers. The manpower for any given fire was entirely dependent on who didn't need to pull a double shift at the chicken factory, and who wasn't stuck overnight on a crabbing boat in the Chesapeake Bay, and who didn't have a baby teething at home, and who could stumble out of bed and race to the fire station in time, leaving pickup trucks askew in station parking lots, and jumping into fire engines that screamed at 130 decibels and shook off any remaining sleep.

"Stations 7, 6, 8, and 18," the dispatcher now said into his headset. The computer-aided system had finished its calculations and provided the closest fire stations, and now, from his cubicle, the dispatcher began to organize emergency response via radio. "Station 7—fire and EMS response. Residential structure fire, Dennis Drive, Parksley," he said into his headset. "Caller has advised apparent abandoned structure, fully involved."

All around the county, heavy black pagers were going off in living rooms and bedrooms, first ringing with the two-noted tone reserved for each particular station, and then coming alive with static-filled instructions. At his home and preparing to eat a slice of cake for his fifty-first birthday, Phil Kelley, the chief of Station 7, the Parksley Fire Department, heard the request for his department to bring both a fire engine and an ambulance. He knew this signified that his station was "first due": although three additional stations would arrive to assist, he would be in charge of controlling the scene. He heard the dispatcher describe the fire as "fully involved," and he knew that, if the description was accurate, it would mean there were flames showing. Fully involved meant the fire was bad.

"Chief 7, en route to station," he radioed in at 10:44 p.m., three minutes after Deborah's 911 call.

"Six-seven, responding par two," responded a truck from Bloxom. "Six" was their station number, "seven" the truck number, and "par two" indicated that the truck contained a pair of firefighters. Bloxom's truck was the first to arrive at the fire, even before Phil Kelley. The Bloxom firefighter holding the radio got out of the truck on Dennis Drive and assessed the situation. "Be advised," he said into his radio, "structure is fully involved."

Kelley, a compact man with a ruddy face and parchment-pale eyebrows, got to the scene and immediately wondered if he might need more water. He was an experienced firefighter. When he wasn't commandeering Parksley's volunteer department, he'd obtained the only kind of paying fire work one could in Accomack County—on Wallops Island, the NASA facility off the Accomack coast in the northern part of the county. There, a team of federally employed firefighters with security clearances obsessively checked and rechecked launch equipment, NASA believing that the best rocket-related fire was one that never happened to begin with. Landing the NASA job had been a life goal for Kelley. He'd grown up in Accomack and had signed up as a support volunteer for the firehouse when he turned fourteen, helping to clean equipment and learning to pack and unpack hoses. Now he was middle-aged, he knew fires, and he sensed that the burning house on Dennis Drive would deplete the water resources on the scene before the fire could be put out. Most of the towns in Accomack County didn't have a municipal water supply, which meant they didn't have fire hydrants. Water was not an unlimited resource. "You pump what you brung" was an old fireman's saying: the volunteer firefighters carried water to scenes in giant metal tankers that held twenty-five hundred gallons each. They pumped the water from their tankers using their engines, and hoped they had enough, or that they'd be close enough to a pond or stream to get more.

"Central, what tankers do I have?" Kelley radioed into the dispatch center, asking for a list of all the trucks present. He listened to the roll call and made a decision. "I need another tanker."

Luckily, one was already on its way.

"Eight-seven, responding par two," said Richie Bridges, a captain with Station 8, the department from the town of Tasley, as he barreled down Lankford Highway in a massive tanker.

Tasley was farther away from the fire than Parksley and Bloxom had been, located ten miles down the Eastern Shore. Tasley had the crummiest firehouse with some of the most lovingly cared-for trucks; members entered them into competitions where they won trophies for their high shine. Tonight, for the Dennis Drive fire, the Tasley company brought two of these vehicles: the tanker driven by Richie, whose sister Shannon Bridges sat in the passenger side, and an engine, driven by the Tasley chief, Jeff Beall. Beall was a tall man with a bristling mustache and a wit as dry as sandpaper. He'd drive thirty miles to loan a friend $20, but whether a person liked him depended on whether they understood that some people showed their love through exacting expectations and constant sarcasm. When Beall's new volunteers told him they were ready to start driving the trucks, he liked to take the aspiring firefighter in a twenty-four-foot-long engine to an empty mansion with a complicated circular driveway and instruct the newbie to drive the engine around it, backward, without touching the grass. It was a little bit of a showboating move, but the Tasley crew were good drivers. Tonight both Bridges and Beall had made it from asleep in their beds to standing in front of a fire, ten miles away, fully suited in protective gear, in less than fifteen minutes.

At Dennis Drive, Kelley saw that Beall's engine had arrived. The two men were friends; they worked together on Wallops Island. They respected and trusted each other, and Kelley immediately ordered Beall's team to fill a two-and-a-half-inch hose with water and start attacking the west side of the building. The plan, he'd decided, would be to put out the fire where it was most virulent, and then force the house to collapse to the ground while they doused the rest of the flames. "Eight-five," he told Beall's engine. "*Charge that line!*"

Three tankers had arrived now, and three engines, and more than a dozen men and women had all come to fight the fire on Dennis Drive.

"Central to Chief 7," the dispatcher back at the 911 Center broke in with a time check. "You are now fifteen minutes into your incident."

"I copy, fifteen minutes," Kelley responded from the front yard where he'd designated a makeshift command post. The air apparatus that each firefighter wore on his or her back carried only forty-five minutes worth of breathable oxygen. Dispatch made sure fire captains were aware of the time.

But right now, Kelley had other considerations besides air supply. He had been right to worry about water: The first tanker to arrive on the scene, the one from Bloxom, was now almost out. So was the tanker that Tasley had brought to the fire. "I'm dry," Beall said into his headset. The fire was cracking like a whip and roaring loudly enough that a headset was the easiest way for men standing just across the yard from each other to communicate.

"I'm out," another firefighter said into his headset, and then a third: "We're out of water."

If the fire cleared the field, it would reach a cluster of houses that stood closer together, with trees that the flames could leap between. It couldn't be allowed to clear the field. Kelley instructed an empty tanker to switch places with a fuller one, sending the empty one to find a place to refill, orchestrating a ballet of heavy equipment easing in and out of the gravel drive. Some fire chiefs didn't mind socializing during fires; they liked when volunteers or neighbors stopped by to ask questions or lament the burning structure. Kelley wasn't one of those chiefs. At a scene, his volunteers knew to give him a wide berth while he figured out the fire. He viewed each one like a puzzle with a unique set of pieces: which hoses to use and where, which access roads needed to stay clear and when. Holding all of those pieces in his head required concentration; he went still and silent while he figured things out.

"Central to Chief 7," the dispatcher interrupted. "You are now thirty minutes into your incident."

The dispatcher asked if they had enough lighting, and Kelley told him the lighting was fine, but the amount of smoke was becoming a problem. Fifteen minutes left on the air packs. If the smoke stayed black for longer than that, he would have to start sending in relief teams or request more backup.

For now, he decided that the best thing to do was continue with what they were already doing: more water, more tankers, more water, putting out the fire in the way that, at its most elemental, was the only way to ever put out fires since the beginning of time.

Communication between the dispatcher and the firefighters on the radio slowed, as Kelley requested face-to-face meetings with his deputies. "Surround and drown," he instructed them, when they met him in the front yard. Get the fire out by attacking it from every direction.

"Central to Chief 7," said the dispatcher. "You are now forty-five minutes into your incident. I got one fresh body coming to you, that's all I got."

The uniforms and equipment that each firefighter wore totaled more than one hundred pounds, and Kelley was starting to feel it. He hesitated before answering the dispatcher: "It's under control."

The fire had finally reached its turning point. Kelley could tell that the mist rising from the house was no longer smoke, but water evaporating as it hit the hot parts of the wood. This was called "steam conversion," and it was how a firefighter knew that he'd reached the seed of the fire and that the fire was almost dead. At any fire, one of the last puzzle pieces to click into place for Kelley was the moment when he stood in front of a house and watched smoke become steam. Now, on Dennis Drive, there was just smoldering embers, charred wood, and ash, and firefighters sweating in their gear, bone weary in a way that the joggers among them would say was closer to marathon exhaustion than wind sprints.

The nice old house was gone. The owner, it would later turn out, had moved to a nursing home and died three years before. Her belongings had all been left behind. The house had been full of them, and they were now scattered in the grass. Papers, clothing, broken dolls, and hardcover books with titles like *The World Since 1914*, a 1933 edition.

With the fire put out, there was no light but the headlamps from the trucks. The firefighters walked the perimeter of the scene, as they did with all fires, making sure that there were no remaining embers, nothing to catch on the nearby trees or to send a fire to the houses across the field. Again, they saw nothing unusual, nothing suspicious. When all of that patrolling was done, Kelley, who never did end up eating his birthday cake, radioed in his last update from the scene at nearly one in the morning of November 13: "Terminating command."

∧ ∧ ∧

MEANWHILE, around the county on the night of November 12:

The sheriff was home with his pager resting on the nightstand, where he left it most nights so he could be awakened in case of emergencies.

The Commonwealth's attorney was at home, preparing for an odd case involving a drunk Navy SEAL.

The ATF and the FBI and the other agencies whose personnel would eventually descend on the county were home, too, but their homes were far away and they were unaware, as of yet, that Accomack even existed.

The regular citizens of the area were quietly doing regular things. Lois Gomez was asleep, preparing for another shift at Perdue, where she would package goose-bumped chicken thighs and wings from a fast-moving conveyor belt, thousands of chickens every day. Helen Hasty was awake, irritated that her dog kept barking, but chalking it up to his age and increasing senility.

Charles Smith, a body shop owner who did precise work at fair prices, who had a self-effacing frankness that most people found endearing—Charlie had lit the fire. But nobody knew that yet, and they wouldn't for a long time.

The firefighters of Accomack County would be called out two more times that night. They would be called out eighty-six times total over the next five months.

The county would grow used to hearing the wail of sirens in the middle of the night, the sound of engines and tankers crunching over gravel. The county would see landmarks go up in flames and neighbors eye one another with suspicion at the grocery store. At night, the roads would transform into a sea of checkpoints and cop cars; citizens trying to get home while Accomack turned into a police state and the county lit up around them. The county went about its business. The county burned down.

Some residents would eventually decide that they needed to take matters into their own hands, and they would form vigilante groups and buy binoculars and guns. Some residents would grow to think, as Deborah Clark did, that this all signified the beginning of the apocalypse and the world must be coming to an end.

CHAPTER 2

"THE SOUTH STARTS HERE"

THE EASTERN SHORE OF VIRGINIA is a hangnail, a hinky peninsula separated from the rest of the state by the Chesapeake Bay and a few hundred years of cultural isolation. It is long and narrow, stretching only fourteen miles at its widest spot but covering hundreds of square miles altogether. The northern border is Maryland at a gas station called Dixieland, which sells Confederate flags and tchotchkes and overstuffed hoagies, and marks the entrance to Accomack with a big sign reading "The South Starts Here." The southern border is the twenty-five-mile-long Chesapeake Bay Bridge-Tunnel, built in 1964 as a triumph of modern transportation, which connects the shore to the mainland for the cost of $12 each way. In between are little towns, clapboard churches, peeling chicken coops, salt-whipped brush, and roads that go miles and miles between streetlights.

The shore is old. It is mostly rural. It is a place that the state senator, Lynwood Lewis, likes to think of as a seventy-mile-long small town where everybody knows everybody, and a place where agricultural traditions convinced the state representative, Robert Bloxom, that when he left the shore for college in the 1980s, he would do so carrying a fifty-pound sack of potatoes along with his suitcase. His grandfather had been a potato farmer, and potatoes had built the shore. Potatoes, but also the railroad, and also a collection of old, old families with names like Bloxom and Lewis and Bundick and Doughty, and a few other shore names that separated the "Born Heres" from the "Come Heres."

The Born Heres were exactly what they sounded like. They were people whose roots went way back in the registers of the Accomack and Northampton courthouses, which had some of the oldest ongoing census records of anywhere in the United States. The Come Heres were recent transplants, many of them folks who had fled Philadelphia or Baltimore in search of cheap waterfront property. They, in a shorthand description provided by one Born Here, organized international film nights and bought their coffee at the independent Book Bin instead of at a Royal Farms gas station. One could easily assess a neighbor's longevity on the Eastern Shore via a short conversation: those whose families went back generations tended to have dense Tidewater accents—"oh's" became "ow's," and "ow's" became "oo's."

A Come Here, even one who had been raised on the shore since toddlerhood, could never hope to be thought of as a Born Here. After putting in several decades, they might eventually gain the status of a Been Here, but only maybe.

The area's original Born Heres, the Accomac, Accohannock, and Mattawames tribes of American Indians, had been gone a long time, forced to sell their land to the ships full of Englishmen who began arriving in 1603. Over the next two hundred years the land was cultivated—potatoes and tomatoes—by farmers and also by slaves who, at the time of the first federal census in 1790, comprised a third of Accomack's population. The county went Confederate during the Civil War, but was occupied by Union troops without much resistance shortly after fighting began.

In the late nineteenth century, executives with the Pennsylvania Railroad were looking for ways to connect customers in northeastern industrial cities to southern farm goods, and they began to notice that the easiest, straightest route was through the Eastern Shore. Shore residents received this news with a mix of excitement and trepidation over the effect of such a modern intrusion. But a straight line was drawn between Norfolk and New York, and in 1884 the railroad opened, bifurcating the peninsula straight up the middle.

The impact on the county was immediate. The arrival of the railroad meant the arrival of railroad towns, planned communities laid out on grids. These towns were followed by the arrival of electricity and then telephone lines. Both were symptoms of the larger economic boom that had arrived to the area. Things that northeasterners wanted—seafood, strawberries, the versatile potato—the Eastern Shore had, and the railroad provided a way to move the goods out of state quickly. The Eastern Shore became a participant in the National Produce Exchange. In this exchange, agents assessed which cities needed which agricultural goods and then immediately put the crops on a train to send them in that direction. Now, instead of supplying just a few regional cities, the Eastern Shore was shipping goods as far west as Kansas City and as far north as Toronto. In the first year of the Produce Exchange, sales on the Eastern Shore were around $750,000. Twenty years later, the sum had grown to $19,269,890. In fact, by this time, in the 1900s and 1910s, Accomack and neighboring Northampton County had the highest valued crops of anywhere in the United States, the third county being Los Angeles. Potato production catapulted from 160,000 bushels a year in 1870 to 1.3 million in 1900. By the time of the 1910 census, those two counties were the wealthiest rural counties in all of America.

Presidents came to see its majesty: Grover Cleveland hunted ducks on the barrier islands off the coast; Benjamin Harrison hunted quail near the town of New Church. One time Harrison visited and ended up having dinner with a local family that had named their youngest son after Cleveland, Harrison's bitter political rival. But Harrison was a good sport about it and gave the boy a ten-dollar bill, at least according to the generations of Eastern Shore storytellers who adopted this anecdote as a favorite.

Wealthy people needed buildings. The farmers who had been living in humble two-room cottages began to use their new fortunes to build houses: A-frames, Cape Cods, colonials. Some of them built smaller houses, and then built bigger houses right next door as soon as they could afford to, and then bigger houses after that. They connected each of the buildings with passageways, producing a maze of rooms that became the shore's most defining architectural silhouette: "big house, little house, colonnade, kitchen."

The Eastern Shore residents built barns and feed stores and restaurants and sheds. To accommodate the tourists who were now coming in on the trains to hunt and take in the scenery, the residents of the Eastern Shore built hotels. In 1931, they built Whispering Pines, a resort complex with a manicured lawn of azaleas, and a restaurant that served oyster stew, chicken salad, cooked tomatoes, pickled beets. It had ninety-five bedrooms, each with a private bath. People came to visit Whispering Pines from all up and down the Eastern Seaboard. They swam in the pristine pool. They admired the grounds. Color fliers were made: "The showplace of the Eastern Shore."

^ ^ ^

THE ECONOMIC BOOM of Accomack County was like the economic boom of farming communities all over the United States, with some measures of uniqueness. And when the economy shifted again, the long, slow bust would be like the one in farming communities all over the United States, with some measures of uniqueness: the railroad had made the Eastern Shore. And, as Eastern Shore historian Brooks Miles Barnes put it, "The internal combustion engine unmade us."

When the railroad had been responsible for shipping out produce, the collective crops of multiple farmers could be held, in freight cars, until prices reached a favorable exchange. But then came the era of the personal automobile. Originally, paved roadways had been seen as a godsend; farmers no longer had to pay a portion of their profits to the railroad in transportation fees. But there were also unintended effects. When farmers began acquiring their own trucks, they began making their own deals, undercutting one another's prices and driving the crop value down. An early bellwether of trouble was in 1928: Farmers that year couldn't get nearly what they once could for a bushel of produce; they couldn't even recoup the cost of production. Those who were accustomed to financing their crops' planting through loans—a typical practice, to be repaid at harvest—found themselves underwater. One year later the Depression began.

As decades crawled on there were other issues, some real and some magnified in the perception of hardworking farmers. Saline levels dropped in the bay, disrupting the marine-life balance that supported the crabbing and fishing industries. Chain grocery stores replaced independent operations; they bought in bulk but paid less for what they bought. Potatoes, once the shore's specialty crop, were now being grown all over the country, with growers nationwide racing one another to the bottom of prices that were difficult to sustain. Consumers began buying crazy new snacks, like the innovative and modern Dorito. "Shit chips," one descendant of potato farmers remembered his father calling these snack foods in the 1950s and 1960s, because it wasn't clear exactly what was in these Doritos and Fritos and Tostitos. Certainly nothing as wholesome as a potato. Farmers were sure it was partially these snacks' fault that their businesses were struggling.

Eventually, beginning in the mid-twentieth century, people left. They went north into Maryland or Delaware, in search of jobs. Or they left for college—the so-called brain drain experienced all over the country—and didn't come back, and the remaining population aged and the shore gradually emptied. In 1958 the passenger railroad left, too: when businesses turned to trucks for their shipping needs and families turned to cars for their vacation needs, there wasn't as much use for a railroad.

For the people who remained, poultry was replacing produce as the county's biggest employer. The chicken magnate Arthur Perdue was from the Eastern Shore, just over the border in Maryland. He'd been a railroad agent who left that industry to grow his family's egg farm into a profitable business in 1920. Eventually he, along with other Eastern Shore farmers, realized that raising broiler chickens could lead to a better profit than raising egg-laying chickens. The land was good for chicken raising: mild climate, sandy soil that facilitated drainage, low building costs. Perdue opened its first mass chicken production factory on the shore in the late 1960s.

By 2012, Perdue and Tyson were the two largest employers in Accomack County. The Delmarva peninsula, which included the Eastern Shore of Virginia as well as parts of Maryland and Delaware, was annually farming 558 million birds, producing 3.6 billion pounds of meat, employing nearly fifteen thousand people (Accomack County, in particular, ranked sixty-fourth of the more than three thousand counties in the United States in terms of its poultry production). Thirteen hundred of those jobs belonged to "growers," the modern term preferred over "farmers" for the workers who housed and fed the chicks until they were big enough for eating. The growers provided the buildings and the manpower; the chicken companies gave them the birds, the feed, the propane, the vaccinations.

The rest of the fifteen thousand worked directly for the poultry companies. They were members of the "catching crew," whose job it was to round up the birds by hand and transport them to the factories. Or they were members of the slaughtering teams, or they were janitors cleaning the machinery in the factories, which smelled pungent and burnt when you drove past them but were

Clorox-clean inside. There were "deboning" jobs, and "trussing" jobs, and "eviscerating" jobs, which required, as qualifications, only the necessity of being eighteen years old with the ability to lift fifty pounds, and a willingness "to stand for several hours . . . work in wet and extreme hot or cold conditions . . . work around dust, feathers and various cleaning chemicals," as one Perdue job ad specified. For this a worker might make $9–$12 an hour. A single person could live on that here, if he scrimped.

Those jobs were steady—people always needed to eat, so they were somewhat recession-proof—but they were precarious in other ways: according to one aspiring politician stumping about the economy on the campaign trail, "We're one bird-flu away from economic destruction."

People held meetings about the environmental impact of these plants, whole standing-room-only meetings about chicken poop run-off, with half the attendees arguing that chickens were polluting the land, and half arguing that chickens created vital work that might not come otherwise. These meetings were about the county's economic future, about the soul of the county, and about an old-fashioned place figuring out the best way to adapt in the modern world.

By November 12, 2012, the same thing had happened on the Eastern Shore that had happened to rural communities all across the country: the shift of family farms to corporate ones. The closing of small businesses and the arrival of big-box stores, which brought much-needed convenience but also left main streets emptying. In the 1910 census, the Eastern Shore population had been fifty-two thousand; in the 2010 census, the population was forty-four thousand, a nearly 20 percent decline.

^ ^ ^

AN AVERAGE PASSERBY wouldn't have known this about Accomack, any of it. Most outsiders who came to the shore at all were vacationers on their way to Chincoteague Island, home of the swimming horses, where Marguerite Henry had set her 1947 Newbery Honor Book, *Misty of Chincoteague*. Or they were on their way to Wallops Island, the NASA facility that employed engineers and rocket scientists and had a visitors center for tourists. If vacationers bothered to drive through the mainland, they likely stayed on the one main road, hopping out of their cars only long enough to buy boiled peanuts from one of the summertime roadside stands.

Which was a shame. Because there were many, many beautiful places on the Eastern Shore: a historic movie theater, a picturesque vineyard, and a donut bakery that would have made Krispy Kreme weep with jealousy, if only anyone off the shore knew about it. There was the Onancock Wharf, where sailboats docked and their inhabitants disembarked to eat crab cakes, and where kids participated in fishing competitions. There was Jaxon's Hardware in the town of Parksley, which sold everything from candy to clothing to butter dishes and ammunition; the kind of authentic general store that posh vacation destinations spend fortunes to reproduce. Not all towns in Accomack were the same, either. Kirk Mariner, a writer who had grown up in the relatively more working-class New Church and then moved to the well-heeled Onancock, liked to demarcate the difference as such: "In New Church, we cut our grass. In Onancock, we mow our lawns." Of Saxis, a tiny fishing community on the western part of the county, Mariner explained, "Saxis isn't the end of the world, but you can see it from there."

Doors went unlocked, bake sales and brisket fund-raisers were well attended, and when two cars passed on the road, both drivers would raise the tips of their fingers off the steering wheel in a wave. The grassy shores and open sky made the land breathtaking—"God's country," people said. There's a reason that the Come Heres want to go there.

But all of the past century's change had resulted in one particular outcome: the Eastern Shore was no longer the richest rural place in

America. It was a place that was falling behind: only 17 percent of adults over age twenty-five had bachelor's degrees, compared with 35 percent in the rest of highly educated Virginia. A fifth of Accomack's residents lived below the poverty line; a quarter of Northampton County's. They were among Virginia's poorest counties.

Route 13, the county's main route, ran the length of the Eastern Shore, and it was the only route that was well lit. The other streets veined away from it, winding off at odd angles or ending abruptly, past hundreds and hundreds of now empty houses that lingered and rotted by the side of the road. At night, hardly anybody went on any of these roads. People went to bed early so they could get up early for work—the agricultural jobs that remained required rising with the sun. Besides, even if someone had the inclination or money for a late evening out, there weren't a whole lot of places to go.

In November of 2012, the Eastern Shore of Virginia was old. It was long. It was isolated. It was emptying of people but full of abandoned houses. It was dark. It was a uniquely perfect place to light a string of fires.

CHAPTER 3

"ORANGE IN THE SKY"

H ELEN HASTY'S LAND exemplified the rise and recession of Accomack County. The acres she lived on used to be known as Smith Brothers Farm. The Smiths were her ancestors. They had grown potatoes, and on Sunday afternoons half a century ago, her grandfather would take the family on long drives to judge whether the crops had been planted in straight lines. In those days, the potatoes on the shore were harvested by migrant workers, who arrived each season and stayed in a labor camp on the property. As a girl, Hasty was afraid of their cussing but still loved accompanying her grandfather when he doled out the farmworkers' weekly paychecks.

Then crop prices dropped and the money for those paychecks started coming in more slowly, until it dried up altogether. The last year of the Smith Brothers' incorporation, Hasty was their only employee. The year after that, the family started leasing the land out to corporate farms. When the corporate farms switched from potatoes to corn and soybeans, which don't need to be picked by hand, the migrant labor camps went unoccupied. Occasionally, tourists stopped by to inquire about the history of the buildings, or amateur photographers who thought the camp had a sort of haunting beauty.

Hasty now found herself part of another defining Accomack story. At half past 1 a.m. on November 13—twelve miles away from where Deborah Clark had called in the first fire three hours before—Hasty went to let out her dog, who wouldn't stop barking, and saw that those old migrant camp buildings were now aflame.

"It's two houses, and it's right on the turn," she told the 911 dispatcher, trying to give directions for the buildings that no longer had an address. "We didn't hear nothing, we didn't see nothing. We let the dogs out—they go in there all the time . . . I mean, the buildings are not insured, they're vacant, they're just old shacks that been there a hundred years. Oh, it's getting bright now, it's lit up both sides of the road. Oh my God. There she *goes*."

The house on Dennis Drive had been the first fire. The one on Helen Hasty's land was the second.

Eight minutes later, another call came into the 911 Center: "I'm down at Arthur Lane," the caller explained. "And there's—the woods are on fire. I was riding by, and it's on fire, and it's spreading. It's two minutes down Arthur Lane at Greenbush."

That was the third fire.

The members of the Tasley Volunteer Fire Department had just pulled back into their station, down on Tasley Road about half a mile from the decaying remains of the esteemed Whispering Pines resort, which hadn't operated as a restaurant in two decades and as a hotel in even longer than that, and which loomed dark and creepy and big by the side of the road.

The firefighters were sweaty and tired from the fire on Dennis Drive, but there were protocols to be followed. They hung up their coats on the assigned hooks lining the wall of the engine room and arranged their boots and suspendered pants on the floor directly below. Their hats went on the shelf above. All of them were yellow or black except for Shannon Bridges's because, when she'd determined that she wanted to become a firefighter, she also determined that she would do so wearing a pink hat. Her brother Richie's hat was the largest in the row and his coat was, too. Richie, twenty-six, had been volunteering with Tasley for seven years, and was built like a refrigerator. The company was always having to order him special-sized uniforms and then even more special sizes when the shoulders of the XXLs were still too tight. He drove a Richie-sized truck, and it was while borrowing this truck one afternoon that Shannon, twenty-eight, decided she would join the fire company like her brother. His equipment had been lying on the floorboard; she kept looking down at it and thinking, *I want to do that.*

After removing their uniforms, the Tasley firefighters climbed on the red and white engine, and began repacking the hose with a precision that most of them would have deployed anyway but upon which Chief Jeff Beall absolutely insisted. Firefighting was his second career. He'd served a full five years in the Air Force and fifteen years in the Coast Guard before moving to the Eastern Shore, and while some of his volunteers thought he was a hard-ass, his military training had taught him that there were right ways to do things and wrong ways, and getting small things correct was the only way to make sure the big things worked when it mattered most.

They had scarcely finished repacking the hoses when the air around them split with noise. It was their pagers, all of them, going off at the same time. They all looked at one another. The brush fire on Arthur Road belonged to them: they were first due.

So it would be one of those nights, Shannon thought, as she grabbed her gear again. Two calls in one night was unusual, but not unheard of, especially in the fall when people began turning on their furnaces or holding bonfires in their backyards. For Shannon, it meant it would be a night when she wouldn't see her husband or her three boys; by now it was after midnight and they were probably asleep. She climbed back into the trucks with everyone else, and Beall called into dispatch to figure out what Tasley was getting into next.

"Chief 8," he identified himself when the 911 Center responded. "Is this reported to be a large wood fire, or what?"

"We've had two calls," the dispatcher answered. "Neither one was able to tell how much woods was burning."

"Okay," he said. "Notify Forestry and have them respond."

Eleven years before, when Beall and his wife, Renee, planned their relocation to the shore after decades of more cosmopolitan posts, Renee, a special education teacher, came in the middle of the summer with their two sons while Beall finished up work back in New York. Beall had found the house earlier, and when Renee saw it in person, she was amused. In every relocation with the Coast Guard, Beall had volunteered with fire companies. It was how he found community. In Accomack, he had yet again chosen a house less than two minutes from the local station. Within a few years he was the chief.

The other thing that had amused Renee was how driving across the bridge felt not so much like entering a different state but entering an interruption in the time space continuum. The small towns, small roads, everyone up in one another's business with small gossip—it felt like the 1950s to her. When Beall started with Tasley, he discovered this time warp carried over to the fire department, too. They were still running fires out of the same building they'd used in 1926, back when eighteen Tasley men had pooled $5 or $20 apiece "for the purpose of a chemical engine," according to the handwritten records of the time. The top floor meeting room perpetually smelled like mildew, and the bottom floor truck bays—designed for hand-drawn fire engines, not motorized ones—were filled with junk. The modern equipment was kept in a newer building next door. And then there was the question of Beall's roster. Some of the older members had been trained not at formal academies but through osmosis, watching their fathers and grandfathers. Memberships at places like Tasley's Volunteer Fire Department went back generations. When Beall wanted something done or something changed, he communicated it in a way that was meant to be frank and direct, but which came across to some of the old heads as insulting. He said "friggin'" a lot, perpetuating regular debate as to whether the word should constitute a quarter in the company swear jar. There was a tiny chasm in the group, between people who appreciated the way Beall was trying to modernize and professionalize the department, and people who thought that Beall, a Come Here, had no respect for tradition.

But this was all behind the scenes. When a fire came, they pulled together and ran. Tonight, all around the county, firefighters were running. The crew from Bloxom had left the fire on Dennis Drive and immediately been called to the one at Helen Hasty's. The crew from Parksley had been called out again, too.

At Parksley, Phil Kelley, like Shannon, was realizing that it was going to be one of those nights, a night where things went wonky; a series of tossed cigarette butts and failed cooking experiments also conspired against the firefighters of Accomack County. But as he drove to his next fire and listened to the types of incidents people were calling in, things started to seem more than regular busy. They started to seem just plain weird. The county was geographically big, but all of these fires were fairly close together. What were the chances of that?

While Kelley crossed the railroad tracks, he kept thinking about Baghdad. When the first Gulf War began, the news kept running clip after clip of the bombing of Baghdad. On television the whole sky looked orange from the light of the buildings that had been hit and gone up in flames. He hadn't been able to picture what that would look like in person. But now, while he was driving toward the reddened sky to get to his fire, he looked north and saw that the sky was red in a different place, too. Multiple big fires, all going at once, in a way he'd never seen before. He thought his county looked a little bit like Baghdad.

Kelley had a friend who ran with the Bloxom Fire Department

just up the road. He pulled out his cell phone to call him. "Do you have an abandoned house fire going on up there?" Kelley asked.

"Yep," the friend said. "What do you got going on?"

"Two house fires," Kelley said. When he hung up the phone he was still thinking. The other number he called was Glenn Neal. Neal was a special agent with the Virginia State Police. He was classified as general assignment, but he and his colleague Rob Barnes had both been specifically trained in fire and bomb investigations—it had been the most pressing need of the VSP at the time they each graduated. It was Neal's and Barnes's jobs to determine the cause of any fires set in the county. Tonight Neal was the one on duty. "Do you know about what's going on here?" Kelley remembering asking when Neal answered his call.

"We're on top of it," Neal said, and hung up the phone.

Houses catch on fire; it doesn't always mean anything. It wasn't unusual for an abandoned house or two to burn down every year. But this had been three in one night. To everyone involved, it was beginning to feel off. It felt, as Jeff Beall would later describe it to friends, like a person arriving home at the end of the day and finding windows open at his house. One open window, and a person might assume that his spouse had done it to air out the kitchen after a cooking mishap. But if all of the windows were open, it became something else, something eerie and malicious.

Fire number four: an abandoned house in Greenbush, called into the 911 Center just twenty-three hours after the first one on Dennis Drive.

Fire number five: an abandoned house in Parksley, called in one hour after fire number four by a man who had stepped outside to smoke a cigarette and heard a bunch of crackles. He looked up and, he told the 911 dispatcher, "All I saw was orange in the sky."

Fire number six: an abandoned house in Hallwood, an hour after fire number five.

At each site, there had been no reports of prowlers or unusual activity, no outward reason for the houses to catch fire. Someone had come in and gone out, and left nothing at all behind.

Six fires.

The first fire had been lit less than thirty hours ago. All around Accomack people were coming to the same conclusion, which they thought to themselves or said to one another.

Kelley had said it to his friend in Bloxom, and Shannon and Richie had said it to each other, and when Neal and Barnes, the investigators, got to the scenes of the burned-out houses and began to pick through the unidentifiable chunks of old house, they would say it to each other. And now on November 13, Jeff Beall, at the end of a long stretch of fires that felt like someone had thrown open all of the windows of his home and left it naked and vulnerable to invaders—he said it, too: "We've got an arsonist."

^ ^ ^

THE NEXT DAY, Barnes and Neal got in Neal's car and set out to examine the scenes of the fires from the two previous nights. Arson inspections were careful business. Investigators began the inspection before they even got out of their vehicles, and then circled methodically inward toward the fire's point of origin. As Barnes and Neal approached the site of the Dennis Drive fire, they paid attention to wind direction and to the vegetation in the area. They noted that there were no sources of power in the house, and confirmed with neighbors that no one had been living there.

In truth, neither of them needed the confirmation, since they were both from the shore. Barnes—tall, broad, dark haired, with the earnest, straight-nosed profile of the former military man he was—drove by the house all the time. He knew nobody had been living in it. The same went for Neal, who was equally tall and whose belly had just the slightest of paunches to indicate that he might be a fun fellow to have a beer with. Barnes's demeanor was the kind of

methodical seriousness that demanded respect; Neal's had a jokey-
ness that caused people to forget, sometimes to his advantage, that he
was law enforcement at all.

Today, they asked neighbors whether any intruders had been
spotted prowling around the house. None had. They interviewed
the firefighters who had put the fire out, asking if they had any information about which direction the fire had been traveling, or which
areas of the house were damaged first—anything that would help
them determine where and how it might have started to begin with.

They moved closer into the scene and stood in the ruins of the
house, which was still smoldering from the night before. At the academy where Neal and Barnes had received their 1033 certification—the
state-level course required to become a licensed fire investigator in
Virginia—the lead instructor, Bobby Bailey, called this part of the
process "sitting on a bucket." It didn't matter if all the furniture in
the house had been burned up. Investigators had to find something
they could sit on, in the middle of the wreckage, and take it all in. Sit
on a bucket. Sit on a shovel. More times than he could count, Bailey liked to tell his students, he'd found himself sitting on a charred
toilet seat in the middle of a demolished house, letting the fire talk
to him: Where was the *V*—the smoke pattern that could likely be
traced back to the fire's point of origin? How high was the soot
line, which could indicate how long and how slow the fire had been
burning? What kind of siding was on the house? Wood and vinyl
burned at different rates. In what direction do the weather reports
say the wind was blowing? Did the fire pattern reflect that? If the
two accounts didn't match up, did the homeowner have a fan running, which might have displaced the wind direction inside?

But at the house on Dennis Drive, there was no bucket, not even
the toilet seat variety. The house was a pile of ashes. No footprints,
no tire treads, no *V*, no fans, no clues.

Barnes had noticed that the county seemed to draw in firebugs
of several different varieties. It wasn't out of the question, for exam-

ple, that a group of teenagers could seek entertainment by building homemade bottle rockets and lobbing them at a beat-up shack. This was a county with one movie theater that played one showing of one movie one time per day, and only on the weekends. The VFW held bingo games, the library had a monthly lecture series, and high school sporting events were well attended—but the opportunities for stir-crazy teens were limited, and bottle rockets were as good as anything.

Nor was it out of the realm of possibility that some farmer might get tired of paying taxes on a bedraggled grain shed that nobody had used in three decades and decide to take care of the problem himself with some makeshift kindling and a match.

So the question was, Were these fires, the ones set on November 12 and 13, like that? A tiny spree that would stop now that the perpetrators had it out of their systems? Or were these fires something else?

There had already been one arsonist in Accomack, David Clifton Parks, a volunteer firefighter who people agreed was as gregarious and likeable a fellow as one could meet, unless he was drinking. When he drank, his instinct was either to punch people or set fires. He'd only lit a few fires in Accomack, though, before spreading his work up to Maryland, which is where he was eventually caught. Now he was in prison, and unless he'd found a way to engineer an out-of-body crime spree from the Jessup Correctional Institute, he wasn't responsible for the latest string. They wouldn't have fit his profile anyway—these houses seemed to have been selected for the fact that they were abandoned; Parks would just light whatever was close by.

Barnes and Neal finished their examination of the house and set to completing the necessary paperwork. There were only certain ways a fire could be coded. This one wasn't nature-made, and it didn't appear to be an accident, like a toppled candle. Eventually, Barnes determined that the fire was "incendiary" in nature. Incendiary meant that someone had probably lit it on purpose, and right now that's all they knew.

^ ^ ^

A FEW MILES down the road, Todd Godwin, the sheriff of Accomack County, was waking up and looking at his phone. He had a computer-aided dispatch app downloaded onto it, which he checked every morning to see what the 911 traffic had looked like the night before. After the three fires the first night, he had been on alert. Now, with three more, he was full-on alarmed. He was protective of his county. People liked that about him, and the fact that he worked hard, pitched in, rolled up his sleeves. Godwin was "a cross between *Walking Tall* and Andy Griffith," as one outsider would think of him the first time they met: "Throw them both in a bag, toss them around a little bit, and Godwin is what you'd get."

He had a graying buzz cut, an easy tenor voice, a face that looked perpetually freshly shaved. Godwin, forty-eight, was a Born Here. He knew most people in the county by first name, always remembered to ask about people's wives or mothers or pets, and doled out ribbing with a wink that made the teasing feel inclusive rather than mean. In return, the people of the county had voted him into office the previous year with a heavy majority, and his wife had gotten used to errands taking twice as long when Godwin was along because of the number of people who would stop to greet him. He was never off duty. He had polo shirts stitched with "Sheriff" on the chest, which he wore on evenings and weekends when he wasn't in uniform.

He was the most visible man in Accomack County. He was also, unlike the state police employees, the only elected law enforcement official in the county. The combination of these two things often meant that he was on the hook if the public wanted someone to blame for a crime that had gone unsolved, a lesson he'd recently learned.

There had already been one string of unsolved crimes in the county that year. Earlier that summer a string of graffiti had begun appearing around the area, mostly on abandoned houses and appearing to target a particular local couple, a man named Jay Floyd and his girlfriend, Danielle. The graffiti accused the pair of being police informants. The tagging ranged from straightforward and benign—"Jay Narc" sprayed on a road sign—to snide and personal: "Jay Floyd, Cops in his pocket and dicks in his bitch," sprayed in two-foot-tall letters on the side of an empty house off a little-traveled road. It had become somewhat of a game, a countywide *Where's Waldo?*, to locate the next spray-painted house. The graffiti wasn't a violent or dangerous crime, but it was an eyesore, and Godwin sensed that people in the county wondered why it was taking so long to apprehend the artists.

Now, at least, there was one fewer of those tagged houses to worry about: the sixth house to burn down in the most recent series had been one of the graffitied structures. The caller who reported that fire had made sure to helpfully identify it when he dialed 911: "This was a Jay Floyd house—a 'narc' house," he told the dispatcher when providing directions to the scene.

The graffiti was driving Godwin crazy.

The arsons wouldn't be under his jurisdiction the way the graffiti was. Though the county used to employ a fire investigator, when that man retired back in 2007 he hadn't been replaced. With no trained investigators on the county staff, the arson investigation would automatically be headed by the state police. But the investigation would undoubtedly end up calling on Godwin's personnel. And it would be happening in Godwin's county, the one he was born in, the place where the only title he'd ever wanted was "sheriff."

Godwin wanted to be ready, and he decided the first thing they needed was a list of potential targets—a way to understand the potential scope of the problem and what, exactly, they could be dealing with here. A request was put forth to a county department for an official roster of all of the abandoned houses on record in Accomack. While they waited for that, the sheriff's deputies and state police investigators brainstormed on their own. It wasn't difficult. Anyone who was from the shore could list those houses for days—they were places kids had told ghost stories about, and teenagers had thrown parties in, and adults had lobbied to either be torn down or returned to their former glory. Houses off Bayside Road. Houses off Seaside Road. The house on the road nobody knew the name of but that always had a goat tied up on the corner. Little shacks. Big shacks. Whispering Pines.

A day or two later, the official list from the county came over. On it were eight hundred addresses. Eight hundred potential targets. To one investigator, that number seemed low: it included only residences that someone was still paying taxes on. It didn't include the houses that were buried deep in the woods or marshland, covered in ivy—the houses that even the Born Heres could stumble upon, surprised. The real number, the investigator thought, was probably in the thousands.

Godwin didn't have thousands of deputies. He thought that, between his own staff and a few borrowed officers from local police departments, he could probably get eight or ten volunteers to keep an eye on a select group of houses. His staff and the Virginia State Police tried to take those eight hundred houses and whittle them down to a few logical guesses. To be candidates for arson, the houses needed to have easy access from the road. Whoever had lit the first fires had done so quickly enough that they'd cleared the area before being spotted. For the same reason, it made sense to focus on houses with multiple access points rather than ones on dead-end roads. The police and sheriff's deputies made their list of houses to be watched: Bayside Road. Orchard Road. Rose Cottage Road. There was a house in Keller that they went back and forth on for a while. It fit all of the criteria. In the end, it was edged out—number six on the list, just below the cutoff. Not because it necessarily seemed worse or better than numbers one through five, but because they had to start somewhere.

Godwin was a hunter, like a lot of men who spent time in the county, going all the way back to Grover Cleveland. It was hard to live here and avoid it: At twilight in these parts, groups of dozens of deer would appear on fields, grazing away at crops. Culling the herds was seen as something of a civic duty. Residents grew up doing it, most of them ate the meat they caught, and a lot of them did the butchering themselves. Here's what deer hunters knew about catching their chosen prey: stalking was not the answer. Deer were too fast, too easily startled. They couldn't be pursued. The way to catch a deer was to figure out where it already planned to go, and get there before it did. Choose a location that had the kind of things deer like to eat, in the kind of environment it likes to eat it in. Wait where the deer couldn't see you. Be still. Be patient. And be certain in your convictions. If a deer didn't show up the first time, come back to the same location again, and again, until it did.

Godwin knew what kind of thing the arsonist liked. He liked abandoned houses. So maybe the thing to do was to find the most delectable abandoned houses in the county. And then wait.

He gave one of his deputies a department credit card and told him to go to the nearest Bass Pro Outlet and buy out their stash of camouflage tents. Portable heaters, too. It was almost Thanksgiving, and the first frost had already descended.

By November 18, while Rob Barnes and Glenn Neal continued doggedly investigating every fire scene, the sheriff had assembled five teams of men in tents. They got in place and they stayed in place, through fires seven, eight, and nine. They arrived before dusk, slinking through the woods when they were sure nobody was watching, and they stayed into the early hours of the morning, when the risk of another fire seemed to die down. They stayed in place while the local paper, the *Eastern Shore News*, ran its first article about the arsons, and then its second, with the headline, "Suspicious Fires

Probed." They stayed through fires ten, eleven, twelve. There was no overtime pay available, so they stayed in place with the promise of comped vacation days that they knew they'd never get around to using, through fires thirteen, fourteen, fifteen.

On the night of December 8, there was a fire at a commercial structure on Seaside Road. It was the one in Keller. Number six on the likely target list, the one they didn't have the bodies to watch. It was the twenty-eighth fire.

Godwin was furious. So were Barnes and Neal, who had been examining every single fire but had, as of yet, come up with nothing in terms of clues. It was the way of fires: evidence burned itself up. The firefighters, who had now been called out nearly every night for a month straight, were exhausted. They were also beginning to wonder if they were dealing with some kind of fucking criminal mastermind.

CHAPTER 4

CHARLIE

CHARLIE SMITH'S LIFE had been a mess, though he was the first to admit it was mostly his own fault, which was one of the things people liked about him. He was perpetually screwing up, but then again, he was perpetually admitting it, too, infused with some kind of relentless honesty. His father had left when he was an infant, but people who had witnessed his parents' marriage agreed that its dissolution might have been a boon for everyone. His mother had remarried a steady man named George Applegate, who treated his new stepchildren well enough that most people knew Charlie as Charlie Applegate and assumed that he was biologically George's.

The public assumptions didn't register much to Charlie, thirty-eight, who still felt like he didn't belong—not in his family, and not in society in general. He never stopped wondering why his dad had left, he never stopped worrying he wasn't loved as much as the kids from his mother's second marriage. He thought a lot about those things as a kid. It was hard for him to know whether the feelings would have gone away on their own, because by the time he was thirteen, he'd found a way to make them go away. A friend gave him some marijuana. He tried it and liked it because it made him laugh and laugh, and it also made him feel like he understood the jokes that seemed to go over his head the rest of the time.

The first time Charlie tried to pass ninth grade, he was too stoned to put in much effort. The second time, he acted up and got kicked out. The third time, he went for "about a half an hour," he estimated, before realizing he didn't know why he was there at all and dropping out for good. He hated school. It didn't come naturally to him and he had trouble imagining a future profession in which formal education was any kind of use.

George fixed cars for a living and taught Charlie to do the same; by the time Charlie was eight, he was spending summers sanding imperfections out of the cars people brought into the family's shop. There were official shop hours posted on the door, but those were guidelines: Cars were worked on until they were finished, and sometimes that meant dawn hours or evening hours, until the light above Eastern Shore Auto was the only one visible on the street. George also volunteered with the Tasley Fire Department, and he taught Charlie to do that, too.

Charlie's voice was on the slow side, his weight was on the roly-poly side, and when he got confused or embarrassed—or when he was amused or flustered or bored or sometimes for reasons even he wasn't sure of—he would burst into a high-pitched giggle that he couldn't control. He was of average height, 5 feet 8 inches, but seemed smaller due to a hunched, folded way of walking. He had close-cropped red hair and wide blue eyes. He was perpetually stoned and, as he got older and marijuana turned to crack, somewhat unpredictable. When people described him, they often swam around for a while in search of the right metaphor: "Not the sharpest crayon in the box." "Not the brightest bulb in the lamp." But even the people who thought he was lacking in book smarts would admit that Charlie knew how to do two things: fix cars and fight fires.

God, could he fix cars, especially the detail-oriented business that came with bodywork. While Charlie was still a teenager, people brought him fender benders, faded pickup trucks, or last-gasp rust heaps that owners were embarrassed to drive but not in a financial position to replace. Charlie, working out of his stepfather's shop, would make them new again. He liked it, the immediacy of it, the fact that he could see what he'd accomplished and then get paid for it.

And firefighting—he'd joined the Tasley crew as a junior member on his twelfth birthday. Pagers didn't exist at that time; volunteers would know there was a fire because a big siren would go off from the middle of town. It went off three times on Charlie's first day as a junior member, and Charlie would always remember how important and vital it felt, to pull up to the scene of a car accident in the fire engine and realize that he knew the injured man inside.

The young volunteers who joined before their eighteenth birthdays got to leave school whenever they were called to a fire, and teachers couldn't do anything about it. Which meant that in the 1980s in Accomack County, at least for the teenage set, being a firefighter was the closest thing to being a demigod.

By the early 1990s, Charlie's drug problem had escalated and begun to interfere with his dreams. He moved in with an uncle he didn't like much, but who at least offered him a place to stay. He then began stealing from that uncle to pay for crack. His uncle looked the other way when Charlie stole a gun, a coin collection, a bicycle—but he couldn't look the other way when Charlie stole his checkbook and began forging checks. They weren't for big amounts, fifty or a hundred bucks each, but there were a lot of them. When Charlie was eventually caught, he was charged with three dozen counts of forgery and sentenced to three years in prison, with most of his time suspended. He got out, relapsed, got clean, relapsed again, and got involved with a robbery in which he and a guy whose last name he wasn't exactly sure of broke into another guy's house and stole a cordless drill, an air compressor, a propane torch, and a battery charger. Police caught him and brought him in for an interview, at which point he confessed. When asked whether there was anything else he wanted to add about the incident, instead of trying to explain away his actions or ask for some kind of deal, he helpfully explained, "The battery charger was for the cordless drill." He went to prison again.

Charlie's probation officer, Roy Custis, dutifully relayed his charge's continued struggles in a series of letters to the local Commonwealth's attorney. Usually, Charlie was where Custis expected him to be for their regular check-ins—with his parents—but sometimes he wasn't. Once, Charlie had disappeared for an extended period of time, then reappeared with bloodshot eyes and sallow skin, telling Custis he didn't need to take a drug test because he'd rather just admit there was crack in his system.

Custis couldn't help but like Charlie, a sentiment that he realized was relative, considering that it mostly meant he liked Charlie more than the other criminals he was employed to spend time with. But he liked the whole Smith-Applegate family. Charlie's mother, Brenda, was unfailingly supportive of her wayward son, and though Charlie's stepfather didn't seem to have quite the same warmth, Custis sensed that any sternness on George's part had to do mostly with worry about Charlie falling off the wagon again. To Custis, Charlie was pleasant and polite. He seemed innocent. Not innocent in the legal sense, but innocent in a sort of guileless hopefulness. Custis hoped he needed just a few more years of growing up before he became a fully functioning member of society.

After his first stint in prison, Charlie had a brief dalliance with an old friend that resulted in a baby girl. The pregnancy had been accidental, but his commitment to fatherhood was steadfast. He suggested marriage; the baby's mother declined but told him he could be as involved in their daughter's life as he liked. He never missed a hockey game or school recital, and volunteered to take his daughter to doctors' appointments and playdates while her mother was at work.

After his second stint in prison, a penitentiary in central Virginia, he went to look for a job at a poultry plant, and when he walked in the door he was spotted by a woman named Mary, who saw him, turned to her friend, and immediately said, "Oh my God, I'll end up with him." There was something about Charlie that Mary just liked. He seemed easygoing. What appealed to her most of all was the way he talked about missing his daughter, and how he wanted to be a good father to her. After he and Mary had been going out for a little while, she agreed to move back with him to Accomack so he could be closer to his child. Her own two children eventually joined them and they settled in a house that Charlie's parents had rented for them just down the block from the fire station.

He did good, they both did. Charlie went to AA meetings and NA meetings, and Mary got a settlement from a job injury that let them do up the kids' birthdays in a big way, and gave her the money to enroll in EMT classes.

And there was the fire department, the other hub in their lives. Despite his criminal record, the leadership of the Tasley department believed what his parole officer believed—that Charlie was a decent guy who was just a little lost. They allowed him back in the department, where his stepfather and half brother, Bryan, were still volunteers.

"Tasley wouldn't have a crew if it weren't for the Applegates," people said sometimes, because Charlie and Bryan showed up so often. Having spent most of their lives learning how to put cars together, they were particularly adept at taking cars apart, and were often called on for vehicle extrication.

Charlie wasn't great at taking charge of a situation, but he was excellent at following precise directions. He would await an assignment from the chief, go off to complete exactly and only that assignment, and then return for his next task. When Tasley was called to car accident scenes, Charlie was brilliant. He could point to exactly which pieces of twisted metal needed to be cut, using which piece of equipment. And he would run into any building, without hesitation. Shortly after Jeff Beall arrived in Accomack, Beall was called out to a burning funeral home. He and Charlie were the first ones in the building. The fire was in the back of the second floor, but the only way to access it was by using the stairs in the front of the first floor. In true Accomack fashion, the building had been constructed piecemeal over time. The hallways zigzagged and joists didn't quite line up, and Beall and Charlie had to belly crawl toward the fire with the hose tucked under their arms, spraying water at the flames that popped and crackled like machine guns. They were laying on the hose, spraying at those flames with full force, but the water wasn't doing anything. The flames kept getting brighter, and finally Beall yelled, "Dude, we gotta go," and they left the hose right on the landing and fumbled downstairs.

By the time they got outside, help had arrived, and one of the other volunteers pulled Beall aside. "We thought the flames were going to catch you," he said. When Beall and Charlie had fought their way down the stairs they passed by a big picture window, the volunteer told Beall. Everyone outside watched through that window as the flames followed the two firefighters down the stairwell, licking the tops of their helmets. "We really thought the flames were going to catch you."

"It was the worse place I've ever been," Beall would say when he told the story. "Me and Charlie."

Friday night poker at the firehouse, weekend barbecues with other volunteers, birthday parties for his daughter at the Tasley firehouse, with little kids trying on all the hats and boots. When the pager went off, Mary would joke about throwing it across the room, but the noise would make Charlie's face light up. She didn't think it was about the fire, particularly—unlike some firefighters, Charlie was just as excited to get called out for a fender bender as he was for a raging blaze. Mary sometimes wondered if what Charlie really liked wasn't the fire aspect at all, but the camaraderie and the sense of being needed.

He liked being needed, especially by women and children. He was always offering to beat people up, not because he was particularly interested in fighting, but because doing it seemed like the honorable thing to do. His friend Saira was with Charlie and some others at a bar when her ex came in. She was furious with her ex and wanted to have words, and while most of her other friends tried to convince her that he wasn't worth her time, Charlie pulled her aside to ask quietly, "Want me to take care of him for you?" No, Saira said. But thanks for asking.

And that seemed to be Charlie in a nutshell, thought the people who knew him—bouts of great heroism mixed with bouts of great boneheadedness. Getting sent to prison but then, while he was there, getting a commendation for his brave actions: one day while he and some other prisoners were being transported to a different location, he saw another car on the road spin out of control. He hollered until the van driver stopped and let him out, and then he ran to administer first aid to the victims—a mother and her young daughter, who were thrown from the car and died at the scene. The memory of this would haunt him for years. One of the bravest things he'd ever done, and it ended up all screwed up.

After Charlie and Mary had been together for nearly a decade, their relationship started to go south. They'd been engaged for a while but could never seem to make it down the aisle. Mary blamed herself. She'd never been with someone who had remained faithful before, and she could never stop worrying that one day Charlie would cheat, too. Eventually, they both decided they couldn't do it anymore, and Mary moved back to the Virginia mainland.

And then people worried about Charlie, whose life so often

seemed like it was held together by the collective effort of several invested parties. Mary had been good for him. She'd kept him off drugs, kept his energies focused in a cozy domesticity. And now she was gone, and things only got worse. Charlie's favorite uncle died, and in a more devastating blow, his mother fell ill shortly after. She had always loved him, always believed and invested in him. He started using drugs again, but this time it didn't seem paired with a desire to get high so much as a desire to get numb.

One night in 2011 he went to a local bar called Shuckers. He was carrying two eight balls of cocaine, though he still didn't know what he intended to do with them. Maybe he would ration out the contents and get high. Maybe he'd overdose. Devastated by the thought of losing his mother, he'd already put a gun to his head once, but found he couldn't pull the trigger.

There was a woman he'd noticed at Shuckers, she was often there when he was, but he was never able to gather more than three words to say to her. He knew he wasn't her only admirer. She was too pretty, she danced too well, and he was certain that opening his mouth would immediately be followed by sticking his foot in it, so he'd decided to keep quiet in her presence. But that night, the night with the eight ball and the self-pity and the confused heart, she happened to talk to him. And his world would briefly turn sparkly and perfect in a way he had heretofore never dreamed, because this is the night he would meet Tonya, who would be the love of his life.

CHAPTER 5

MONOMANIE INCENDIAIRE

A RSON IS A WEIRD CRIME.
It doesn't make its perpetrators any richer, unless it's an insurance-related plot. It's not like stealing; it doesn't result in nicer things. It doesn't, to simplify murder to its most basic element, get rid of someone you hate. It doesn't even usually make people famous: researchers have assessed that less than 20 percent of arsons lead to an arrest. Another way of looking at this percentage is to infer that any research employed on arsonists is employed on the unlucky ones. The skilled, careful, or otherwise lucky arsonists are never caught. It's a crime in which the weapon is nature, and the end result is the destruction of a thing, the changing of a landscape, the carving of a charred signature onto a dead piece of earth. Ultimately, the visible remnants of an arson are not what it has left behind but what it has taken away.

It's also a property crime, inherently less compelling than crimes against living things. An arsonist might not even make the news cycle, unless someone is injured in the fire. Serial killer David Berkowitz was an arsonist. People forget that, because the fires were overshadowed by his more heinous crimes of murdering New Yorkers under the moniker "Son of Sam" in the 1970s. But he lit fourteen hundred fires, according to a log book he kept of his activities, and it was one of these fires that ultimately led to his arrest: after he started a blaze outside of his neighbor's door, the neighbor suggested police investigate Berkowitz, who he thought behaved oddly.

The Boston Belfry Murderer was an arsonist, too. Thomas Piper, who assaulted and killed four young women in 1870s Boston—and who, after a witness spotted him in a long black opera cloak, caused the men of the city to abandon wearing the popular clothing item altogether—later admitted that he would set fires as a means of relieving tension when he wasn't attacking girls.

It is not a new crime. There are references to arson in the Bible, like King Absalom instructing his men to burn Joab's fields. There might have been arsonists living in caves—patient arsonists using flint rocks and small twigs, because the invention of maliciously setting fires first required the invention of mastering fire, making arson an unlikely signpost of humanity's evolution.

But the way we think of arson is new. The way arsonists have been perceived and studied is continually evolving. German scientists were the first to study it, beginning in the late 1700s. They believed, based on anecdotal evidence and prurient wishful thinking, that fires were set predominantly by young peasant women. The suspected cause was puberty—the trauma of menstruation, a sexual development gone awry. Fire starting was an illness of tragic, hysterical, impoverished women who lacked coping skills and were victims of the unpredictability of female biology. *The Morbid Anatomy of the Brain*, a medical textbook from 1815, describes one case study as such:

"A servant girl in the country, happy in her situation and liked by her master and mistress, one day while making a toast for the tea was overcome with the propensity to set fire to the barnyard—instantly went out and committed the act, for which she was hanged."

Any underlying causes to this "sudden propensity" are not explored. Was the servant girl truly "happy in her situation," or only according to her master and mistress? Was she "liked" by her master—or was she harassed by him, or abused by him, or any number of other possibilities that were not explored by the textbook author?

In later years, the German researchers' conclusions would be proven to have no scientific basis—in every other study, the vast majority of arsonists have been men. Most of those men reflect the racial demographics of the area they live in: a predominantly black neighborhood would be more likely to have a black arsonist, a white neighborhood would have a white arsonist, and so on. A majority of arsonists have IQs below the range considered normal. A disproportionately high percentage of them struggle with substance abuse or have been diagnosed with schizophrenia; a disproportionately high percentage of them are adolescents or young adults.

Research on female arsonists is incomplete at best, though the research that does exist suggests that female fire setters are more likely than males to do so with a revenge motive in mind, and more likely to set fire to buildings with emotional meaning rather than to random structures. Ugandan spiritual leader Credonia Mwerinde once set fire to the possessions of a man who had spurned her, and then later instructed some of her followers to burn down the home of a man who had refused to join her cult, and then later, after her predictions about the end of the world did not come to pass in 2000, brought six hundred members of her cult into a church filled with gas cans, locked them in, and left them to perish in a fire. (There are disputes as to whether she actually lit the match in that instance.) In some studies, the percentage of female arsonists was as high as 35 percent, in others, women were as low as 4 percent, but they do not appear as the majority in any recent study.

In time, scientists began realizing that all women got periods, not just peasants and not just arsonists, and so perhaps a better explanation was needed to explain arson. Sigmund Freud suggested, as he was prone to do, that people who set fires did so for reasons related to phalluses. Flames themselves were reminiscent in shape and movement to penises, Freud argued, and thus attraction to them could represent homosexual impulses in men and heterosexual impulses in women. Of course, the same attraction could be used to describe not only arsonists but also aspiring firefighters: "It is as if primitive man had the impulse, when he came into contact with fire, to gratify an infantile pleasure with respect to it and put it out with a stream of urination," he wrote in a 1930 essay. "Putting a fire out by urination represented a sexual act in man."

Aside from the German and Freudian research, a French scientist named Charles Chrétian Henri Marc contributed his own thoughts to the field in the mid-1830s. A compulsive setting of fires was, he decided, merely a problem of impulse control. At the time of his research, there was a subset of crimes that fell under the umbrella category of "monomania." Crimes under this umbrella term were, Marc described, "against nature, so monstrous and without reason as to be explicable only through insanity, yet perpetrated by subjects apparently in full possession of sanity."

Arson, he decided, deserved to be a special subset of these illnesses. He first called it *monomanie incendiaire*, and then, a term familiar even to twenty-first-century readers, "pyromania."

Americans were not sure at first how they felt about pyromania as a psychiatric illness. The term crossed the pond around the same time as the assassination of President James Garfield in 1881. The assailant had been a delusional man who believed he was responsible for Garfield's presidential victory and owed a Cabinet post. America was uneasy with the idea that criminals could use mental illness as an excuse for bad behavior, as psychiatrist Jeffrey Geller chronicles in a history of American fire setting. In the late nineteenth century, the thinking was that things ought to be black and white. Either some-one shot the president, or he didn't. Either someone lit a fire, or he didn't. The reason why shouldn't matter.

But current researchers realize there are lots of fathomable, logical reasons people light fires, even if that logic is sometimes profoundly twisted. The Center for Arson Research, run by a psy-chologist named Dian Williams, has divided fire setters into catego-ries. Experimental fire setters, usually children, who light fires once and then never do it again. Thought-disordered fire setters, whose arson is a symptom of greater mental illness—the kind of arsonist who might believe, for example, that his fires are a message from a voice only he can hear. Communicative fire setters, who use their fire to convey a message they find themselves unable to otherwise convey. (Jeffrey Geller writes about one such patient—a forty-three-year-old woman who'd spent her adult life at a mental hospital after trying to burn down her family's house as a teenager. Whenever she grew unhappy with her living situation and wanted to be moved, she lit another fire.)

It's not unheard of—in fact, it's practically become a trope—for firefighters to become arsonists in an attempt to become heroes, lighting fires and then racing to the scene to put them out. Wil-liams puts these arsonists in the "thrill-seeking" category. The most famous American arsonist, John Leonard Orr, was a thrill-seeking arsonist. His day job was a fire captain and investigator for the Glen-dale Fire Department in California. On his own time, he lit hun-dreds of fires, one of which killed four people. He even wrote a novel called *Points of Origin*, about a serial arsonist in Southern California. *Points of Origin*, he swore after he was caught, proved nothing about his own acts. Those who were obsessed with the Orr case could not help but notice, however, that the protagonist's name, Aaron Stiles, could be arranged into a particular anagram: "I set L.A. arsons."

The people in the preceding examples were all arsonists, but some of them might not necessarily have been pyromaniacs, at least not by the modern definition. "Pyromania" is an overused term. A group of psychiatrists in the *Journal of the American Academy of Psychiatry and the Law* once explained it this way: "Firesetting is a behavior. Arson is a crime. Pyromania is a psychiatric diagnosis."

"Arson" does not exist in the American Psychological Association's *Diagnostic and Statistical Manual of Mental Disorders*. But pyromania does. It is the only subset of fire setting that is explicitly included in the DSM. It is defined as "experiencing tension or affective arousal before setting a fire, and feelings of pleasure, gratification, or relief during or after fire-starting."

A pyromaniac does not light just one fire, like an experimental fire setter; a true pyromaniac will light several. He does not do them because he is drunk or psychotic or because he believes he is being instructed to light fires by a voice or a god or devil or monster, like a thought-disordered fire setter. He does not do them because he wants to be a hero, like some firefighter arsonists, nor for the practical reason of gaining insurance money, or covering up the evidence of a different crime.

For a true pyromaniac, the fire itself is the motive. An act that becomes its own purifying absolution, its own reason for being. He lights fires because something about lighting fires gives him a sense of release. A pyromaniac is like Thomas Sweatt, a Washington, D.C., fast-food manager and arsonist. His first fire, in 1985, had a perverse logic to it: he wanted so badly to again see a man he had found attractive that he decided the best way to do it was to burn down the man's house, which he did by following him home one night and pouring two liters of gasoline underneath the front door. The man's wife died and his two daughters were injured. But Sweatt, as he watched the scene from a distance, was pleased to see the object of his affection appear on the street wearing only his underwear. He discovered such a feeling of pleasure and release from the experience that he went on to light an approximated three hundred more fires, several of them fatal. When he was eventually caught in 2005, he received a life sentence.

To talk about arson is to talk about buildings burning down. To talk about the term "pyromania" is really to talk about the unfathomable mysteries of the human brain and the human heart: Why do we do things? Why do we want things? What moves us, and stirs us, and why are some people moved by the things that the rest of us find inexplicable or abhorrent?

Some arsonists go into treatment and are cured, though those are often the arsonists whose fire setting was a by-product of another mental illness. Some arsonists take well to the therapy, pronounce themselves cured, and then leave treatment and immediately burn down another house. No one really knows why. Because, despite all of the research and studying that scientists have put into understanding arsonists over the years, there's a piece of the puzzle that remains inexplicable:

Some people light things on fire because they feel like they have to.

CHAPTER 6

TONYA

E VE WITH THE APPLE, IN THE GARDEN. Hester Prynne
with a scarlet *A*.

Later, after all this, people would have stories about Tonya
Bundick. They would conflate vague memories with speculations
and folklore, and they would decide Tonya had been a bad girl. Or a
sociopath, not deliberately bad but lacking the moral compass most
people had. Or that she had sorceresslike powers over men. They
would make her into what they each needed her to be in order to
make sense of everything that happened, and they would peel and
peel away at her, never knowing if they were to the center.

People who didn't know Tonya at all knew her family name.
Bundick was a Born Here name, a good one, with roots tracing back
to Richard Bundick, a colonist who had arrived in 1647, farmed
hundreds of acres, and died with enough land and tobacco to make
his wife and children comfortable for the rest of their lives. Now,
Bundicks were everywhere; the name appeared on law offices,
HVAC companies, government IDs.

People who knew her in person knew her mostly from school functions—she was a single mom with two sons—or from the bar Shuckers. Tonya, forty, was very pretty, with a fine-boned face and big blue eyes that had the flat, bored look of an Egyptian statue. She tanned all the time. She was so tan she was orange, and people would see her at multiple tanning salons in a single day, switching locations when she hit the maximum allowed time. Her legs were shapely, and at the bar she wore clothes to show them off. On at least one night (As a joke? A costume?) she went to the bar wearing a magenta lingerie set—bra, panties, garter belt—and nothing else.

In the context of Shuckers, which in 2012 was at the height of its popularity, this was less of a shocking sartorial choice than it might have been elsewhere. One of the bar's frequent attendees, a woman named Terri, described the place as "sort of like Studio 54," if the famous New York nightclub was located in rural Virginia, with a parking lot full of pickup trucks and a clientele that occasionally broke out in brawls. (Another Shucker's patron noted that he mostly tried to stay away because of the fights. But that if he was in the mood to see a fight, as one was from time to time, then Shuckers was the perfect place to go.)

Anyway, the Studio 54 comparison was really about social hierarchy: a place with a definitive sense of who was in and who was out. There were some female customers who danced on the bar or on the stage at Shuckers to show off, and some women who watched them. Terri had been one of the watchers until one day she was told by one of the dancers that she should come dance on the stage, too. The woman who told her that was Tonya Bundick.

To Terri, who was a little older than a lot of the twenty- and thirtysomething clientele, and who hadn't been out of the house much recently due to a chronic illness, Tonya telling her to get on the stage to dance made her feel as though she'd been embraced by the cool kids at the lunch table.

Tonya was fun, and always seemed to have a lot of people paying attention to her. If the clothes she wore were provocative, no one could deny she had the body for them. She'd even inspired her own fashion following. One Accomack resident remembered seeing Tonya "peacocking" around the bar in a tube top befitting, in size and design, a Barbie doll. Trailing behind her was a cluster of other women, similarly tube-topped, but none of them with quite the figure or presence to pull off the ensemble. The parade reminded the onlooker of the movie *Multiplicity*, where the main character makes a series of clones, which become more defective with every copy. Tonya wasn't ever catty about it, though. She was the type of person to seem genuinely happy when she received compliments from other women, and happy to return them as well, offering fashion or makeup advice. She made an impact. A former Shucker's employee remembered Tonya as the kind of woman who "never bought her own drinks or had to bring her own money." Another Shucker's regular was a bit more circumspect. "One of those girls who if you just look at her, you assume she's trashy," the regular said. "But she actually seemed shy. People were just quick to judge her."

One of the remarkable things about Tonya's popularity was the fact that she had become popular at all. Growing up just north of Parksley, she'd been a bit of an outcast. Her eyeglasses were huge and round. She was bullied, especially on the school bus. She rode the bus several times a day: Arcadia, the high school she attended, had a lot of vocational tech programs in the early 1990s: Future Farmers of America, or Future Mechanics. Tonya, along with a small group of other girls, was a member of the Health Occupations Student Association, a group of students who took regular school classes in the morning and then got on a bus in the afternoon to take classes in home health care, allowing them to graduate as certified nursing assistants.

The kids in that program were smart, recalled one student who went through it with Tonya, but moreover, they were practical and realistic about their future options. Their families didn't have the money to pay for college. These students expected to graduate high school and then immediately go to work, so they spent their teenage years learning to turn patients to prevent bedsores, or lift heavy objects without lower back strain. It was a pathway for girls to get the kind of work that would be useful in Accomack, a place with an aging population where the demand for home health aides was regularly listed as a "growth occupation" in the Virginia Employment Commission's annual report. It was that way across the United States.

For Tonya, the work did seem to come from a place of genuine interest rather than just a practical fallback. Her mother, Susan, had studied to be a nurse before marriage. She'd never officially entered the profession, but she'd kept her old textbooks. Susan was a gentle person, the kind of friend who would see a good deal on cantaloupes in the grocery store and pick up an extra for a neighbor, or who would hand out homemade preserves as gifts. Tonya's father had been a farmer, mostly working other people's land. People thought that Carroll was an odd man. He had an unpredictable temper, as one man whose family employed him remembered. Certain strains of Bundick men were ornery. It came with the blood.

The blood also ran through Tonya, who herself gained a reputation for orneriness, though of a different kind. The people who remembered how she'd been teased also remembered how she'd taken it: When people teased her on the bus, she never cried and she never accepted it. She fought back, schoolmates remembered, even when the perpetrators were twice her size.

She graduated from high school and she did become a nursing assistant. She moved to the nearby island of Chincoteague and ended up pregnant by a local landscaper who specialized in bringing southern palm trees to Eastern Shore front lawns. He was black, resulting in the kind of union that, even in the late 1990s, made a good portion of Accomack County take notice. Accomack was about 61 percent white and 29 percent black. The chair of the Board of County Supervisors was black, and so was the clerk of the court, and the population was too small for the two public high schools to be anything but integrated—all of the neighborhoods went to them—but like a lot of the South and like a lot of America, there was a difference between who people worked with and who they socialized with. Tonya and the landscaper weren't ever officially together, though, and after the birth of their second son, she took the children and moved back to the mainland without him.

She got another nursing job, at a residential house for mentally disabled adults where she arrived by 6 a.m. to make beds and help residents through their wake-up call and breakfast. Her colleagues liked her, thought she was a fast learner and unflinching in the face of messy, intimate work. It was hard, and it didn't pay particularly well. In that job, she almost never made more than $15,000 a year. When she talked about her private life with her colleagues, it was about her boys, whom she doted on. She complained, sometimes, that the boys' father didn't send regular child support, but she made do. She baked cupcakes for school fund-raisers, she bought the boys clothes from Peebles, a local department store with precisely hung jeans and collared shirts, instead of from Walmart or Rose's, the discount chain where clothing was always sliding off hangers and sometimes had holes.

In 2006, Tonya's mother, Susan, collapsed in her own backyard. She died instantly. Tonya was the one who found her, out near the clothing line like she'd been getting ready to hang some laundry. A short while after that, Tonya moved with her two boys back into the house in which she had been raised, a white ranch-style home on a two-lane road in an unincorporated locale called Hopeton. The house had been left to both Tonya and her sister, Anjee, but the two had decided upon an arrangement. Anjee would sign over the rights to their parents' house for the sum of one dollar, plus, as they decided to word it in the transfer of deeds, "natural love and affection and other good and valuable consideration." In exchange, when their still-healthy grandmother eventually passed away, Tonya would similarly sign her rights to that house over to Anjee.

At nights to unwind, she'd started going to Shuckers. Old acquaintances saw her, people who had never left the mainland, and they were stunned because somehow, in between the two kids and the hard job, and the move to Chincoteague and back, she'd become beautiful. The glasses were gone. Her hair—whether she was wearing it blonde and spiky or brunette and curly—was meticulously styled. Her makeup, frosty lips and dark eyeliner, was expertly applied.

Some folks didn't even recognize her. One man, who had gone to high school with her and whose wife had counted herself as one of Tonya's only friends, spent several minutes chatting with Tonya before she laughed and said, "You have no idea who I am, do you?"

Gradually, this new Tonya replaced the old Tonya in people's minds. At Shuckers, she found the popularity she never had in high school. One night she invited a coworker from the residential facility to come out to Shuckers with her. The colleague hadn't ever been there before—she was black and thought of it as a place where mostly white people hung out. But she went and was surprised by how much fun she had, and even more surprised at how popular her coworker was. "The queen of her own little world."

So that was Tonya, or a version of her. The version that anyone who had lived in Accomack for more than a decade would have gleaned just through idle grocery store chatter. Sometimes there would be grace notes added to the story—people gossiping over the parentage of her kids, or saying that women who had children shouldn't leave the house dressed as she dressed, or marveling at the orange color of her skin.

But set all of that gossip aside and there was still a clean narrative: There was a girl. She was plain and unpopular. She moved away. When she came back, she was beautiful. Both when she was plain and when she was beautiful, she had a spark to her, the kind of spark that led her to stand up to bullies or, as one person who knew her socially remembered, arm herself with a preemptive beer bottle when another female patron was getting up in her face.

By day she was a hardworking nurse and terrific mother, by night she got dressed up and went to Shuckers, and that was the other part of Tonya's story people could agree on: it was here that she met a funny guy, a firefighter with a drug problem who everyone said had a big heart, and they got to talking.

CHAPTER 7

"LIKE A GHOST"

IN THE MIDDLE OF THE NIGHT on December 15, 2012, Lois Gomez sat up in bed. She thought she heard something. She listened. Nothing. Maybe she was wrong, maybe she hadn't heard anything. She went to the kitchen for a drink of water. It was two or three in the morning, only a few hours before her shift at Perdue and her husband's shift at Tyson. Now she definitely heard something. A banging on her front door—which in itself was odd; friends and family knew they always used the side entrance—and someone yelling: "Your garage is on fire! I've already called 911!"

She stood frozen in the kitchen trying to process the information. *Christmas lights*, she thought. Her outdoor Christmas lights were halfway up, but she and her husband had recently decided to visit his family in Texas for the holiday and she'd been trying to figure out whether to bother with the rest of the decorations, which were meanwhile stored in the family's detached garage, which was now on fire. Christmas lights, along with the expensive music equipment for her son's rock band.

It had been a rough couple of months. For one thing, she wasn't getting along with her next-door neighbors. She'd been close with the woman who'd owned that house before, Susan Bundick. They brought each other dinner sometimes, or stood and chatted in their backyards. But one Sunday afternoon, Lois was outside emptying the aboveground backyard pool to close out the summer season, and she saw the police were at Susan's house. They told Lois her neighbor had died. Now, Susan's daughter lived in her mother's old house and things weren't as pleasant. Tonya was fine, kept to herself, but Lois had a few run-ins with Tonya's new boyfriend, a squirrelly redheaded guy whose name she didn't know. He'd done a few little things, like dumping a bunch of branches on their lawn instead of disposing of them like he was supposed to. Once he'd accused her of making racial slurs against Tonya's kids. The accusation was ridiculous. Lois's husband was from Mexico, and her four grandchildren were partly black.

She'd also been having nightmares about the arsonist. In one dream, she went into her kitchen late at night and saw someone racing through the yard, an intruder wearing dark-colored sweatpants and hoodie. "What are you doing?" she called. The figure turned and looked at her but she still couldn't see his face, and he eventually disappeared behind her detached garage. She woke up and realized it wasn't real.

This night wasn't a dream, though.

She went outside, where flames were leaping from the garage. She watched the dissolution of her Christmas ornaments, and her son's band equipment, and all the other things people stick in garages and toolsheds when they don't want to get rid of something but aren't ready to say good-bye. Numbly, she realized that whoever had lit the garage on fire had also taken the time to let out the chickens. They had been kept in a pen attached to the building and they were now running all over the lawn at three in the morning.

It was the thirtieth fire.

By now, it was a strange time to live in the neighborhood.

Reports of arsons were appearing almost daily on the local TV news as reporters strained their thesauruses looking for new words to describe fire, and ended up just saying "blazed" a lot. The newspapers, the *Eastern Shore News* and the *Eastern Shore Post*, operated with shoestring staffs, a handful of reporters apiece who covered everything from local politics to local basketball games in print editions that had been reduced to twice a week. Now they were covering the biggest news of the decade.

By the time Lois and Miguel's garage lit up, they already had friends whose properties had burned, in what was becoming a real fear for anyone who owned a structure that looked even slightly decrepit. People were filled with—well, "paranoia" wasn't the right word for it, not exactly, because paranoia meant that the thing you feared wasn't likely to actually happen. These fires could happen, did happen, every night, all the time.

It was hard to pinpoint one moment when people realized what a big deal the serial arsonist was. Was it fire number seventeen, a big rental house worth $95,000, a lot of money for the Eastern Shore? Was it fire number thirty-four, the house on Front Street? That one was abandoned, but it wasn't isolated like the others. It was right in downtown Accomac, just a few blocks from the courthouse. If the wind had gone the wrong way, that fire could have taken out the whole town.

Maybe it was fire number fifteen, a little house directly across the street from state police investigators Rob Barnes's and Glenn Neal's offices. That fire wasn't even called into 911—Neal saw it himself as he was driving back from an interdepartmental meeting about the arsons. He was on his cell phone, talking to the director of the 911 Center about how the meeting had gone, and said, "Well, shit, man, the house is on fire. I gotta go." It was so blatant. fire fifteen had a message, and the message seemed like it was *Screw you*.

After a little while, watching the fires was akin to seeing a set of china stacked precariously on the edge of a table and knowing it would fall but not knowing when. Or watching someone squeeze and squeeze a balloon and trying to prepare for the inevitable pop. Every single place people shopped or worked or went for coffee or got the car repaired, they would wonder if the arsonist was standing next to them in line. Facebook pages developed: "Who is trying to burn down Accomack County?" and "Arson in Accomack" and "Who is setting these fires? And how will they be stopped?"

On one of those pages, somebody reported that there was a scanner app that could be downloaded onto smartphones, so that listeners could hear about 911 calls at the same time the cops did. Everybody took that advice, and shortly after, somebody else noticed a different thing: one of the features of the app was that it showed users which cities it was most popular in, a top ten list. There was a period of time in late 2012 and early 2013 when number three was New York City and number two was Los Angeles, and the number one place where people were listening for crime data on their phones was Accomack County, Virginia.

The national news media had arrived, eventually. The story beckoned because of the sheer vastness of it—the almost comically large number of incidents taking place in a locale that brought with it a ready-made atmosphere. To journalists and professional storytellers, crimes are always more interesting when they happen in folksy, safe communities than when they happen in big cities; there's a reason that *Twin Peaks* was set in a small Washington State logging community and not in New York.

But there were other reasons why the Accomack fires were so appealing to the American public at large. Big-name crimes have a way of becoming big name not only because of the crimes themselves but because of the story they tell about the country at the moment. The infamous bank robbers of the 1930s—Charles "Pretty Boy" Floyd, Frank "Jelly" Nash—were stealing money at a time when hardly anyone had any, when Dust Bowl poverty made such thefts seem, if not justified, then at least understandable. The 1920s jazz killers—women who murdered their husbands and blamed it on the music—did so in an era where the country was grappling with rapidly loosening morals and a newly liberated female populace, which had just gotten the vote.

And now here were arsons, happening in the type of rural environment that had been figuratively burning down for several decades, whether in the midwestern Rust Belt or the southern Bible Belt, or the hills of Appalachia. Underrepresented in television shows and media. Left behind when industries changed or factories moved. Residents in places like these represented the "real America" that national politicians always seemed to talk about when they wanted votes. The America that had just recently caused President Obama to found the White House Rural Council, to "promote economic prosperity and quality of life in rural communities." Obama had recently been elected into office for a second term, but the vast majority of people in rural places—61 percent—hadn't voted for him. The United States was still recovering from a crippling recession that had bitterly divided the nation in terms of where its money should go. Should the country continue farm subsidies, which sent billions of dollars every year to less-populated counties? (Between 1995 and 2014, Accomack received nearly $68 million.) How much money should go to supporting affordable housing in rural areas? In 2010, the government-backed 502 Direct Loan program, which provided funds to buy or rehabilitate rural dwellings, was funded at $2.1 billion; three years later the number was $828 million.

This was not the story of Accomack. This was the story of America. In 1910, back in the peak of the Eastern Shore's wealth, more than 70 percent of Americans lived in rural counties. It was the norm, it was the standard. Now, rural counties contained only 15 percent of the nation's population.

The people who did stay in rural places got older. The median age of a United States citizen was thirty-seven in the 2010 census; in Accomack it was forty-four. There were counties out in the western part of the country—big, cowboy counties—where the median age now approached sixty, populated by residents who didn't want to leave but who knew they didn't have the amenities to make younger folks stay. "It's time for us to have an adult conversation with the folks in rural America," U.S. secretary of agriculture Tom Vilsack had just recently said in a December 2012 speech. "Rural America, with a shrinking population, is becoming less and less relevant to the politics of this country, and we better recognize it and we better begin to reverse it."

Rural America was a theoretical place that took up a large, romantic space in the American imagination. The people who lived there had cultivated the nation. They had fed the nation and nurtured its soul. Thoreau had to go find the countryside to write *Walden*. The poet Elinor Wylie had to go find the countryside to write "Wild Peaches" in 1925. In fact, she had to go find the Eastern Shore: "When the world turns completely upside down," she wrote, "you say we'll emigrate to the Eastern Shore."

> *You'll wear a coonskin cap, and I a gown*
> *Homespun, dyed butternut's dark gold color*
> *Lost, like your lotus-eating ancestor*
> *We'll swim in milk and honey till we drown.*

The imagery was beautiful, it was wistful, it was evocative, it was eerie. But what did it mean in real life? What did it mean in the modern world? What things were worth holding on to and what things had to be relinquished? America fretted about its rural parts, and the arsons were an ideal criminal metaphor for 2012.

^ ^ ^

CHARLIE ROSE was about as national as you could get, a newscaster with *CBS This Morning*. He'd sent down a reporter from his show to get the story on the ground. "Someone is waging war on rural

Virginia," Rose said to his viewing audience, from behind his desk in New York. "Their weapon of choice is fire. Chip Reid is in the town of Tasley on Virginia's Eastern Shore. Chip, good morning."

Chip Reid, a reporter with *CBS This Morning*, had come to Accomack with a camera crew. He interviewed the pizza maker at the Club Car Cafe and asked lunching locals how the fires had changed their lives. He visited the Parksley fire station with Phil Kelley, who had been dispatched as a local fireman representative. Before the cameras were even rolling, Reid and Kelley drove around together, Kelley in a carefully selected sweatshirt with the fire company's logo, and Reid in an expensive-looking, tundra-ready parka. Kelley pointed out the locations of some fires and explained the equipment and terminology of firefighting, and Reid made Kelley feel comfortable by conducting a pre-interview, a casual conversation to ready Kelley with the kinds of questions he could expect to be asked when the camera was on.

"The arsonist is almost like a ghost," Kelley offered, thinking of the way nobody had seen him slip into or out of any buildings yet. Reid's eyes lit up, as Kelley remembered, and he told Kelley that the ghost metaphor was a really good one. Then the camera man started to film.

"What's your biggest worry?" Reid asked Kelley on air.

"My big worry is, of course, my people first," Kelley said. "I mean, there's no need to risk somebody's life for an abandoned building. But then, how far is this going to escalate?"

"When you arrive on these scenes, what goes through your mind?" Reid asked.

"Total amazement," Kelley said.

"Amazement?"

"Amazement. No one's seen him. It's like," he paused, trying to pretend it had come to him just now, naturally. "It's like a ghost."

"Like a *ghost*?" Reid said.

"Like a ghost."

Nobody would deny that it was an awful time to be a firefighter—relentless late nights and permanent dark circles under the eyes. But it wasn't all bad. They'd suddenly become heroes; famous in a way people from Accomack never expected to become famous and in a way most of them never would be again.

Over at the fire department in Tasley, Jeff Beall had gone on the local broadcasts so many times it had become rote. He gave good quotes, and he had a frank, matter-of-fact speaking style that appealed to journalists. Shannon Bridges got used to turning on the morning news and seeing the recording of her work from the previous night, her sooty pink helmet, bobbing in the background of wherever was the latest burning.

For decades in this county, firehouses had been the center of social life. Fire stations held fall chili cook-offs, summer barbecues, year-round bingo tournaments. Every October, the Tasley station had taken a donated patch of woods and turned it into a haunted forest, with hay wagons full of passengers being slowly pulled past ghosts and zombies. It was the highlight of the Halloween season.

But that way of life had been hard to hold on to, not just in Accomack but all around the country. Enrollment in volunteer fire departments had declined nationwide with 11 percent fewer volunteers than in the 1980s. It was a money issue and a time issue: Volunteers who used to learn on the job alongside their fathers were now required to complete hundreds of hours of coursework before they could become certified, often at their own expense. As fire safety improved, the cost of equipment had ballooned (one self-contained breathing apparatus cost $5,000) and the time dedicated to fund-raising for that equipment had ballooned, too, with volunteer departments nationwide spending an estimated 60 percent of their time raising money. For all of the myriad reasons that young men and women set out to join fire departments—excitement, public service, community, a sense of duty—it was difficult to believe that any of them would have cited, as a primary reason, "bake sale." One study by the U.S. Fire Administration, about retention rates among volunteer firefighters, found a few factors unique to rural places, one being the replacement of small Main Street businesses with larger department stores. It was easier to hang a "Be back soon—fire duty" sign on the front of an independent shop than it was to get spur-of-the-moment permission to leave a shift at, say, a Best Buy or Costco.

In Accomack, C. Ray Pruitt, the director of public safety, personally had several explanations for the decline of fire volunteers, all of which mirrored the national data on enrollment decline. Pruitt's department was responsible for maintaining the volunteer firefighter rosters and organizing the annual training. He'd also been a firefighter himself, because his father was, and his grandfather was. He could remember when volunteers were so abundant that it wasn't unusual to have twenty-five or thirty men respond to a single fire call. In his youth, people went to the firehouses the way they went to bars, as places to unwind, gossip, feel plugged into the community. The problem, as Pruitt saw it, was that people were now plugged into everything else: iPhones, iPads, Xboxes, Netflix. People got their community through Facebook and their jolts of adrenaline through World of WarCraft. They didn't need to risk their lives, unpaid, with a fire department. And he saw people today taking on second or third jobs just to make ends meet. He saw them too busy to coach their children's Little League games, and too busy to volunteer with the PTA, and if they were too busy for those things, they were too busy to volunteer to be roused from bed in the middle of the night to drive to the fire station. Instead of twenty-five men per company for a fire, Pruitt might see six or seven.

But now, here it was in 2012, and suddenly, firehouses were again at the center of Accomack County's social life. Each night as the fires mounted, parades of thankful citizens stopped by with cases of Gatorade, packets of instant coffee and hot chocolate, endless boxes of Nature Valley granola bars, and, once they learned that firefighters used it to clean the hoses—endless bottles of Mr. Clean dish soap.

November had barely passed when the young men of the Tasley station decided that their regular way of doing things needed to be revisited. It didn't make sense for them to all go to sleep in their own beds when they knew they would just be wakened by their pagers again a few hours later. There were fires almost every night. What would make more sense would be to just sleep at the firehouse.

There were several young men of Tasley: Bryan, who was George Applegate's son and Charlie Smith's half-brother, who repaired cars and coached a youth hockey league. Richie, the extra-large brother of Shannon, who hadn't ever meant to become a firefighter. He'd only gone through the training to keep a friend company, but the friend lost interest and Richie, more and more, liked the idea of having something meaningful to do. A guy named Chris. A guy everyone called "Kitchens."

Richie and Shannon were both born on the Eastern Shore. Their parents had been, too, but they'd moved to Massachusetts for a spell when Richie was in high school and when they moved back, it was right in the stage of life where everyone Richie had grown up with seemed to have either paired off already, or be interested primarily in going to bars to facilitate pairing off. Richie didn't drink—he'd never been a fan of the way alcohol made him feel, and he was painfully shy around girls. He hated when people fought or didn't get along, as they were prone to do at bars. The Tasley Fire Company seemed like a cure for all of this. Instant camaraderie, with people who wanted to volunteer to do good, and a place to go, and engines to fix, and equipment to maintain, and essentially a way of life, ready-made, that would happily suck up as much time as Richie was willing to put into it.

He lived in Onancock, about a five-minute drive away, but he volunteered with Tasley because he knew the people better. After a week of arsons, racing up Tasley Road in the middle of the night to drive the tankers and engines, Richie was the first to move in, with a laundry basket full of clothes. A few days later, Chris and Kitchens and a couple other guys started staying there, too, with their own laundry baskets.

Some of the firehouses had nice bunk rooms, with little night-stands next to twin beds with hospital corners. These were mostly the firehouses that also housed paid EMTs, with a guaranteed round-the-clock ambulance response. Tasley didn't have EMTs, Tasley's bunk room was a crawl space with four-foot-tall ceilings, which was mostly used for storage but into which somebody had, at one point, crammed a few camp beds in a hopeful attempt at accommodations.

The Tasley boys slept there a few nights, acquired more than a few bruises on their heads, and determined that instead of sleeping in the closet, they'd just bring sleeping bags into the main meeting space. It had mildewed blue carpeting and a heating system whose two settings were frigid or boiling, and whose walls were plastered, inch by inch, with photographs and placards of the firefighters who had been serving Tasley for eighty-five years.

They ran out of couch space and some of them started sleeping in chairs. The group would arrive together, and sleep together, and if they needed something to eat, they would try to do that together, too, so that when a call came through they would already be in the same car. Waitresses at Panzetti's Pizza and Waffles got used to see-ing large groups of tired men scramble away from the table, pies untouched, bill unpaid, promising to come back the next day to settle up. There were a few movies at the firehouse, stuffed in a filing cabinet. Someone brought over a copy of *Backdraft*, a movie about a serial arsonist and the firefighters trying to stop him, but it was decided that the 1991 Ron Howard film hadn't held up so well. They really preferred *Ladder 49*, a 2004 film starring Joaquin Phoe-nix as a firefighter trapped in a burning building and John Travolta as the colleague trying to save him. Richie had a PlayStation that he brought in along with a selection of video games, mostly fighting related, or about war.

In the outside world, this was an era of forwarded viral videos. Particularly the Harlem Shake, in which a quiet room of people would suddenly, on a particular musical cue, erupt in Bacchanalian dancing. Versions of the Harlem Shake filmed in office buildings, swimming pools, and department stores flooded the Internet. One night the firefighters of Tasley set up a camera, put on their fire helmets, turned on all the sirens, and filmed a spirited rendition of the Tasley Shake, complete with a person wearing the company's Dalmatian mascot suit, which was usually reserved for parades.

This, for a group of twentysomething men, became their own personal arson schedule: come to the fire house, play video games, get called for a fire, play more video games, post something on Facebook or YouTube, get called for another fire. It was easier not to sleep sometimes, to instead remain in a perpetual state of wiry adrenaline. They played video games in teams, in which the group of guys from Tasley could challenge a group of guys from somewhere else in the country. It got to the point where nobody wanted to play them because nobody could beat them because nobody else's minds had melded like theirs. In war-themed games, Bryan Applegate became known for always carrying a Bouncing Betty, a landmine that launched into the air and detonated three feet off the ground, killing his adversaries. The other players would hear the telltale click and say, "GodDAMN it!"

So one offshoot of the arsons was that the firefighters in town came the closest they ever would to an exalted state of holy heroism; the other offshoot was that the men of Tasley became singularly good at playing Call of Duty.

^ ^ ^

IN THE MIDDLE OF ALL OF THIS, there were fires. There was the fire that was two fires, across the street from each other, one a raging beast that the firemen put out only to realize that the second had been quietly burning the whole time, too. There was the fire where the engine Jeff Beall was driving got there first and Beall, having a fire hose but no way to fill it with water, left the back end of the hose tied around the tree, awaiting a tanker for it to attach to. "I wrapped my hose around a tree!" he kept bellowing into the radio to the men from Onancock, who were a few miles behind and who broke into giggles when they got to the scene and saw the tree tied up like a birthday present. There was the fire where the chief from the Onley Department finished dinner with his family, looked at the clock, picked up his pager and jokingly declared, "Now's the time!" and the pager went off in his hand.

The stockpiles of Gatorade got bigger, and the sense of community outrage and pride got larger, and the firefighters became intimately acquainted with the baking skills of every sympathetic household on the Eastern Shore. And an airplane hangar burned down, and a big pile of tires burned down, and an old empty restaurant burned down, and abandoned house after abandoned house, and there was always something burning.

There was only one thing to be grateful for, and that was that the arsonist hadn't tried to burn down Whispering Pines. That old resort complex was just down the street from the Tasley Fire Department, and over the years it had gone from being an abandoned eyesore to a bona fide structural hazard and the ghost of Accomack's past, symbolizing everything the county once had. The original owners had sold it in the early 1970s. It had changed hands several times until it closed, and the most recent owner had accrued more than $10,000 in back taxes. A church held services in one of the meeting halls, but the sewage system was declared unsafe. Finally, a few months before the arsons began, a small cluster of people had gathered near the steps of the courthouse. Two county employees set up a folding card table in the crisp early spring air. It was a public auction. Whispering Pines was the only item on the auction block. The place that had once hosted the Glenn Miller orchestra, where Diana Ross of the Supremes had once ordered a Chinese dish in the dining room, where a generation of Accomack teenagers earned their first paychecks as dishwashers in the back, now sold at auction for $28,000. The whole hotel, all of the land, sold for pennies on the dollar to a man who did not have an Eastern Shore name.

Now, the townspeople joked about Whispering Pines: "One of these days, they should burn down that shit heap." Put it out of its misery. But the firefighters knew that the actuality of that fire would be monstrous. Bigger than anything any of them had ever seen, in all their combined years of work. Awesome and terrible and biblical, almost.

Christmas Eve came and there was a big fire in a garage that happened to have a propane tank in it, and that fire lit the sky. Christmas Day came, and Sheriff Todd Godwin had encouraged most of his deputies to take the day off. He spent the evening riding around with Scott Wade, a special agent with the Virginia State Police who normally worked with the drug task force. Godwin and Wade stopped at a Royal Farms gas station for a cup of coffee and when they got inside it was mostly empty but for a few people.

Two of the people were Charlie Smith and Tonya Bundick. Godwin and Wade slid into the booth across from them, shooting the breeze, idling away a lonely Christmas. Godwin asked about Tonya's boys and Wade asked about Charlie's family, and they talked a little about the arsons.

"Y'all must be busy, with all the fires going on," Charlie said.

"Yes," Godwin and Wade said with weariness. They were busy and exhausted. The two pairs finished their coffee and went back out into the dark, empty county, but there was no fire that night and Christmas was, mercifully, quiet.

CHAPTER 8

"TELL US WHAT YOU
KNOW ABOUT THAT"

DISCREETLY, SO AS NOT TO STIR RUMORS OR GOSSIP, the police began developing an initial list of suspects. State police investigators Rob Barnes and Glenn Neal had started with a few criteria: people who had previously set fires, people who had previously been in jail and released within the past year, and—the intersection of the Venn diagram—everyone who had done both.

For a spare set of hands, they called in Bobby Bailey. Bailey was a division chief in the Virginia Fire Marshal Academy. He was also the man who had taught and certified both Barnes and Neal as fire inspectors, in a four-week intensive course that culminated with Bailey decorating a large trailer like an apartment—sofa, coffee table, Christmas tree, stuffed animal—then putting on a flame-retardant space suit and going inside to light the whole thing on fire. The students' job was to figure out how and where the fire had begun; Bailey would video the whole thing with thermal-protected cameras to show them whether they'd gotten it right.

In addition to heading the Fire Marshal Academy in Richmond,

Bailey also taught classes on arson investigation at the local university, and coauthored papers with titles like, "The Use of Liquid Latex for Soot Removal from Fire Scenes and Attempted Fingerprint Development with Ninhydrin." He was both boastful and dismissive of his academic accomplishments, his personality being less fusty arson professor and more Marlboro arson poet. He was short, muscular, with a wiry mustache and a low, deep drawl. He'd been a cop and a firefighter, and because of those experiences he looked at fire scenes holistically.

For example, were there dead bodies in the room where the fire was? "You walk into a scene and you find a person facedown, that's normal," he would explain to his students. "They're trying to breathe. They'd be crawling on their hands and knees and eventually they'd pass out, and when they did they'd be on their stomachs." But if there was a body lying faceup, that would be suspicious. That would indicate that the person hadn't died from smoke inhalation, but rather a heart attack, or foul play.

Essentially, his continued fascination with fire boiled down to this. Other kinds of crimes left evidence: fingerprints, stab wounds, footprints. They were, as police called them, "behavior-rich crime scenes." Arson wasn't. It washed all of the behavior and evidence away. It was ultimately unknowable. He believed fire was a living, breathing thing, and he said that to students: "Fire is a living, breathing thing. It pushes. It pulses."

He was a little intense. But this was, people allowed, to be expected of someone who loved a job about fire as much as Bailey.

And now that he was on board with the Accomack fire investigations, Neal and Barnes had a spare set of eyes to conduct the inspections, and also to help with the other things they had decided were necessary to an investigation.

Bailey had arranged to bring an armful of motion-sensored wildlife cameras over the bridge with him from Richmond. One night he went out with Sheriff Todd Godwin and one of Godwin's deputies to put them up around the county. The trim, agile Godwin balanced on his deputy's shoulders as they positioned the equipment high in trees, trained on houses they suspected would be targets.

Occasionally, if the house was across the street from an occupied dwelling, they might ask the dwelling's owner for assistance.

"How would you like to help?" Bailey asked. "I want to put one of those cameras in your mailbox. But you can't tell nobody, because we don't know who the arsonist is."

"Oh, this is going to be cool—I'm CSI!" the resident agreed, promising secrecy and then promptly telling enough people that the story flew around the county: *The police are putting surveillance equipment in your neighbor's mailboxes.*

Meanwhile, Neal had begun pursuing a different line of investigation. Aside from Bobby, he had another friend in Richmond, named Kenneth Morris. Morris also worked for the Virginia State Police, and Neal asked if he minded coming out to the shore for a few days to have a look around. Morris said he wouldn't mind at all, and thus kicked off the beginning of a psychological exploration into the arsonist's mind.

Morris was a criminal profiler. He'd worked arson cases with Neal in the past, and before he became a profiler, he was an arson investigator himself. Though he wouldn't ultimately be the lead profiler on the Accomack arsons—he was approaching retirement and beginning to wind down his career—Neal knew and trusted him and wanted his opinion.

On this first visit, Morris and Neal drove around to each of the sites, just as Neal and Barnes had been doing for weeks, so that Morris could get a sense of the environment surrounding the fires. In between sites, they talked.

The thing that surprised Morris most, he told Neal, was that in spite of how many fires the arsonist had set, he actually didn't seem to be very good at it. "If I'm an arsonist, I'm going to make sure that when I'm done, the houses are a black hole in the ground," he explained. "But a lot of these aren't." In one house, the arsonist had started the fire by lighting some materials that were on top of a table, which was far less efficient than if he'd lit something on the floor. As a result, the house was left singed and smoking, but not annihilated. Morris decided that the motive didn't appear to be profit; if the arsonist was after insurance money, he'd want the structure to burn completely. It didn't appear to be a religious or political extremist either. "Looks to me like he's motivated by vandalism," Morris told Neal. "Like he has a vendetta against the county."

By the end of the arson investigation, at least four criminal profilers would be brought in to assist on the case. Morris, Isaac Van Patten—who was not with law enforcement, but a university psychologist—Ron Tunkel from the federal Bureau of Alcohol, Tobacco, Firearms and Explosives, and Jon Cromer with the Virginia State Police.

It was an occupational hazard of criminal profilers that the general public thought of them as either useless frauds or all-knowing wizards, with not a lot of room in between. What they actually excelled at was both more concrete and more boring than was generally understood. They knew statistical trends of various types of criminals. They knew general behavioral patterns. They knew, for example, that it was common for arsonists to return to the scenes of their fires. With this knowledge, they could help detectives write reports to their superiors, requesting extra staffing and surveillance for those locations. It wasn't romantic, but it was useful.

Morris was the only one who was familiar with the Eastern Shore. The ATF profiler, Ron Tunkel, had previously worked as a profiler on the Olympic bombings in 1996. One of his strengths was working with the police on how to devise the most effective media strategy and public communication. Tunkel knew there were two kinds of witnesses: those who had seen something and understood the significance of what they'd seen, and those who had seen something and didn't even know it was important. With as many fires as there had been, Tunkel figured there had to be people in the latter category. Someone had finished making dinner and gone outside to dump the leftover cooking grease and had spotted a person walking through a field. The key was to create a public message in a way that would jog people's memories without disclosing any proprietary information or leading all potential witnesses.

Eventually, they all submitted psychological profiles of the arsonist to the Virginia State Police. Morris reiterated his belief that the arsonist's primary motive was vandalism; he also suggested that the arsonist likely had an immature personality, and that it would be wise to look into people who had vendettas against the police or fire departments. Tunkel's report touched on the notion that people who committed arson were often people who felt powerless and were trying to regain authority in their own lives. He wrote, "The year 2012 was probably not a very good one in the life of the offender."

A general synopsis of the profiles was provided to the media, and Carol Vaughn, a reporter for the *Eastern Shore News*, wrote a front-page article titled "Police Describe Arsonist's Profile." (Given that the *Eastern Shore News* had only three reporters on staff at the time, the overworked Vaughn was also responsible for two of the other three articles that appeared on the front page of that edition: "West Point Jacket, Unearthed on N.J. Beach after Hurricane, Returned to Owner's Widow" and "Community Raises Money for Arcadia Chorus.") "We feel certain that the person or persons responsible for these fires is a resident of Accomack County," a captain from the Chesapeake Field Office was quoted as saying. The article also warned readers that the arsonist "likely talks frequently about the fires" and may "show an unusual pattern of leaving home during the night." Privately, police had decided that the arsonist was likely not a teenager: someone so young would be noticed if he slipped out of the house at night. They were looking for someone who didn't have to account for his whereabouts to a guardian.

Locals devoured the information and reposted it on social networks, but it also made them scoff. *Of course* the arsonist was likely talking frequently about the fires. They all were. It was the one thing everyone in the county was talking about. And *of course* the arsonist was a resident of Accomack County. Who would bother to drive all the way to a remote area of the United States just to burn it down?

^ ^ ^

MEANWHILE, lead profiler Jon Cromer was deciding how to accomplish a necessary but delicate task: interviewing the firefighters. Nobody could deny that there was a chance that the arsonist was a firefighter. At the same time, being the one to raise that suspicion was bad for community relations.

Cromer was a soft-spoken man with a gentle southern accent, the kind that made him sound, even when he was interrogating hardened criminals, like he was interviewing a four-year-old about the location of a missing cookie. But rather than talking to each of the firemen individually, Cromer decided the best thing to do in this situation was to go station by station and pass out a structured questionnaire, to each of the hundreds of firefighters.

He started with the company in Bloxom. That town was in the middle of the county, centrally located to the fires. Once everyone was seated around tables in the meeting room, Cromer and Kenneth Morris passed out the questionnaires and a bunch of pens. They told the firefighters that the reason for the surveys was because the firefighters were themselves invaluable resources: they may know things that they hadn't previously thought to share. The volunteers found the explanations insulting. The police could pretend all they wanted that the purpose of the questionnaire was to get their valuable input, but most of them were pretty sure they knew the real purpose. A few of them refused to fill it out, others felt free to tell Cromer and Morris exactly how they felt about the questionnaire: it was complete bullshit.

The profilers remained calm. It was possible that the person they were trying to find was in that room. And if so, that he would give himself away with clues he wasn't even aware of.

On the first page of the questionnaire, Cromer briefly recapped all of the fires that had been happening on the shore. He explained that he was on the shore with the state police as part of an investigation. "Tell us what you know about that," the writing prompt said. It was left ambiguous, so respondents could say what they knew about either the fires or the investigation. The second page instructed the participants to "List the five most important things that could have created this situation." Again, it was up to participants to decide how to interpret "situation." The final page asked participants to put themselves in the shoes of law enforcement: "If you were in charge of investigating the fires, how would you do it?"

The ambiguity of the questions was important. When Cromer had given a similar survey to a police department that had experienced thefts from the evidence room, seventy-four of the seventy-six respondents offered similar rationales for what could have created the situation: the evidence room was sloppily run and often left unlocked. But two of the respondents offered explanations that had nothing to do with management: "Maybe someone needed money," they said. "Maybe someone had a drug problem." Those answers in themselves weren't any kind of admission to guilt, but they were different enough to get Cromer's attention.

The order of the questions was important, too. Each question was designed to prompt a different mind-set that would set up the next question. The order had been especially useful in child abuse cases. Often a parent, when asked to speculate what could have caused burning or bruising on a child, would blame external factors—a playground fall, a rough hour of recess. But when the parents were asked how they would investigate the situation themselves, the responses wouldn't follow at all from the previous question. "I think you should talk to the family and see if anybody has a bad temper," they might write—an investigating tactic that made no sense if the culprit had been a swing set. If the parent truly believed the child was being injured on the school playground, their proposed solution should have involved advocating for better recess supervision, or removing dangerous equipment. Their minds would not have immediately leapt to anger management issues at home.

It was almost, Cromer analogized, like a grade schooler trying to use the test in order to beat the test. They might be able to come up with plausible answers to one question, but when asked to come at the answer from a different direction, they would falter.

Cromer had all of this in mind when he passed out the surveys, first to the fire company in Bloxom and then later to the one in Parksley. Most of the responses were what he expected them to be, blaming punk kids or vindictive insurance seekers. One of the responses came back a little different. On the last page, in response to how she would investigate the arsons, the firefighter had written, "I would start with the fire service".

But instead of a period, she'd ended the statement with a colon. "I would start with the fire service:" It was the colon that was interesting to Cromer. Had she merely run out of time? Or was she about to elaborate on her suggestion with specific names, before thinking better of it? Cromer recommended the woman be brought in for questioning. It didn't lead anywhere. As it turned out, none of the structured questionnaires did. But this was the nature of the investigation at this time. The investigators were willing to try anything, even open themselves up to the possibility that the entire case could hinge on an inexplicable piece of punctuation.

Cromer's other contribution to the investigation was immediately suggesting that his superiors call Isaac Van Patten.

Van Patten, like Cromer and Morris, was a profiler. Unlike those two, both career police who had become law enforcement first and then profilers, Van Patten was an academic. He had a PhD in marriage and family therapy, and his official employer was Radford

University in central western Virginia, where he was a professor in the behavioral science department. But he consulted with the Virginia State Police, too, and after years of focusing on therapeutic approaches to treating offenders and on the psychological aspects of criminal profiling, Van Patten had developed an interest in a burgeoning field of study. This field of study was the other thing that set him apart from the profilers already on the case, and the reason Cromer so badly wanted him to join the effort.

Van Patten's specialty was called geographic profiling. It was a discipline based not on psychology but on data. Geographic profilers mapped the locations of crimes, and in doing so, mapped the criminal's mind.

The laymen's explanation that Van Patten found most helpful, and that he frequently referred people to, came from the pilot episode of the crime-solving drama *Numb3rs*. In it, a detective goes to his mathematician brother, searching for a way to predict a serial rapist's next target. The task, the brother tells him, would be nearly impossible. Think of a lawn sprinkler: even with all the mathematical models in the world, there would be too many variables—change in wind direction, mechanical glitches—to predict with absolute certainty where each droplet would fall. But it *was* possible to work backward and go in the other direction. With enough fallen droplets, one could develop an algorithm to trace each one back to their common point of origin. Given the droplets, you could find the sprinkler. Find the sprinkler, find the criminal. The idea was that repeat offenders, even the ones who believe they are choosing their crime scenes completely randomly, are actually subconsciously employing patterns. They orient their actions around a home base, like a residence or place of work. Van Patten, with luck, could use a computer algorithm to point toward the home base.

Because geographic profiling was based solely on location data, the type of crime wasn't important. It worked the same for a serial rapist as for a serial burglar or serial murderer. The only ingredients necessary were addresses, the more of them the better. In late November, the Virginia State Police had arranged for Van Patten to be sent the addresses of all of the fires so far. There were about twelve at that point, more than enough for an initial profile, with the idea that additional sites could be added in the future. Analyzing these incidents, Van Patten developed a report, which he submitted to the police in December 2012.

The beginning of the report summarized the time patterns of the fires: Most of them had been clustered between 10 p.m. and midnight—which indicated, if nothing else, that the arsonist must not work a night shift. The report also looked at the topographical spread of the fires, and where each one lay within the county. So far, though the arsonist had flirted with both county borders, he hadn't left Accomack.

These were all observations that could have been made by any armchair detective with an Excel spreadsheet. For the second part of the analysis, an algorithm was needed. Van Patten was careful as he input the addresses, input being the most likely occasion for human error to poison the data. What Van Patten's computer screen first showed him looked simply like a messy series of overlapping ovals and circles on a map, all roughly clustered toward the center of Accomack County. This was just the raw data. Van Patten needed to interpret and streamline it so it would make sense to human eyes. When he finished doing that, the results came back a second time. This time, the computer screen showed him one neat circle, a quarter mile in diameter, beginning just north of Parksley and ending just south of Bloxom. Somewhere within this circle, Van Patten hypothesized, was the home or workplace of Accomack's arsonist.

Van Patten included an image of that map on the memo he submitted to the Virginia State Police, with his recommendation for what should be done with the data:

"As an investigative strategy, it would be advisable to conduct knock-and-talks with as many of the homes in Hopeton as possible," he wrote. "In particular, priority for this canvas should be the Matthews Drive/Dennis Drive axis."

Matthews Road was a quiet, rural street, mostly filled with one-story houses on medium-sized lots. It was a good place to raise a family, which might have been why Tonya Bundick chose to return to her childhood home there, after her mother died. She and Charlie lived in a white ranch house on Matthews. About five houses down from the intersection of Dennis Drive.

CHAPTER 9

CHARLIE AND TONYA

CHARLIE HAD SEEN HER BEFORE. Since his ex-girlfriend had moved out with her kids, he'd been spending more evenings at Shuckers, and he'd noticed Tonya. More particularly, he'd noticed the tattoo on her lower back, and how good she looked when she danced, and he'd come to the conclusion that she was out of his league. Thus, he avoided her on purpose. Women like that, he always ended up making himself a fool in front of, and it seemed safer to stay away entirely.

But they had a pair of mutual friends, Jay Floyd and his girlfriend, Danielle, and on this night, the night Charlie had an eight ball of cocaine in his pocket and a vague plan to kill himself, Danielle came over and said Tonya wanted to know why Charlie never said more than three words to her. She'd seen him looking. "Are you interested or not?" Danielle, as Tonya's emissary, asked Charlie.

Later that night, she came over again. "Tonya wants you to have her number in your phone," she said.

Charlie and Tonya ended up talking that night in the parking lot.

He told her about his past struggles, the thefts and the prison time and the drugs he wanted to shake but couldn't. She told him about her sons, how important they were and how hard she worked at being a single mom. She said that she couldn't have people around her kids who did drugs, it was a deal breaker for her. It was a talk that both of them would remember and tell other people about, one of those conversations that seemed to cover everything that had ever been important in their lives. Charlie kept laughing, first because he was nervous, and then because he was happy. At the end of the night, he excused himself, went back into the bar, and flushed his cocaine down the toilet.

^ ^ ^

THEIR FIRST DATE wasn't one, really. She asked if he would come to her house and help her kids set up a PlayStation. When he got there, the boys' father was there, too. Charlie felt awkward and spent the afternoon pretending to make calls on his cell phone until he finally made up an excuse to leave. In the days that followed, Tonya kept texting him. "Do you miss me?" she asked. And he did miss her. She was the prettiest girl who had ever been interested in him, and she seemed smart and funny, too. He never imagined a relationship coming out of any of this, though. In the beginning, they'd both decided to keep things purely physical. But after a little while, he realized what he was most looking forward to with Tonya was when they were just hanging out.

By the time he'd decided, one night in bed, to tell her he was falling in love with her, Tonya already suspected a declaration was coming, and she teased him about his nerves. She told him herself a few days later, via text message, as Charlie remembered, while he was repairing his outdoor steps. His phone buzzed, and the text was only one letter: I. The L followed in the next message, and the O after that, then the V. By the time Verizon had sent him the whole "I love you," he had close to sawed off his finger in excitement.

He took her out on a proper date, and then again after that. After a little while, she started talking about having troubles finding baby-sitters. He sensed the real problem was that she couldn't afford them on her hourly salary but was too embarrassed to admit it. "Why don't I just come over?" he suggested. "I really don't do much when I'm not with you, anyway."

In truth, the arrangement delighted him. He'd always wished he could be a full-time parent to his own daughter, and he liked being around kids again. Tonya was close with her boys—homemade lunches, cupcakes for school fund-raisers—but Charlie's and Tonya's lives weren't all domestic: they still went out, and she still looked good and wanted him to look good, helping him pick out clothing that would coordinate with hers. "But not better than me," she would tease.

Eventually, he moved in with her and the boys. The location and the relationship kept him too busy to volunteer with Tasley any-more. They merged their social media accounts into one on Face-book—"TeeChar," an amalgamation of their names—and a picture of the two of them, Charlie smiling at the camera and Tonya kissing his cheek.

Tonya posted more often, but sometimes using the same account, Charlie would post a response, differentiating his own messages by specifying, "It's Char."

"Having teriyaki chicken and veggies straight from the oven for dinna," she wrote.

"It's Char. You make the best teriyaki chicken I have ever tasted yumyumyum."

Tonya was something of a poet and developed a near-daily rit-ual of posting either rhymes or homespun aphorisms that she called "Tonya-isms," as in, "A little Tonya-ism to brighten your day."

"Tonya-ism," she posted one day. "everywhere i go i try to make someone laugh . . . walmart is a good place to do this . . . also mcdonalds drive thru . . . i feel if i made someone laugh for a minute or forget their problems . . . i did a good deed . . . it does work u shud try it sometime."

"It's Char," he posted in response. "A lot of times when I'm stressed or just had a bad day, Tee takes me to Walmart and just does some of the craziest things and most of the time it makes me forget the stresses and worries of life."

That was the thing about Tonya. To Charlie, she could make anything interesting. They'd go to the children's department and play with the toys, or she'd open the tester nail polish bottles in the makeup aisle and paint each fingernail with a different color. Or, knowing how much he appreciated her posterior, she would walk a few paces ahead of him and wiggle. Sometimes it was as simple as that.

Her Tonya-isms were sometimes poems, silly or cheekily dirty.

"i love to feel the cold air . . . blowin thru my hair," she wrote in preparation for a coming rainstorm. "lazy day of hoverin . . . underneath the coverin."

A few days later the storm arrived: "its raining its pouring . . . the old lady ben out whoring . . . she dribblin done her chin . . . wonder where dat mouth been . . . she skirt is torn . . . she lookin real wore . . . he tapped that ass . . . she probaly got gas . . . poor ole soul ben freaked in da hole . . . she cant sit down . . . she look like a clown."

"You are very talented with words," a friend responded.

^ ^ ^

WHEN THEY MET, Tonya was still working as a nursing assistant and Charlie out of his stepdad's shop. Several months into their relationship, though, George told him he thought it was time for Charlie to strike out on his own. Charlie would keep the customers that he'd accrued, but start working out of a different shop. He wondered if the separation was a test. George was getting older—if

Charlie could successfully run his own outpost for a couple of years, then maybe George would retire and leave the big business to him.

So Charlie did move out, but not very far. He took over the lease on a building just across the street, the old post office, and turned it into his own body shop. The space meant for the manager's office was bigger than anything Charlie could imagine needing for himself, so he suggested that Tonya, who had recently decided to leave her nursing job, take it over and come up with a business for herself. She seemed to love the idea. After a while, she came up with a plan to open a kind of clothing boutique. Going-out clothes, she told people, at inexpensive prices. She said she thought a store like that would really flourish on the shore, as there weren't any other places to buy the sorts of club attire she had in mind. Charlie hung some drywall and built a little hallway to separate his repair business from her store. When the first shipment of clothing came in from the wholesale vendor, Charlie remembered, they laid them all out for display and then laughed that they hadn't ordered nearly enough merchandise. What had seemed like a big shipment barely covered the racks and tables she'd spread through the room. But they were still learning how to run businesses and they could both grow, they decided, so they went ahead and had a sign painted. On top, "Charlie's," and beneath, "A Tiny Taste of Toot," after the nickname Tonya's father used to call her.

"Lilac bling dress size medium $19," she wrote on the Facebook page she created for the store, above a strapless purple dress with silver sequins embellishing the bust. "Perfect for Easter."

She posted pictures of white platform pleather boots, gold-studded backpacks, tank tops with the Playboy bunny insignia, Apple Bottom dresses, designer or knockoff handbags: "Prada. Baby blue. They don't last long when in stock."

The name was a little confusing to people. Some people thought it sounded more like a children's store. The name actually caused a rift between Charlie and the mother of his daughter, who wondered if "toot" was a reference that meant Charlie was using again. But some people liked having a little spot to go to. It was nice to have an open business in the otherwise barren downtown of Tasley. Ever since the general store had closed, the only places to buy anything were Charlie's stepdad's shop, where you could get a quart of motor oil, or the vending machines alongside the fire station, where neighbors would walk to buy a can of Pepsi.

Charlie worked on cars in the back, and Tonya sold clothes in the front, and occasionally Charlie would wander in while customers were browsing the racks—it was a tiny little place, only room for a few people at once—and she would have to explain that women didn't like looking at clothes near a man in greasy coveralls. She would hold little promos sometimes—bring a bag of hard candy to feed her sweet tooth, get a free piece of jewelry.

They dressed up for Easter, in bunny costumes for a children's party. They dressed up for Halloween, he as a zombie and she as a vampire. For this occasion, she composed and posted on Facebook a special edition of a Tonya-ism: "Char has a date . . . he won't be late . . . I might put him on my plate . . . he might get ate . . . I lookin' for fresh meat . . . like a dog in heat . . . like a dog and a bone . . . a kid with a cone . . . I'm going to the dark side . . . wonder if he can handle the ride . . ."

"LOL, it's Char," Charlie wrote in response. "I'm hanging on for dear life with this ride."

People had been surprised by their relationship at first. Perhaps because Tonya's kids' father was black, people assumed that she was only interested in dating black men. And yet here she was with doughy, bashful Charlie Applegate, whiter than white, and she seemed happy about the relationship. The couple snuggled in bed and drank root beers, or took late night drives to McDonalds for coffee, or grilled burgers outside, or attended to their pets, which had grown to include not only dogs but also chickens and pigs and goats that lived in a pen in the backyard. With Charlie's acquiescence, they repainted the bedroom in girlish pinks and purples—a gesture that, to those who knew them, seemed both sweet and a little nutty, the idea of adults wanting to live in a Hello Kitty color palette.

"Some people think I have it all," Tonya wrote on Facebook after they'd been together a little more than a year. "I own my own house, I own two vehicles, I have a farmload of animals, I have two wonderful children, a wonderful man, a closet full of clothes, shoes, two businesses, health, and sanity."

And there it was, a parable of love in Accomack County, a modern romance of limited budgets and modest expectations and the simplest of pleasures. Still. In the middle of this domestic bliss, there were worries. There were parts of Tonya that Charlie felt he couldn't access. She almost never talked about her childhood. When stories about her past would come out, they would do so in pieces, halting. She told Charlie, as he remembered, that even those fragments were more than she'd ever shared with anyone else. She didn't seem to want anyone else to know the parts of her that were soft or vulnerable. She got upset when the house wasn't spotless, or when she wasn't put together. He never saw her without makeup or styled hair. She almost never talked about how she felt, about anything, really. Charlie noticed there was a wall built around her and it bothered him.

On the other hand, he was happy he'd been let in as far as he had. The quiet, mysterious hardness that surrounded Tonya—these things seemed like reasonable trade-offs, in order to be with a woman he'd once been too afraid to even talk to in a bar.

One afternoon in late 2011, he suggested they meet for lunch. He took her to the Sage Diner, a place that served all-day breakfast but also proper entrees that came with a salad and dinner roll. He had words planned but couldn't get them out; he kept having to excuse himself to walk around the parking lot until he could calm his nerves.

"What have you got to say? I know you got to say something," she said when he came back inside.

He pulled out the silver ring he'd purchased from Walmart. "Will you marry me?"

He'd planned to get down on one knee, but the restaurant was busier than he'd expected and he felt so awkward there in front of the other patrons that he ended up just passing the ring to her under the table.

She said yes, but had an idea: Perhaps they should keep this development a secret. People might be jealous of their happiness. She wanted to let the idea of the engagement sit a while, and then redo it in a bigger way, later on.

Charlie waited until her birthday and proposed again, this time at Shuckers, this time with a cake, borrowing the microphone from the evening's band, who quieted everyone in the bar by saying, "We got an announcement."

People remembered that proposal. The way Charlie had stopped the band and gallantly said, "This is the first place I ever saw you in, so I decided this was the proper place to ask you to marry me. Ever since I met you, my life has changed. I've never loved any women but my daughter and my mother, but now I want to spend the rest of my life with you."

He got down on one knee, he took her left hand in both of his, he really did the whole thing up right, everyone thought so.

At first Tonya shook her head like she was going to say no, but then she jumped up and down and said yes, as he knew she would. They'd coordinated everything for the night, including their yellow outfits to match the yellow cake that Charlie had arranged to be served upon her acceptance.

The cake was a vertical affair. The top of it was a Barbie doll, waist up, as Charlie remembered. The bottom half was the cake part, a big billowing frosting-dress. Charlie and Tonya decided on it because Charlie sometimes told Tonya that with the way she always did up her hair and makeup, she looked just like a Barbie. She took it as the highest compliment.

So now there they were, engaged.

CHAPTER 10

SCHRÖDINGER'S EVIDENCE

SCOTT WADE PULLED HIS CAR onto Matthews Road. The state police special agent was one of several investigators and patrolmen who had been sent out to complete this particular task: canvas the area that profiler Isaac Van Patten had identified in his geographic profile of the arsonist's likely home base. The circle encompassed the region just north and west of Parksley. Officers, some in teams, had spent several days canvassing those streets, going door to door, seeing if anybody had noticed anything suspicious about their friends or neighbors.

The stretch that Wade had covered this day had already been impacted by the arsons. Just around the corner, the arsonist had burned down a shed belonging to a woman who'd relocated to the shore to move in with her ailing mother. All of her worldly possessions had been stored inside. When she first saw the light from the fire she assumed that her neighbor must have bought a flood light for security, that's how bright the flames were. A little farther down on

Matthews Road, an old truck was lit on fire. Shortly after that was the Gomez residence, where Lois and Miguel had plans to eventually rebuild their garage but hadn't yet.

The Gomez residence was the first house Wade knocked at where anyone was home. Later, he wouldn't recall their names, but would remember them as the frightened older couple who, after the burning of their garage, kept a rifle leaning in the corner for safety.

He left and headed next door. His second house that night belonged to Tonya Bundick. She spotted him coming across the yard and stepped out on her stoop to meet him. He thought she looked familiar and after a few seconds placed her: Christmas night at the Royal Farms, when he and Sheriff Todd Godwin had sat and chatted with Tonya and her boyfriend, and everyone had been glad there were no fires that night. Now he reintroduced himself and explained what he was out doing.

She didn't have anything to add, she told him. She mentioned a Facebook page that Accomack residents used to gossip and speculate over the arsons. She told Wade that if he wanted to know who was doing it, he should visit that page. She was pretty sure that whoever was doing the arsons was probably hanging out there.

Wade moved on to the next house.

^ ^ ^

THINGS THAT HAD BEEN TRIED, but hadn't yet led anywhere, in the investigation of the arsons of Accomack County:

Members of the drug task force were working their informants to see if they'd heard anyone with a big mouth bragging about the fires.

Virginia fire marshal instructor Bobby Bailey's cameras were still trained on the potential arson sites. They were special cameras. When they detected motion, they'd automatically text the photos to preprogrammed numbers. Bailey arranged for any captured images to be immediately sent to himself, Sheriff Godwin, and the investigators Neal and Barnes. On his own phone, he gave each location a different ringtone. If the camera labeled Cashville Road was triggered, he'd get a ding-dong, or if the camera from Groton Road was triggered, he'd get a woo-woo-woo, or a siren for Johnson Road. The roads were literally calling to him.

The first night the cell phones went off, the four men grabbed them eagerly only to see a blurry picture of a squirrel crossing the field. The next time, it was a bird. One night they caught an image of a cat chasing a mouse. The symbolism in that seemed rich, but it didn't bring them any closer to an investigative victory. One time, it was a fuzzy image of a hand that appeared to be reaching toward the camera. There was great excitement over this, but they didn't know if it belonged to the arsonist or just a curious hiker.

There were men in cars, a whole alphabet soup of men from the ATF and the FBI and the VSP, who patrolled every night within their assigned jurisdictions, burning rubber to get to the site of each fire as soon as the 911 call came in with the goal of one day getting there before the arsonist left.

There was a man in an airplane, a sheriff's deputy who got in a tiny Cessna flown by a state police pilot every night and soared up and down the length of the county, tailing cars that had been radioed in as suspicious, or just observing the streets where, from the air, streetlights cast a glow that was pale and yellow, and fires cast one that was deep amber. "On a clear night on the shore, you can see a long, long way," he said.

There were still the men in tents, freezing their butts off, arriving in rotating shipments from counties around the state who had loaned in personnel. These western Virginia mountain men or D.C.-area suburbanites would get debriefed on the Eastern Shore, be issued a tent, a heater, some night-vision goggles, and a radio, and would then be driven to their assigned abandoned house, where they would leap out of the car when nobody was looking and then lie in wait.

And there was forensic evidence being collected, all the time. There was the set of two shoe prints that were discovered, to great fanfare, at a fire on Pungoteague Road, fire number fifty-two. The investigators celebrated, and marked the print by sticking little evidence flags into the ground in order to protect it until a stone cast could be made. There was a tire imprint at another.

Casts were made of the tire and the shoe prints. These casts were packaged up and sent to the Virginia Department of Forensic Science branch across the bay in Chesapeake, where forensic scientists tried to determine a match.

The tire impression was determined to belong to "BFGoodrich or any other brand of tire with similar tread design," according to the forensic report. This was less than helpful: Goodrich was one of the most common tire brands in the United States. The shoe print was determined to belong to "Nike, or any other brand of footwear with a similar outsole design." This was less than helpful.

Even if the forensic scientists had been able to identify the exact make and model of the exact shoe worn by the arsonist, Neal and Barnes found themselves wondering exactly where that would get them. So what if they had a perfect shoe print—were they going to obtain search warrants for the closets of every man in Accomack County? Require a shoes-off policy for all public spaces, so that each person's footwear could be examined before they were allowed entry? Lacking a suspect to compare the prints to, the prints became essentially useless.

The same was true for a wadded-up rag found at one scene:

"No hairs suitable for nuclear DNA analysis were recovered," read the forensic report.

And another rag:

"It is not suitable for PCR analysis and no further testing was conducted on this sample."

And another:

"No DNA profile consistent with this profile was found."

The only other potential evidence that could be tested was what was drawn from the fire itself: the shards of wood debris that had been collected from each fire's point of origin. Those shards might have remnants of the accelerant used to light the fires, which, if identified, could turn out to be clues.

The forensic scientist in charge of this testing received the samples of wood debris in an empty paint can. This was protocol; the can helped seal in vapors and prevent contamination. The first procedure she performed was called "passive adsorption elution." She suspended a piece of a charcoal strip from the inside lid of the paint can and placed the can in a precisely heated oven for sixteen hours. The goal was to draw any present vapors from the wood debris to the charcoal strip, which could then be tested for the presence of various flammable substances that might have been used in the ignition of the fires. Next, she washed the charcoal strip in a solution, transforming the vapors into a liquid solution. The whole thing was a bit like the Schrödinger's cat analogy: through every step of the process, the analyst had to treat the samples as if they included an accelerant, when in fact, it was possible that the paint can she was heating and the liquids she was separating actually contained nothing at all.

Next, she moved on to a different process, called "gas chromatography." The purpose of this was to separate the liquid and break it down into compounds, and then see if any of the discovered compounds matched known ignitable liquids. There was a whole database for this kind of work, the National Center for Forensic Science's Ignitable Liquids Database. The database included the compounds for starter fluids, paint thinners, gasolines—anything an arsonist might latch on to as a signature accelerant. Often, the present compounds would come back and be something mundane like household lighter fluid, the kind that every American with a grill had in his or her garage. But sometimes you got lucky and found a history buff arsonist who was lighting a whole town up with Civil War-era lamp oil.

The Department of Forensic Science received its first batch of charred wood samples on February 13, and sent responses back two weeks later.

"Item 1 was extracted using a passive adsorption-elution technique and was examined using Gas Chromatography-Mass Spectrometry (GC-MS)," the report read. "No ignitable liquids were identified in the Item 1 extract. The evidence is being retained for personal pickup."

In other words, Schrödinger's cat was never even in the box to begin with. The forensic scientist had been looking, scientifically speaking, for something that didn't exist at all.

^ ^ ^

ACROSS THE BRIDGE in Accomack, the slog of the rest of the investigation pressed on. A series of roadblocks were set up on the county's three main roads. This was an area in which the isolation of the county became useful: It was impossible to get anywhere in Accomack without using one of these three roads, and therefore possible to quarantine the whole county just by blocking them off. They didn't catch the arsonist using the roadblocks, but when word about them spread, people were careful to make sure they weren't caught cruising with an open beer.

In fact, to the deputies of the sheriff's department, it seemed that other crimes had drastically decreased. Nobody was driving drunk, nobody was burgling. It was simply too risky, now that the streets were overrun with law enforcement officers. One law enforcement officer, after noticing an unfamiliar car suspiciously loitering by the side of the road, knocked on the car's window to check things out. The man inside said he was from out of town, just passing through, and had pulled over to read a map. But he seemed confused. "You're the third cop who has stopped by to check on me in ten minutes," he said. Accomack County felt the safest it had ever been, except that it was in the middle of the biggest crime spree in its four hundred-year history.

And the graffiti that had plagued the county before the arsons started—the ones that had so aggrieved Todd Godwin and the sheriff's department—had, for reasons unknown, completely come to a stop.

CHAPTER 11

THE EASTERN SHORE
ARSONIST HUNTERS

MEANWHILE, THE RESIDENTS OF THE COUNTY were collectively losing their minds.

On Ash Wednesday, in the middle of February, a Methodist church was set on fire. It didn't completely burn down, and the charred wood was discovered the next day when a repairman pulled into the gravel parking lot to eat his lunch. Leatherbury United Methodist was a small but devoted community. The minister was a man named Jon Woodburn, a circuit preacher who also served two other congregations: he would preach in Riverview at 8:30 a.m., then make it to Leatherbury by 9:45 and then Cashville by 11:00.

The burning of a church triggered the arrival of the Feds: the ATF and the FBI. The following Sunday, Woodburn tried to make his sermon about hope rather than despair. "It didn't burn down," he told his congregants. "There was no reason for it not to burn down, but it didn't."

Nationally, Methodist congregations were grouped by size: small, medium, large. The Eastern Shore churches were all tiny. "They're small, smaller, smallest," Woodburn liked to joke. They were just chapels, with double-digit congregations and maybe a tiny fellowship hall. The burning of a community church, on a holy holiday, raised the panic level of the entire shore. Satanists? Atheists? Someone with a vendetta against religion?

Ministers organized prayer vigils trying to quell their congregants' nerves: "Do not fret because of evildoers or be envious of those who do wrong," a Baptist pastor from Onley read to his congregation from Psalm 37 at one such vigil. A Presbyterian minister urged attendees to pray for the arsonist, who must be struggling, and for his repentance.

The Facebook pages, "Who is trying to burn down Accomack?" and "ESVA fires," had become crazed with gossip and speculation, with several thousand members apiece. A few people tried to keep things civil and helpful. Tonya Bundick was one.

"One would have to ask, with all the migrant houses burned, where will they stay this year?" she wrote on one occasion.

"I myself am not afraid, just cautious," she wrote on another. "I am always on the lookout when my animals start barking and when my livestock start making noise. Make yourself aware of the little things."

A third time, she scoffed that a recently burned food truck didn't seem to fit the pattern of the other arsons: "Seems to me some of the properties being burned are people who are taking advantage of an arsonist bein' on the loose . . . so they are burnin' their own properties . . . mmmmmm . . . Jus a thought."

Another person who was very active on Facebook at this time was Matt Hart.

Hart was a searcher, a doer, a young man with big dreams that he wanted to achieve. He wasn't comfortable if he wasn't moving forward, finding a new challenge or fixing a new problem. By the age of thirty-two, Hart had been through a stint in the Army, he'd obtained his real estate license, and most recently he'd started up his own construction company, purchasing billboards around the county to advertise his construction services. He also owned several rental properties. He was also studying for his bachelor's degree online and thought he might try to get his masters when he was done with that. He was also training for a marathon. He also had a dream of one day opening a coffee shop in Onley, near his real estate offices.

Until the arsons, Matt's primary online activities had been two-fold: he talked about his favorite sport, football, or about his beagle, Parker. During the arsons, he posted about the fires. The fires as a source of speculation. Of mystery. Of a macabre kind of entertainment based on the idea that the county had become a dartboard at which an arsonist was randomly throwing darts.

"Question of the day," Matt posted one evening: "Where will the next fire be? I need to make some cold cash."

"I'm going with two picks tonight: Melfa and Wachapreague," one of his friends wrote. "I think it's going to be a double header. He isn't coming to Chincoteague. Our fire department has only a small area to cover; they would be on the scene before he left."

"I like those picks," Matt approved. "I'm impressed, you must be doing your homework." To another friend, whose predicted burning houses hadn't burned, he wrote, "We are sorry to inform you that your picks are invalid. Thank you for playing arsonist lottery. Better luck next time."

Sometimes the speculation turned paranoid. "I wish they would let us have a damn drone," someone wrote on Matt's wall, thinking that a loaner drone would make it easier to catch the arsonists in the act. "Maybe if they just threatened to drop a bomb on any abandoned structures that were burning, we would get lucky."

There were people on the shore who thought that maybe the fires were being set *by* drones. Or they were being set by military special forces, and observed by drones. In the world at large, the NSA was spying on citizens and a government contractor named

Edward Snowden was about to reveal it. It didn't seem out of the realm of possibility that the U.S. government—which already had a NASA rocket-launching facility up the road, thank you very much—would be testing out new tools of warfare and would be doing so in Accomack County.

Matt had more of a vested interest than most people in following the arson proceedings. He'd just purchased a rental house in the town of Cashville. It wasn't fixed up and it didn't yet have tenants, so he was scared it might be targeted as abandoned. One night he grabbed a folding chair and set it up in the rental's living room, staying up all night, looking out into the cornfields. It was, he realized, a little crazy. But he also got a small thrill out of it. It was so definitive, such a tangible course of action to take in the face of something so big and unwieldy.

Law enforcement had originally put forth a $5,000 reward for information leading to the arrests of the arsonist. They later quintupled it, to $25,000. On the shore, this was a huge amount of money—as Sheriff Godwin put it, "On the shore, I will tell on my mom for $5,000."

The reward escalation gave Matt, the man who was never happy unless he had a project, a new endeavor: catch the arsonists.

It started mostly as a joke, with a simple posting on Facebook one night. They were talking about the regular arson matters. One of his friends made a suggestion: "I say we get twenty-five people together and go out one weekend," the friend wrote. "Tell law enforcement where we will be and what we are driving so they know. Each takes an area of the county that keeps getting hit. Catch them and split the money. I would settle for a grand."

"No offense to any law enforcement," the friend continued in a second message, "but if they had this, there wouldn't be a twenty-five thousand dollar reward."

Matt thought the idea sounded funny and went with it. "Haha, okay. Where will we hold our group meeting? Bring camouflage, face paint, and stun gun?"

"I'm with a twenty-five-person posse," wrote a second friend.

"I always wanted to be a detective," wrote a third.

The concept percolated in Matt's brain until it started to seem like a good idea. They were at more than fifty fires by this point and his first friend had been right—it wasn't like law enforcement was getting anywhere, even though they were swarming the county and the Holiday Inn had become a sea of patrol cars as troopers were brought in from all over the state. Maybe they needed a hand.

Matt spread the word that there would be a meeting at his house, for anyone interested. And, being a man accustomed to running his own business and having to think about advertising, Matt realized the first thing they needed was some branding.

He called up his friend Seth Matthews, who was a graphic designer, and the two quickly came up with a design concept: over the front left chest, a small flame, and on the back, a big flame. Over both, a logo: Eastern Shore Arsonist Hunters. T-shirts, available for $22.

The inaugural meeting of ESAH was held in Matt's living room. Three guys showed up: Michael Stefano, a fellow real estate agent whose car had been parked so close to one of the fires that the paint was melted clean off, and Sutton Perry, who had returned to the shore after college and was biding his time working as a technician for an eye doctor while he decided whether to join the military. Seth Matthews, the graphic designer, also showed up. He was recently divorced and had begun to stay up late in his new bachelor pad, listening to the scanner and adjusting to the quietude of his new, single life. He'd tried the bar scene, a little. One night he took a snapshot of some acquaintances, Charlie Smith and Tonya Bundick, and they liked it so well they asked if he would be the photographer for their upcoming wedding.

The four men brought their laptops to Matt's house and pulled up a Google Earth map that the local news had run recently, which plotted all of the fires. Now all they had to do was figure out where the arsonist was going to strike next. He seemed to strike a lot in the central part of the county, they could see that. He was in Tasley a lot, and Parksley, too. As a real estate and construction person, Matt was familiar with many of the properties in those areas, abandoned or otherwise.

Michael Stefano knew the houses, too, but at some point during this meeting, he started to think the whole idea was a little ridiculous. The other guys were young and unencumbered; he was a fifty-seven-year-old businessman and father of two who was now sitting in some vague acquaintance's living room pointing to random locations on a map and talking like he knew what he was doing. "It was all very Colonel Mustard in the library with the candlestick," he would say later about the experience. He didn't go to any more meetings.

But for the others, the idea of finding the arsonist started to mean something. At the end of the meeting, in a way not too different from how the police and sheriff's department had done it, the Eastern Shore Arsonist Hunters came up with their own list of potential targets.

They started by again staking out the house Matt owned down in Cashville. Matt and Sutton set up a couple of lawn chairs behind the big picture window, opened a couple of beers and set to waiting. It was a quiet night on an empty road, and in the hours they sat there only one car passed: a dark-colored Pontiac Grand Am. A little while later it passed again, going in the opposite direction, returning from whatever errand its driver had been running. Right after that, Matt's scanner app went off.

He and Sutton looked at each other. The arson address given on the scanner was less than a mile away. Taking the logical route, the arsonist would have had to drive right past Matt's Cashville house to get to the fire. And there was only one car that had driven in and out, the whole time they were sitting there: a dark-colored Pontiac.

They could feel adrenaline coursing through them, tinged with a disappointing realization. "We can't go driving after them now," Matt pointed out. They'd each had a few drinks. And if they left the house, there would be another problem. To get ready for this stake-out, both men had elected to wear camouflage and carry firearms. Which had seemed prudent earlier, but which now, Matt was realizing, just made them look like crazy arsonists.

They phoned the police to let them know about the car but then watched helplessly as it drove away. The next day, Matt was in the Food Lion parking lot when he saw a guy—tattooed, pierced, carrying a Zippo lighter—walk back to his car, which was a dark-colored Pontiac.

Oh my god, it's him, Matt thought, fumbling for a pen to write down the license plate while dialing Seth on his cell phone. "We found him," he hissed into the phone, getting into his own car and trying to appear nonchalant as he followed the Grand Am out of the parking lot and turned right onto Route 13.

"I think he knew we were following him," Matt would admit later. "I mean, we're not used to following people." For miles, they were on one long, straight road. It hadn't occurred to Matt to do anything like adjust his speed or leave another car in between. Basically, if this guy had looked in his rearview mirror at any point whatsoever he would have seen Matt inching along behind him. Matt stayed with him for a good half hour, at least, until finally he realized they were almost to the Bay Bridge, halfway into Northampton County where the arsonist had never struck. He called it quits and went home.

They didn't give up, though. Matt decided that the T-shirts Seth had designed should be available to all of the public and put them on sale for $22. The proceeds, he announced, would go to the local fire departments. "Buy a shirt, help the fire companies!" he wrote, posting pictures that users had submitted of themselves in the clothes. He also decided they needed to put up some cameras. He didn't know about the ones Bobby Bailey from the fire marshal's office had set up around the county and believed the idea to be entirely new.

There was an abandoned old place down in Tasley, where the arsonist hunters knew the owner and thought he'd be okay with—that he might even appreciate—having a few cameras on his property. One night, late, Matt and Seth pulled up to the entrance, dropping Sutton and quickly driving off so as not to give away their plan.

Sutton tiptoed around the perimeter carrying the camera, trying to find a tree branch with the right height and angle to attach it. After strapping the camera on, he had begun to pick his way back through the woods when he looked up and saw it: another camera, pointing directly at him. It appeared to be much nicer and more professional than the one Sutton had just jerry-rigged to the other tree, and he realized that it must belong to law enforcement. All of the hundreds of abandoned houses on the Eastern Shore, and he, Matt, and Seth had picked the same one as the professionals. He felt a small thrill of pride, and then he started to panic.

These guys are going to think I'm the fucking arsonist, Sutton thought as he ran, panting, back through the woods. *They're going to think, "I know that kid, there's Sutton Perry, he's the arsonist."*

And then he started to think, what if the actual arsonist was there, too, watching him. *What if the arsonist has a gun?* Pant, pant, pant. *We're on the Eastern Shore. Most people have guns. We have cameras and phones.* Pant, pant, pant.

Sutton got back to the car and told Matt and Seth what happened. "I'm not going back to get those trail cams," he said furiously. "If you want them, you can go back and get them."

Matt did go back, tramping through the woods. When he found the law enforcement camera Sutton had described, he tried to figure out which way it was pointing and wave his arms in front of it, mouthing, "I'm not the arsonist. I'm not the arsonist." Then he took down his own camera and he and Sutton and Seth drove away.

Nobody would realize it, but it was possible that the ghostly hand the investigators had seen reaching toward the camera wasn't the arsonist at all; it was Matt Hart embarking on another one of his schemes.

CHAPTER 12

"I'VE SEEN ENOUGH
ASS TO KNOW"

T HEY WERE A LITTLE EXUBERANT, the Eastern Shore
Arsonist Hunters. But then, how do you measure crazy behavior when it was really, perhaps, a normal reaction to a crazy situation? People turned on their friends and neighbors. They just did, it
was the sort of thing you couldn't help doing after enough sleepless
nights. Matt got funny looks from people who thought that anyone
that interested in the case must be trying to hide something. Seth
did, too. One night he got pulled over for speeding, the same night
there had been two big fires in the Fox Grove neighborhood, from
which he had just come.

"Man, I saw the truck with a FoxGrov license plate on the back
and I knew it was you," laughed the state trooper, who turned out to
be a friend Seth had known since they were twelve. He questioned
Seth about his comings and goings, swept his flashlight around the
interior to make sure there were no gas cans, and then let him go.

Seth had no idea that his childhood friend would privately consider him to be a person of interest until much later, after everything was over.

One evening state police investigator Glenn Neal asked an acquaintance to come out and drive around with him. Neal wanted to explore the field where a fire had earlier been set. The acquaintance had some brushes with the law in the past, but he knew those fields really well and he was basically a decent guy. While they were out patrolling, another fire was set and Neal's cell phone rang: a tip from a concerned citizen. The fire that had been set that night, they were sure they knew who had set it. They told him who.

"Are you sure?" Neal asked. The caller said they were sure. "Huh," Neal said, "because he's sitting right next to me."

Everyone had a building that burned, or knew someone who did. Everyone made a 911 call, or knew someone who did. The callers couldn't help but insert the stories of their own day into the emergency calls, as if the fires belonged to all of them, the narrative of a county and its destruction and its fear. "I was just out trying to fix my phone wire," the callers said. Or "I had just come outside to my car." Or "I had just met two state police going down to Saxis." Or "I just left Evergreen Church and I'm on the road from Pungoteague to the Pungoteague School, and there's a house, and it's on fire, and its empty, and I've got cold chills."

"What's the address?" the dispatcher asked the caller from the Pungoteague fire.

"I really don't want to go near that area," the caller said, afraid the arsonist might still be lurking nearby.

The dispatcher paused. "I don't blame you."

On Valentine's day, a call came through that was different from all the others, because it wasn't an abandoned house. The house was occupied by J. D. Shreaves, a single father who ran out for twenty minutes to drop his daughters off at their grandmother's a few miles away. When he came back, he thought he smelled smoke, but after walking from room to room, he figured there must just be a cigarette in the ashtray. But when he picked up his daughters a few hours later, his girls said they smelled something burning, too. This time he went outside and patrolled the perimeter. Under a loose siding panel, someone had stuffed a lit rag and it was still smoldering. Someone had known he'd left the house, and timed the fire accordingly. Someone had been watching. "Girls, calm down," he told his crying daughters as he waited for the dispatcher to send the police. "Your daddy's with you."

One night the arsonist burned a pickup truck carrying wood flooring that its owner hadn't gotten around to installing. Neal was sent to investigate, and when he got there, he realized that the fire was only a few houses down from where his friend Charlie and Charlie's girlfriend, Tonya, lived. Neal was closer with Charlie's brother Bryan, but he knew Charlie, too. As Charlie remembered, they'd first met when Neal pulled him over for a traffic infraction. Charlie, incensed at the ticket, had stormed into Bryan's house ready to complain about the jerk cop he'd just met only to find the cop sitting in his brother's living room. They laughed about it and ended up occasional drinking buddies.

"Let's ride across the street and talk to Charlie and Tonya," Neal suggested to the patrolman he was circling with that night. "I know they'll talk to us."

Charlie seemed a little fidgety when Neal and his patrol partner knocked on the door—at least Charlie himself remembered seeming a little fidgety—but then again, to other people he often seemed that way. After he'd kicked drugs he'd acquired a caffeine habit; those who would see him at the body shop remembered him leaving every hour, on the hour, to run to the gas station for twenty-four-ounce cups of coffee until he was bouncing off the wall like a cartoon chipmunk. "All that coffee is going to kill him," his stepdad would remark, and Neal, who knew Charlie's backstory, once replied, "Yeah. But it's better than what he used to do."

Neal stood in the living room and asked Charlie and Tonya if they were sure they hadn't noticed anything unusual on the night the truck was burned.

"C'mon, man—you can't tell me you didn't see anything," Neal said.

"Naw, man. I ain't seen nothing," Charlie said. "Damn, I wish I'd gotten some parts off of it, because I need parts for a Ford Ranger."

"I'm sure you could get them for cheap now," Neal joked.

"Maybe I should go over and talk to them."

Neal moved on to the next house, another friend he had on the road, and that friend hadn't seen anything either.

Each time a new fire was reported, the geographic profiler Isaac Van Patten plugged the location into his algorithm, hoping to generate a more specific profile. Instead of the circle getting smaller, though, it appeared to stay roughly the same size, just moving slowly southward. By the time Van Patten ran the algorithm several weeks later, the intersection at Matthews Road was no longer a part of the targeted area at all.

^ ^ ^

BY MARCH 5, Bobby Bailey's cameras, the high-tech ones that automatically sent pictures to the investigators' phones, had amassed quite a collection. In addition to the cat chasing the mouse and the ghostly hand, there was also an assortment of birds and wildlife. But he still hadn't caught the arsonist, and this was getting to him on a psychological level. He was supposed to be the guy. The teacher. The fire mastermind. And he hadn't gotten any further with the investigation than his students.

One of Bailey's advantages in this investigation had been that he wasn't tied to it. Not personally—he had no family or friends on the shore—and not professionally, either. While the sheriff's department and the state police all had to operate in a complicated bureaucracy and hierarchy, Bobby was the sole representative on loan from the fire marshal's office. If he wanted to work odd hours, he could work odd hours. If he wanted to requisition extra equipment, it wasn't hard for him to do that either. Best of all, if he wanted to move about anonymously, listen in on strangers' conversations to see if they were talking about the arsons, he could do that without anyone realizing he was law enforcement. Eventually, Facebook began to ruin his advantage, though. Every time he took out his big white truck to examine a fire scene or for some other investigative purpose, the arson groups would immediately take note. They would go online and post the time and the location of his truck, which they'd dubbed the "White Elephant." To mitigate this, Bailey acquired a farming license plate for the vehicle, to disguise its true purpose. It worked, but it added the complication that people now believed he was a farmer. During breakfasts at the Hardee's, Bailey got used to being approached by laborers who heard he might be looking to hire.

"I know you. You got a big chicken farm in Northhampton?" they asked.

"Naw, I'm into small grains," he said, having done his research into Northhampton farming.

"Are you hiring? I heard you pay good."

"Well, now, what things can you do?"

Bailey, in jeans and a cotton shirt, hunched with purpose over his solitary biscuit breakfast, would dutifully interview laborers about their work experience and take down their phone numbers before sending them along. He felt bad about it, but he wasn't sure what else to do. By the time he left Accomack, he figured he could have staffed a medium-sized soybean farm full of reliable workers.

He took to driving the length of the county every night before bed. Starting in Exmore, just south of the Accomack border, where he was staying at the Hampton Inn, and all the way up to the Maryland border, looking and thinking about what he saw. He'd just stepped out of the shower after one of these jaunts on March 5, when he finally caught a break. He heard the sound of a doorbell. It was coming from his phone. More accurately, it was coming from Old Church Road, where he had placed a camera high in the branches of a spindly tree. Bailey glanced at the photograph. Not a squirrel. Not a cat. A shadowy human figure, near an abandoned house.

"Son of a *bitch*," Bailey yelled, pulling on his clothes even as he speed-dialed Neal. "It's rolling, right now!" he said, grabbing his truck keys and hauling ass back up Route 13. In the truck, he got Sheriff Godwin on the radio, who was already en route himself, closing in on Church Road from the other direction. Was tonight the night? Were they finally going to catch him?

"Sheriff, the camera's in the tree!" Bailey screamed into the radio. "In the backyard, there's a locust tree next to a shed. Get to the shed. GET UP IN THE TREE!"

Pulling up to Old Church Road, sirens blazing, Godwin saw the tree Bailey was talking about. He also saw that it was dangerously close to being engulfed in flames from the burning house. Without hesitating, he shimmied up the tree *like a spider monkey*, thought the other deputies who had arrived, while Bobby Bailey, over the radio, screamed, "You got to get that camera!"

"I can't reach the thing!" Godwin yelled back. "It's hot as hell over here!"

"You got to!"

He finally got it down, tossing it like a hot potato, until the investigators could sit down and watch it. When they did, they learned two things.

First, investigators determined that the fire had been going for forty or fifty minutes before it was even called in to 911. They could see the tiny flame on the camera, staying tiny as minutes ticked by. That's how slowly the flames had grown. For months, law enforcement had been breaking their necks to speed to fire sites, assuming every time that they'd just missed the arsonist driving away. But if the fires were growing that slowly, it was possible that the arsonist was already home in bed by the time the police even got to the scene. All of that neck-breaking speed had been for nothing.

They discovered something else, too. For a little while, some of the investigators and profilers had been suspecting that the arsonist could in fact be two people. There were a couple of reasons why. First, at the site where they'd found shoe prints, there had appeared to be two different sets of footwear. Second, and more importantly, some of the properties hit were pretty far back in the woods. If a single arsonist had left a car in the road while he picked through the trees to light the fire, the abandoned car would have been noticed. There were just too many officers on the lookout for suspicious-looking vehicles. But if two people were working together, one could drop the other off in a matter of seconds and arrange for a pickup later. It had to be two people with a close bond and genuine trust in each other, or one of them would have talked. Godwin thought he might be looking for two brothers, or maybe a father and son.

They looked at the photo. It was blurry and hard to tell much. The figure was facing away from the camera, and appeared to be wearing a hoodie, which made identification even more difficult. *Sasquatch*, Bailey thought, thinking of all those blurry photos people posted online that they claimed were of Bigfoot. *The hooded thing that's out there in the abyss but you can't ever really see it.*

And there was another thing about the photo, something all of them noticed but had a hard time putting their fingers on. Something about the tilt of the figure as they'd captured it, midstep, or maybe about the figure's shape. As Bailey remembered, he was the first to articulate what they were struggling to put into words.

"I've seen enough ass to know," Bailey said. "That's a woman."

Some people thought that meant they should consider—at least, consider—the possibility that the arsonist could be female. Other people thought it was only proof that the camera hadn't captured the arsonist after all—it had just snapped a picture of a lady cutting across the field on her way home. Either way, it was the first and only real break they would receive in the case.

^ ^ ^

THEY BARELY HAD ANY TIME to think about what this clue meant.

Seven days later, on March 12, a call came into the 911 Center at 9:27 p.m. "Hi, how you doing?" the caller said to the 911 dispatcher. "I'm over here at the old hotel, and I think you have a fire over here at this particular building. In the rear?"

"So, you did see fire?" the dispatcher asked.

"I see a lot of smoke pouring out of one of the buildings."

"Did you see anybody around?"

"No ma'am, I didn't," the caller said. "I just happened—I live down a little bit on the block, and I smelled it."

While the caller gave his name and phone number in case they got disconnected, the dispatcher was already typing an address into her automated system, to send as many firemen as she could get toward Tasley Road. Whispering Pines was fully involved.

CHAPTER 13

"LIKE HELL WAS COMING UP THROUGH THE GROUND"

OVER IN TASLEY, the firehouse sprang into action. There was no need to wait for volunteers to get to the station—they had been sleeping there for months, in their tangles of sleeping bags and PlayStation controllers. By 9:28, one minute after the 911 call, they were already rolling the engine out of the bay. Bryan Applegate radioed in with their progress as they sped toward the sprawling, abandoned Whispering Pines resort complex, less than a mile away. "Engine eight-five responding," Bryan said. "Engine eight-five par five."

"Flames are showing," the dispatcher warned the crew. "All units responding—another caller advised structure fully involved."

"Eight-five on scene," Bryan radioed in again a moment later as the engine pulled in front of the hotel. "I have command."

At his home three quarters of a mile away, Tasley chief Jeff Beall had just fallen asleep in his recliner when he heard the two-toned alert of his pager. The 911 dispatcher repeating the location of the fire turned out to be completely unnecessary; by the time Beall got to his driveway, he could already see the flames shooting into the sky. "Fuck," he said.

As he barreled down the road toward Whispering Pines, he tried to think of a particular word, a word that meant something was one's destiny, an ultimate goal that one would eventually reach whether they wanted to or not. *Nirvana*, he thought. Later he would realize that it wasn't quite the word he was looking for. Destiny, fate, Everest—all of those would have been more appropriate. But right then, as the firefighter drove to the biggest fire of his career, that was the phrase that kept coming to mind. *This is my Nirvana.*

Whispering Pines was his company's first due. They would be in charge, or more specifically, Beall would. He passed his own team's fire engine on the way to the station, changed into his gear, hopped into a smaller truck, and drove himself to the scene. His heart dropped into his stomach. In front of him, more than half of the Whispering Pines outbuildings had all caught on fire. Darkness had turned to daylight. Embers the size of softballs were leaping off the buildings, toward the front lawns of the little bungalows across the street. Those yards were guarded by pine trees, and the roofs of the houses were covered in four inches of dry pine needles. It would take only one unlucky fireball before the whole neighborhood burst into flames.

Beall scanned the other buildings, the ones that hadn't yet caught fire. Normal protocol would have been to send firefighters into or around those buildings—the closest access point to the active flames. But they were hazardous, on the verge of collapsing even when their structural integrity hadn't been threatened by the presence of nearby flames. Sending volunteers in there meant putting lives in certain danger.

"Chief 8 to central," he radioed in. "We're going to be setting up a defensive system here." He paused. "We're obviously going to be here for a while. Give me two more tankers and have them stage north of the scene."

"Eleven and twelve, bring in your tankers," the dispatcher radioed to Wachapreague and Painter, two stations from farther south in the county, which were on their way with support vehicles.

"And go ahead and have electric respond up here," Beall said, worried about the power lines that crossed Tasley Road.

"We're getting them up here," dispatch said.

"Might want to send two trucks. It's going to be a big operation."

More tankers and engines were arriving on the scene. In addition to the ones from Painter and Wachapreague, there were ones from Onancock, Parksley, and Melfa. The neighbors across the street were all awake, standing in their yards and watching the embers pop out of the hotel's second floor and lob toward their houses.

Beall sent the Wachapreague volunteers, who had just pulled up in their pale yellow truck, across the road to douse the Tasley homes with water. "Have them get out their garden hoses," he called out. It was mostly precautionary, and to give the terrified homeowners a sense of control, but there it was: the homeowners of Tasley were frantically pulling their garden hoses out of summer storage and using them to defend their own homes.

Beall called the remaining fire chiefs on the scene over for an impromptu meeting in front of the dying building: "There's not enough water on the shore to put this fire out," he said.

They needed a new plan and quickly devised one: the goal was no longer to put the fire out. The goal was to use enough water to contain the fire, boxing it in until it devoured everything flammable inside the box, exhausting itself and going out on its own.

Beall sent Bryan Applegate around to the back of the property to monitor the spread. Flames weren't traveling that way yet, but they could.

"How you doing back there?" he radioed back to Bryan, and kept doing so every few minutes. "How's it looking back there? Is it spreading to any other building?"

"It's burned all the way over to this last building," Bryan said. "It still hasn't made it to the roof."

"How you looking, Bryan?" Beall called a few minutes later.

"It's getting pretty hot."

"Make sure eleven knows I want them to stop on Tasley Road, and I want them to be in position so that if this jumps and goes in the woods, I want them to be our first line of defense."

"Let me know when it's under control, for our records," the dispatcher asked, when it became clear that there was nothing more that could be offered from the 911 Center where he was located.

"It won't be under control for several more hours," Beall said.

∧ ∧ ∧

THE NIGHT that Whispering Pines burned down, the county came together. State police investigators Barnes and Neal had office space in the nearby Virginia Department of Forestry; if Neal had been in his office at the time, he would have been able to see flames from his desk. Local teachers and nursery owners and waitresses all heard the warnings on the radio to stay away because traffic was being diverted, and then they all got in their cars and drove precisely to the spot they had been instructed to avoid, just to see it. Pete Blackwell, the DJ who had agreed to work Charlie and Tonya's wedding, happened to be driving nearby and saw flames, and the way the whole landscape seemed to ooze with fire. "It looked," he would later say, "like hell was coming up through the ground."

The fire happened, an article in the local news by reporter Carol Vaughn would later point out, "within yards of an electronic sign on Route 13 advertising a $25,000 reward for information leading to the arrest and conviction of the arsonists." The sign was later changed, warning motorists about heavy smoke in the area.

The news article offered other pieces of information: how one of the onlookers, Charlie Russell, watched the fire because in 1931 his grandfather had constructed the hotel dining room's knotty pine walls that were, in 2013, the first thing to burn. How the grand-

Tonya Bundick and Charlie Smith celebrate Halloween at Shuckers, the site of their meeting and courtship. *(Photo courtesy of Seth Matthews)*

Firefighters work to control one of the larger arsons, a fire at the former Mallards Restaurant near Onancock, Virginia, in March 2013. *(Photo courtesy of Jay Diem)*

Tasley fire chief Jeff Beall and captain Richie Bridges, a volunteer with the company, rest after fighting another fire. *(Photo courtesy of Don Amadeo, Tasley Volunteer Fire Company)*

A vintage postcard depicts Whispering Pines in its heyday as the Eastern Shore's premier resort. *(The Tichnor Brothers Postcard Collection, courtesy of the Trustees of the Boston Public Library)*

Whispering Pines, already in disrepair, became a burned shell after fire destroyed it in March 2013. *(© 2014, Bonnie Jo Mount / The Washington Post)*

Charlie's auto shop and Tonya's clothing store shared a small, weather-beaten storefront in downtown Tasley. *(Photo courtesy of Don Amadeo, Tasley Volunteer Fire Company)*

OPPOSITE, TOP: The Tasley firehouse, where Charlie had volunteered since his twelfth birthday. The Tasley Volunteer Fire Company was called out for more arson fires than any other Accomack fire department. *(Photo by Lydia Outland)*

OPPOSITE, BOTTOM: Accomack County Sheriff Todd Godwin works a police checkpoint on U.S. Route 13 in Tasley, Virginia, on March 8, 2013. *(Photo courtesy of Jay Diem)*

Charlie is interviewed by Todd Godwin and Rob Barnes on the night of his arrest, April 1, 2013.

Charlie's and Tonya's mugshots, taken on the night of their arrest, April 1, 2013, at Accomack County Jail. *(Accomack County Jail)*

Tonya consults with one of her attorneys, Christopher Zaleski, on the first day of her first trial in January 2014. *(Vicki Cronis-Nohe* / Virginia-Pilot *via Associated Press)*

Charlie wipes away tears with cuffed hands as he testifies against Tonya on the stand during one of her trials. *(Vicki Cronis-Nohe /* Virginia-Pilot *via Associated Press)*

father, Charles F. Russell, had offered a prize of a ten-dollar gold piece to the area resident who came up with the winning name for the soon-to-open hotel. How the winner had been a girl named Pearl Bryan, a senior at Accomack High School, who suggested the name "Whispering Pines Tourist Camp." A gala dinner and dance had celebrated the opening of what was the Delmarva peninsula's first modern resort. The parking lot was always full, and the Russell family ran the resort until 1972 when they sold it to a man named Ralph Powers, who shortly thereafter died in front of the building when the truck he was fixing accidentally slipped into gear and ran over him.

Some people were glad to see it go, knowing that it had been an unsafe eyesore. But it was still a sad thing. The fires were causing the county's past to vanish: landmarks gone, horizons changed.

The firefighters of Accomack County fought that fire with the same diligence and care that they fought every fire. Objectively, it wasn't the worst fire of anyone's career. Nobody's life was in danger, nobody needed to fight their way up a burning stairwell, the way Beall and Charlie once did in that burning funeral home. But it was the essential fire. It was the fire they had dreaded and the fire they would talk about. It exhausted them.

"We just did a walk around; everything's clear," said one firefighter into his radio, as March 12 slid into the dark hours of March 13.

"We're outta here," said the chief from Wachapreague, as his volunteers finished up their assigned duties. "Good luck. Call us if you need us."

As time dragged on, radio updates became less frequent, there was nothing to do but wait as planned for the fire to wear itself down. The beginnings of fires were always filled with adrenaline and anticipation. The ends of them were soot and weariness and fire hoses that needed to be cleaned. The ground was hot and the wood wasn't wood anymore. The parts of the hotel that hadn't burned—the rooms with the blue furniture and gold-filigree wallpaper—would be so doused in water as to retain a permanent stench of mildew. Fire killed one part of the hotel, water killed another, and eventually, months later, the earth would snake up through the collapsed beams, saplings and vines snaking through the fallen architecture, and in this way the old hotel was completely given over to the elements, ashes to ashes, dust to dust.

"We're done. Let's shut everything down, baby," Beall finally said into his radio. It was 2:51 a.m.

The Whispering Pines hotel took nearly six hours to burn down, causing $300,000 worth of damage. When it was finally under control, the news reporters, who had positioned their trucks around the perimeter, establishing their live shots and doing sound checks, began to approach the soot-covered volunteers, beckoning them to position themselves near the gutted-out front entrance of the hotel, where the devastation was the most severe and the shot was the most dramatic.

A reporter from the Salisbury Fox affiliate latched herself onto Beall and asked if he would do an interview. He said okay. He was getting good at sound bites by this point; he'd given enough interviews. "We all have jobs. We all have families. We all have lives," he told the camera. "This has cut into everything. Our fuel cost is tripled. We're going through a lot of equipment. The biggest toll it's taking is on personnel. We're all volunteers, and it's really taking its toll."

After the interview, the reporter, Cleo Greene, had to wait for her next live shot. Beall thought she looked cold and sleepy and he was right; she lived ninety minutes away and had driven down to the fire scene as soon as the scanner app went off on her own phone. Beall said if she had more interview questions, they could go sit in his truck where it was warmer. He must have drifted off midsentence, and the reporter must have followed suit soon after, because the next thing he knew, the news station's cameraman was tapping on the glass and pointing at his watch. They had to get back up to

Maryland to file their piece. "Is there a message you'd like to send to the arsonist?" Greene asked.

"Take a break," Beall said. "I need one."

The news reporter asked him what his plans were for the rest of the day, now that the Whispering Pines fire was put out.

"I'm going to go home and take a shower and come right back," he told her.

"Why are you going to come back?" he remembered her asking.

"Because this is my fucking fire."

∧ ∧ ∧

FINALLY, IT HAD TO BE OVER. There could have been no better metaphor and no better final message for the arsonist than burning down Whispering Pines. If he had burned down Whispering Pines and then stopped, he would have burned down sixty-six build-ings and he never would have been caught. That would have been a more appropriate end to the story, an unsolved mystery, a blaze of glory. But the pagers went off the next night, and it wasn't over quite yet.

CHAPTER 14

TONYA AND CHARLIE

T HE WEDDING PLANNING was moving along.

Tonya told friends she was envisioning a large affair, more than three hundred guests, the party of the year, since neither she nor Charlie had ever been married before. They had decided the reception would be at Shuckers, the place of their meeting, courtship, and engagement. "Announcement will be in paper in January," they posted in October on their shared Facebook page, but they encouraged interested guests to RSVP right away, via e-mail. They needed to be able to estimate food and drink costs, plus, "security will be tight," they warned. Some folks were surprised that they would even have three hundred people to invite. In the 2010 census, the entire population of Tasley was three hundred people.

Word also got around that the wedding would have a theme: "November Rain," like the 1991 Guns N' Roses power ballad, and that Tonya would be wearing a dress like model Stephanie Seymour had worn in the music video, short in the front but with a long train in the back. This, too, seemed a little odd—in the video, Seymour is an unhappy bride who dies at the end—but it was a first marriage for both of them, so they could be excused for being a little full of it. Still, security at a wedding? Who did Charlie and Tonya think they were?

Jeff Beall heard Charlie was scrounging around for extra jobs, so he could afford the dress Tonya had in mind. Charlie told him it would run in the thousands. Beall had always tried to throw auto-repair work Charlie's way, but he was horrified by the expense of the wedding. He tried to make his feelings known: he didn't like Tonya. Something seemed weird about her. Something seemed weird about the whole situation. Charlie was upset at the suggestion that the wedding was an extravagantly delusional fantasy. The men's friendship dissolved.

^ ^ ^

WHEN THINGS FALL APART, it sometimes happens quickly, and it sometimes happens slowly, and it sometimes happens so that you find yourself in the middle of a big pile of shit that is so deep and all-encompassing that you don't even realize you're in it.

The first thing that started to go wrong, Charlie thought later, when he would look back on it, had to do with Tonya's older son. Charlie had fallen hard for those boys, just like he had for their mother. But it was apparent to him that the older boy, now thirteen, was troubled. He was acting out at school, he was acting out at home. He took a swing at Charlie once, with the sharp edge of a skateboard; it sliced Charlie's back from shoulder to waist. He jumped out of their moving car one afternoon when he was being taken somewhere he didn't want to go. Tonya was sick about it, and Charlie was sick about her, and neither one of them knew the best way to deal with the behavior. Out of desperation, Charlie tried calling his old friend with the state police, Glenn Neal. "Can you come over and scare the shit out of him?" he asked, "because this kid is acting up in school."

"I'm not going to do that—I don't want him to be afraid of the police," Neal said. "But I will come over and talk to him with you." Neal went over and sat in the living room and tried to have a heart-to-heart with Tonya's oldest boy. Neal told him to listen to the teachers, and if he didn't agree with them, to come home and talk to Tonya so she could fight his battle for him. He thought the kid seemed a little more troubled than a typical kid, but hoped that it was still probably nothing he wouldn't grow out of. "Don't put your mama through this," he finished. "She's trying as hard as she can."

Doctors threw a storm of diagnoses at them, but nobody really knew for sure what was going on. The boy was a good kid, sick and apologetic about his own behavior. But it wore on them. When he acted out at school, Tonya or Charlie would be called to pick him up, and after they'd both missed too many shifts, they decided it would be better for Tonya to quit her job and dedicate herself full time to his care. After the problems got worse, they decided to remove him from school entirely and start a homeschooling program. That was the unspoken reason why they decided Tonya should open up her clothing shop. Working her own hours was the only way to guarantee that she'd be able to be around for her kids.

Charlie's relationship with his own daughter was disintegrating in a different way. Her once frequent visits to the house had slowed and then stopped; Charlie told himself it was because she was getting older and would rather hang out with her friends than her dad, but later he heard that the girl's mother didn't trust him, didn't trust Tonya, and thought they were both on drugs.

All of this might have been bearable except that in May of 2012, Charlie's mother died. It was the same cancer that had already taken her sister and brother, Charlie's favorite uncle. The blow was staggering. Charlie's mother had not only been his unfailing supporter, but also the string that bound him to the rest of the family, his stepfather and half-siblings. Without them, Tonya was his only family. And because Tonya's own mother had died, and her sister was estranged, he was hers.

And all of this might have been bearable, or even solvable, if they'd had any money to put toward fixing it. But Tonya had quit her nursing job so she could be more available for her kids, and the clothing store wasn't making any profits. The payments on the furniture sets they'd purchased in optimism were due now, and they didn't have the money. Charlie was picking up the jobs he could, but Accomack's perpetual recession left other people's wallets thin, too, and there were only so many cars he could repaint. Charlie knew the deli counter guy at Food Lion. He sometimes passed Charlie recently expired meat, which Charlie used to feed their animals. The meat was perfectly fine, the guy had told Charlie—it was just government regulations that forced him to throw the food out. One night Charlie found himself picking through the dumpsters behind Food Lion looking for perfectly fine meat, not for the pets, but for his family.

Even the house seemed to be turning against them. Tonya had always been fanatical about keeping up with cleaning—she'd holler if the forks were put in the knife tray or vice versa; she said her dad had been that way, too, which was one of the few things Charlie had ever heard her say about her father. But they'd acquired a Chihuahua that kept pooping on the floor, and it made the house stink, and the very space seemed like it was collapsing in on them.

They couldn't ask anyone for help. Charlie thought Tonya didn't want to. She said that if they displayed any kind of weakness, other people were likely to use it against them. Their good friends Jay and Danielle were recently less a part of their lives. Danielle, after trying to match them together, had decided they weren't good together and was trying to break them up. She said Charlie wasn't good enough for Tonya. It made the couple furious.

And all of that might have been bearable, except for this other Thing, this big Thing. This other, big, embarrassing Thing that

Charlie didn't know how to deal with. This Thing had started to make him feel like he wasn't good enough for Tonya and afraid others would think so, too. He was afraid she would leave him any day.

He needed to talk to somebody about the Thing, so one day he showed up at the office of John Burr, a local Baptist minister who had comforted Charlie's family when his mother died. Burr didn't know Charlie well, but he was a patient, unflappable listener. He encouraged Charlie to come to Bible study, which Charlie did, and also to bring Tonya into his office so they could all talk about the Thing together. At one of those meetings, Charlie and Tonya asked Burr if he would be the minister at their wedding. Burr thought about it and decided he couldn't; it would go against his beliefs to marry two people who were already living together. In order for him to perform the ceremony, Charlie would need to first move out so they could recommit themselves to doing things the right way. Charlie was angry.

"Calm down," Tonya told him in the presence of the minister. "It's okay."

It didn't feel okay. None of it did. It felt like their world used to be beautiful and now it was shit.

The strange, surreal aspect about all of this is that nobody else knew how bad it had gotten. Both Tonya and Charlie had told a few people that they were struggling with the kids, but others assumed it was just normal growing pains. People knew vaguely that there were money troubles—though they believed them to just be wedding related, the way weddings stretched many couple's budgets. Only a few people seemed to start to see the cracks. An old friend noticed that Charlie seemed more withdrawn than usual. At work, Bryan Applegate thought his brother seemed sadder and sadder, for lack of a better way to describe it. He thought Charlie's relationship might be to blame, but he never brought it up; it didn't seem like the kind of thing a younger brother should mention.

Tonya and Charlie were still going out for dinners, and making it to the bar once or twice a week, because keeping up appearances seemed so deeply important to Tonya, Charlie thought, and because despite everything, neither of them was able to fully accept what was painfully obvious: in the span of six months, their lives had fallen apart.

A respite from all of this was driving, out at night, after the kids were safely asleep. They drove to McDonalds or to Walmart, the place where Tonya had always been able to make Charlie laugh. Or they drove out to nowhere in particular. Miles of empty roads in Accomack meant hours of time to blow off steam.

And then one night, they were driving around the county like they always did, trying to sort through their lives like they always did. Charlie remembered Tonya telling him how grateful she was that he was in her life. Maybe God had put him there for a reason, to help her with her son and to show her that it was possible for a troubled kid to grow up and be a good man. She knew it hadn't been easy on Charlie, and she wanted him to know that he could leave if he needed to, no hard feelings. On this night, she said that just as they were driving past an old abandoned house on Dennis Drive. It was November 12, 2012.

"I'm in it for the long haul," Charlie said. "I'll do whatever it takes for you to be happy."

Tonya said, as Charlie remembered, "Get out and set that house on fire."

Charlie looked up. It was such a non sequitur to anything they'd been discussing, he wondered if he'd misheard something.

They'd already driven once past an old white house set back in the field, and now Tonya, who was driving, looped back again and had pulled to a stop.

"I want you to set that house on fire," she repeated. Charlie laughed. He realized he'd heard right, but now assumed it was some kind of joke, Tonya messing around, like she did at Walmart or McDonalds to put them in better moods.

Keeping up with the joke, he got out of the car. He walked

through the field, into the house, and stood around for a while, wondering how far he was supposed to take the prank. She pulled away with the car, and few minutes later, she called him on his cell phone. "Have you done it?" she asked.

"Yeah," he teased back. "I done it."

After a few minutes, the car pulled back around. When Charlie got inside, he was surprised. It didn't seem like Tonya. It seemed like a different version of Tonya: a lighter, happier version he hadn't seen in months. That's when he realized she'd been serious. She wasn't in a better mood because she'd been joking about the house. She was in a better mood because she'd been serious, and she thought he'd done as she asked. She was a beautiful, mysterious woman that he still, after several years, at some level didn't know at all.

The realization made him worried and confused. But it was mixed with relief. After months of feeling like he was a disappointment to Tonya, like she was on the verge of leaving him, he had finally done something that made her happy.

They drove around and it was just like old times, like Tonya was imagining all the bad stuff had gone up in the smoke of that ugly house on Dennis Drive that nobody lived in anymore anyway.

After an hour, she wanted to go back and see the burning house. They did, but it wasn't burning. Charlie made up an excuse about how it could take a while for the flames to show because he'd set the fire in a small closet. They drove past it again and again, and Tonya kept asking why she didn't see any flames yet. Eventually, Charlie couldn't think of any other excuses. He had to tell her he'd lied. He hadn't actually lit anything on fire.

She didn't seem mad, really. Just a little exasperated that she'd entrusted Charlie with a task he clearly wasn't up to. "Never send a man to do a woman's job," he remembered her teasing, but almost in a friendly, flirtatious way.

They went back, and they burned that house down, Charlie says, and then they burned sixty-six more after it.

CHAPTER 15

"THEY'RE NOT
HUNTERS AT ALL"

APRIL I.
 The team of criminal profilers—Isaac van Patten, Jon Cromer, Ron Tunkel, Ken Morris—had been coordinating the psychological part of the investigation from afar for too long. Five and a half months into the fires and they still hadn't all been to Accomack at the same time. Tunkel had come down once around Christmas, but that was a period when the fires came to a stop for a couple of weeks. At the time everyone had hoped they were done for good, so Tunkel had gone back home. Isaac Van Patten hadn't been there at all.

On this day, April Fools' Day, they'd managed to all get there. They hoped that having their shoes on the ground would give them new insights into the man or men they were trying to catch. There were things you couldn't know until you were there in person.

Tunkel was asked to give a presentation to some of the fire investigators who were desperate for something, anything, that could help forward their psychological understanding of the arsonist. Jon

Cromer remembered sitting in the audience and being impressed with his colleague's work, and the way he vividly described how to best embolden witnesses to come forward. "He will make a mistake," Tunkel said. Police should trigger citizens' memories by encouraging them to trust their instincts and be on alert for anything out of the ordinary.

One person at the meeting, a police supervisor, had a question for further down the line: When they did catch the guy or guys, how should they question him? What should be the protocol?

Tunkel demurred—he was hesitant to offer a boilerplate protocol when every situation required nuance. The questioner pressed on: "Listen," he said, "my boys might catch him tonight, and we won't have time to get up with you." They needed something general they could work with if push came to shove.

Tunkel tried to formulate something general that would be of use. He talked about power. "Arson is a means of power. Fire setting is a means of demonstrating power," he said. "Serial arsonists tend to be unempowered people. These aren't captains of industry or successful businessmen."

On television, police interrogations often involved an officer browbeating a suspect, or two of them ganging up until the suspect finally cracked. That wouldn't be the way to go in this case, he explained. The person or persons lighting the fires were already having a bad year, some of the people in the room remembered him saying. The way to get him to talk wouldn't be to berate him, but to be gentle. Make it clear the investigators understood where the arsonist was coming from. Make it feel like some of the power was being returned to him.

"We know there's some goodness in you," Tunkel suggested saying to the arsonist. "We know that whatever was going on in your life, there was a lot of stress. We appreciate the fact that most of the buildings were unoccupied." Tunkel suggested reminding the arsonist of the chickens at the Gomez house. Remind him how he made sure to let them out before lighting the garage on fire. He didn't have to do that, but when he was given the opportunity to be compassionate, he chose to be compassionate.

"Anyway," Tunkel concluded, "these are common suggestions. If we were to write an interview strategy, we would most likely talk about these things."

Either after or before the presentation for law enforcement—it was hard to remember—the psychological profilers all got in a few cars and took a tour of the county.

As they drove through the unfamiliar place for the first time together, Ron Tunkel's heart began to sink. One of the concepts that he'd always held firm on was the idea of the unknowing witness—the assumption that, with this many fires, someone would have seen something. With this theory, if the police could only trigger the memory of that unintentional witness, they would have a break-through in solving the crime. Now that he was looking at the land-scape, he realized that assumption might not hold. The landscape was more barren than he had imagined. The houses were farther apart, the streets weren't well lit, the shops closed up earlier. *There's* nobody *out here at night*, he thought. Had one of his premises been wrong? Suddenly, it seemed completely plausible to him that some-one could light seventy or eighty fires without anyone else seeing.

Isaac Van Patten felt a similar sense of frustration. Looking at the case from back home in western Virginia, the sheer number of fires had led him to believe that the arsonists were likely to be either exceptionally skilled or exceptionally audacious. Now he, like Tunkel, saw that these arsons hadn't necessarily required smarts or bravery. The county he was looking at was isolated and dark. *They're not hunters at all*, he thought to himself. *They're like a duck hunter who is sitting on his boat and the entire flock just happens to land around him.*

That night, around the county, the usual arson-catching appara-tus was slipping into gear like a well-oiled machine. The men in tents were settling in for the night, on an evening that felt uncommonly cold. The men in cars were refueling, making sure they had enough coffee and gas to get them through their shifts. The firefighters were getting home and getting to bed early, before dusk. Daylight savings time had begun a few weeks before and made it even harder to get enough sleep. Scott Wade, the detective who had run into Tonya in the Royal Farms and visited her house during his canvassing, was also home asleep. Rob Barnes was at the state police office in Melfa, wading through backlogged paperwork. Glenn Neal had just arrived in Atlantic City, having finally accepted a superior's advice that he needed to get away for a long weekend and clear his head.

The psychological profilers went out to a late dinner, to talk over the day and come up with strategies. They were filled with a sense of renewed anticipation: Now that they understood the landscape, now that all of their brains were in one room, they might at last have the tools they needed to understand who the arsonist was. The anticipation was tempered by dread. What if they were even further off than they'd realized? What if they never caught him?

But they would. Sooner than they thought.

CHAPTER 16

"I DIDN'T LIGHT THEM ALL"

S TATE TROOPERS WILLIE BURKE AND TROY JOHNSON
had been in position since just after sundown, in their camouflage pup tent with a tiny little space heater set up fifty yards behind
the little bungalow on Airport Road. The address belonged to an
older man who now lived on the mainland of Virginia but wanted
a weekend house for when he came back to the shore to visit family. This owner had just put on a new roof and new windows,
but the building still looked dilapidated enough that it had been
placed on law enforcement's watch list of abandoned properties.
It had a little porch. To its right was a field and then some woods
and then, far beyond that, a little post office, and then the little
town of Melfa. To its left was a field and then the entrance to the
airport the road was named after, which was small and used only
by private planes. The nearest house was a quarter mile away. It
was everything the arsonist seemed to like: abandoned-feeling, set
back from the road, accessible from multiple access points. Burke
and Johnson had been sitting behind it for two weeks. "Post 6,"

the house had been dubbed, one of ten or twelve houses equipped with twenty or twenty-four sheriff's deputies and state troopers among them.

Burke and Johnson had known each other a long time, having previously worked in neighboring counties. The two men made sure to sit next to each other at orientation when they first arrived, and had volunteered to be posted at the same house. The first day of their post, a superior joked, "Y'all gonna catch this guy this weekend or what?" and Johnson had answered that he hoped so.

But instead it had been two weeks of damp and boredom, hanging around the hotel or going to the diner during the day, folding themselves into a hunter's tent each night, switching off responsibilities for the radio and the night-vision goggles. Other fires had been set those two weeks, but none that had been guarded by men in tents. Tonight was Burke and Johnson's last night before they would each be returned to their respective home counties. It was also Johnson's birthday and he was glad to be going home. It was hard to keep your eyes fresh for that many hours, staring at the same stretch of two-lane road and eyeballing every infrequent car that passed and trying to keep their voices low. They just had another couple of hours in their shift until it would all be over.

At 11:45 p.m., Burke suddenly cut off: "There's a vehicle," he whispered, "pulling up." Johnson clamped his own mouth shut. The vehicle was a van. It rolled to a stop in front of the house and, in the dark, a figure leaped out of the passenger side.

Instinctively, both men reached to turn off the space heater, to dim the orange glow it produced. The figure was running at a dead sprint toward the house, and the van that had just dropped him—it appeared to be a him—pulled away.

It was Johnson's evening for the night-vision goggles. He pulled them out now.

"He's running, he's running to the back side of the house," he whispered to Burke, who had pulled out the radio. Fifty yards away, the figure sprinted to the back of Post 6 and made a series of rapid motions, stuffing what appeared to be a piece of cloth in the doorjamb. Three or four times, Johnson could make out a brief flicker that would quickly extinguish again. In the green glow of the night-vision goggles, the figure and the flames were both a sickly chartreuse.

"He's lighting it," Johnson told Burke. "He's stuffing some material in and lighting it."

The house has to catch on fire, Johnson thought, forcing himself to stay in position even while he was itching to go get the guy. If he and Burke didn't let the arsonist try to burn down the house, all they had on their hands was a trespassing charge.

Johnson narrated everything he was seeing to his partner, who quietly radioed it into central command and to their support vehicle, a sheriff's deputy who was circling nearby, ready to swoop in.

It seemed to Johnson like time had slowed. The adrenaline in his veins caused every second of the scene in front of him to pause and crystalize, even though he knew he couldn't have been watching for more than a couple of minutes. Suddenly, the rag caught fire in a shower of sparks and the figure started running again, back around the house in the direction he had first come from.

Johnson and Burke threw the tent off, running toward the clearing through a patch of woods so rocky and pitted they would later be surprised one of them hadn't twisted something in the process. "State police, stop!" Johnson yelled. "Stop!"

The man didn't even seem to realize he'd been spotted. He appeared to be talking to somebody, maybe through a cell phone they couldn't make out in the dark. The two officers had barely cleared the woods when, in what seemed to Johnson like perfect timing, the minivan reappeared and the man jumped into it, speeding off toward the county's only main road, Route 13.

The two men stared helplessly after the van. They'd been dropped off and didn't have a vehicle at the ready, but they kept their eyes on it as long as they could, while Burke narrated the receding van's location to the support vehicles in their vicinity. The van had gotten a good distance, maybe a mile, down the road. But the street was straight and they could see it stop at the intersection of Route 13. A second later a marked Dodge Charger—the sheriff's deputy who had picked up Burke's radio for help—appeared behind the van and quietly waited.

The driver of that car was a sergeant who had heard the words "Location 6" and "van" on his radio and immediately began scanning the road for the car in question. It wasn't hard. When the vehicle appeared, it was the only one on the road besides him. The light turned green and the van started to pull through it. He knew other deputies had been alerted and that backup was on the way, but for now he was alone. He turned on his siren. The van in front of him stopped and the passenger door opened. The sergeant, afraid that his suspect was about to run, immediately got out of his own vehicle. In the dark, the passenger raised his hands in a position of surrender and stepped into the light of the squad car's headlamps.

And it was Charlie Smith.

Charlie Smith. A man the sergeant had known for fifteen years and seen most mornings getting coffee at The Wine Rack.

Charlie.

Another vehicle pulled up. Inside was a young state trooper named Martin Kriz. When Kriz saw that the sheriff's deputy had turned on his blue lights and parked near the passenger's side, Kriz put on his own lights and pulled near the driver's. He drew his weapon as he slowly approached the car. Behind the wheel was Tonya Bundick, hair messy, wearing a sweatshirt and jeans. He didn't know her. He didn't know Charlie, either. Like the other two state troopers a half mile down the road, Kriz had never laid eyes on Accomack before that week when he'd been loaned out from his home base in Goochland County near the center of the state.

"Do you have any weapons?" Kriz asked.

"There's a ChapStick in my bra," Tonya told him, and he removed it from the strap and escorted Tonya to his squad car.

There were maybe twenty cars around by that point: troopers and deputies who had been assigned to the Airport Road jurisdiction, troopers and deputies who were on duty elsewhere but had heard the arsonists had been caught, troopers and deputies who weren't on duty at all. Everyone who had access to a police scanner had come, from all around the county, to offer assistance or just to look, at the ghost they'd been chasing since the middle of November.

Between December 1, when the Virginia State Police began collecting data on its arson investigation, and mid-April, police personnel dedicated 26,378 work hours and 14,924 overtime hours to solving the arsons.

All of the cameras they'd placed. All of the forensic evidence they had submitted. All of those rumors about the police closing in on a suspect. All of that meant nothing. Until Charles Smith wandered onto the property of Airport Road with a lighter, law enforcement had been no closer to catching him than they were five and a half months ago.

The firefighters of the Tasley department were called out for the fire, but then called back at the last minute. The flames hadn't fully involved the house, and the Melfa and Onley departments were already on the way and thought they could handle it. The Tasley members got close enough to the scene only to register that there seemed to be more police cars than usual, then Jeff Beall turned the engine around and most of the firefighters went home, grateful for the night off.

One of the firefighters from Tasley, Bryan Applegate, didn't immediately go back to the station when the call was canceled. The scene commander at the burning house decided he still needed a tanker. Bryan was driving one, with another volunteer next to him, so he continued to the scene. As they got closer to the fire, Bryan noticed that all of the cop cars seemed to be clustered around a particular vehicle. At the same time Bryan realized the cops might have finally caught the arsonist, he also realized that the surrounded vehicle looked just like his brother Charlie's new minivan.

"Did I just see what I thought I saw?" he asked the friend sitting next to him.

"I don't know," the friend said, but his voice sounded like he knew.

Once they got to the burning house, Bryan recognized the chief in command as a friend. "You got an airpack?" the chief asked him. "I need another firefighter after all."

This house was going to be different, Bryan learned. The fire companies couldn't just let it burn to the ground because it might be used for evidence in a trial. Someone needed to actually go inside and put the fire out, and the chief was asking that one of those people be Bryan. He suited up. Inside the smoky, half-redone house there were wood pilings and construction beams, flammable renovation materials that needed to be cleared away. The few firemen present attacked the flames with an inch and three-quarter water line, spraying water up into the rafters, an attack that lasted eight minutes, from 11:54 p.m. to 12:02 a.m. Afterward, a police officer asked Bryan if he could stay around for a few more minutes. He needed Bryan to sign a statement saying what he'd done in the house, so it could be incorporated as evidence. Bryan paced and waited for the form. There were a lot of minivans in Accomack.

He signed the paperwork, took the tanker back to the station, and then immediately got in his own car and started driving north toward Hopeton and Charlie's house. He just wanted to get there and see the van, parked safely in the driveway, porch lights off, everyone asleep, and learn that it had all been a mistake. Bryan crawled up Bayside Road until he got to the point where it intersected with Matthews Road. He couldn't even turn onto it. The whole street was blocked off with police cars. Bryan turned around, drove home, and never talked to Charlie again.

Back at the scene of the fire, someone radioed Todd Godwin,

who had been out patrolling the roads, as he had been every night for the past five and a half months. When he heard the arsonist had been arrested, he started driving toward the scene in his own marked car. At Airport Road, Charlie asked to see him, so Godwin went to the police car where Charlie was handcuffed, waiting to be taken in for questioning.

"Todd," said Charlie, because everyone called the sheriff "Todd," because everyone knew everyone here in Accomack County, "I'm sorry. But I didn't light them all."

CHAPTER 17

"SOMEDAY THEY'LL GO DOWN TOGETHER"

W E NEED TO ADDRESS, for a moment, Bonnie and Clyde. The American gangsters, the country's most photogenic public enemies, for whom only first names are needed.

They met, by most accounts, in 1930 when Bonnie Parker was twenty and Clyde Barrow was a year older, at a friend's house in West Dallas. By then, Clyde had already been arrested a few times for petty misdeeds—possession of a truckload of stolen turkeys, in one instance. He and Bonnie fell in love, and then they fell into crime. Later, after Faye Dunaway and Warren Beatty had played them in cinematic glory, they would be known for their bank robberies and getaways. But most of their holdups were actually at rural gas stations or small-town general stores. The Barrow gang, which also included Clyde's brother and his wife, would walk in, demand money, shoot anyone who got in the way during their escape, and then move on to the next town, the next motel hideout, the next caper.

They were violent—in the process of their crimes they killed at least nine police officers and civilians—but they were also glamorous. Clyde was tall and strong; Bonnie was petite with piercing eyes and a bow-shaped mouth. Her leg had been permanently disfigured in a car accident and it was difficult for her to walk, so Clyde often carried her. In a pile of photographs discovered at one of their hideouts, which newspapers printed and reprinted, one image showed Clyde holding Bonnie aloft with one arm, their faces pressed cheek to cheek. In other pictures, they playfully pointed firearms at each other, smoked cigars, mugged for the camera. Bonnie wrote poetry about their exploits—rhyming ballads that went on for dozens of stanzas and were memorable and recitable, if slightly clunky:

> They call them cold-blooded killers
> They say they are heartless and mean
> But I say this with pride, I once knew Clyde
> When he was honest and upright and clean.

Bonnie and Clyde became, in other words, the ur-template for American crime-spree couples: repellent, but also alluring and, above all else, in love. Their crimes felt uniquely American. Not merely because they happened in the dust and heat of the United States south and southwest, but because these crimes were viewed by much of the American public as a reaction to the Great Depression. "Gaunt, dazed men roamed the city streets seeking jobs," writes historian E. R. Milner in *The Lives and Times of Bonnie and Clyde*. "Breadlines and soup kitchens became jammed, foreclosures forced more than 38 percent of farmers from their lands . . . by the time Bonnie and Clyde became well-known, many felt that the capitalistic system had been abused by big business and government officials. Now here were Bonnie and Clyde striking back."

They were products of their times, and they defined how generations of Americans would view and interpret lovers who broke the law. And when they died, they died together in a rain of bullets, faithful to each other until their end.

There's a French term, *folie à deux*, which literally means "madness of two." It refers to a psychiatric disorder where two patients share the same delusion, cultivating it together and transmitting it back and forth between each other. A husband and wife might grow to both believe, for example, that the federal government is bugging their home, or a mother and daughter might come down with the same psychosomatic symptoms and blame them on the same nonexistent illness. There is no comparable term for an evilness of two, wherein two people jointly decide to commit crimes. But it happens.

How else to explain Paul Bernardo and Karla Homolka, for example, who became known as the Ken and Barbie killers because of their clean-cut good looks and preppie clothing? In the early 1990s, they together raped and murdered three girls in the Canadian province of Ontario. The victims included Karla's fifteen-year-old sister, whose drugged assault the couple filmed and later re-created in a different home movie. Karla, in the re-creation, play-acted the role of the deceased teenager as she and Paul had sex on her sister's bed.

How else to explain Nathan Leopold and Richard Loeb, two brilliant young friends and occasional lovers who, in the shadow of Chicago's 1924 jazz obsession and under the thrall of the German philosopher Friedrich Nietzsche, decided that they were living examples of Nietzsche's "supermen," superior beings unbound by the pedestrian rules that governed the rest of humanity? After conspiring on a few burglaries, they came up with the idea to put their intelligence to the test with an intellectual challenge: committing the perfect murder. They chose their fourteen-year-old victim at random—he was a cousin of Loeb's but no personal offense was intended, they insisted—stopping him on his way home from school and bludgeoning him to death before they'd driven more than two blocks.

Romantic partners have staged kidnappings, holding prisoners in their basements and garages. They have robbed banks and stolen cars. They have forged $45 million worth of art, in the case of Wolfgang and Helene Beltracchi, who conspired to reproduce the works of more than fifty artists before being captured in 2011.

The public is fascinated by these couples, these incidences of crazy love put prominently on display, these people who had found quite literal ways to answer the quintessential romantic thought experiment, "Do you love me enough to do something mad? To die for me? To kill for me?" Hollywood has made not one but seven movies inspired by Charles Starkweather and Caril Ann Fugate, teenage lovers—Caril Ann was only fourteen in 1958 at the time of their crimes—who, after killing Caril's disapproving family, then embarked on a two-monthlong murder spree that left a total of eleven people dead. A Caril Ann-based character was played by Sissy Spacek in 1973 (*Badlands*), then Juliette Lewis in 1993 (*Kalifornia*), then Juliette Lewis again in 1994 (*Natural Born Killers*). *Badlands*, the most critically successful of the filmed versions, was heralded a masterpiece of its time: "A cool, sometimes brilliant, always ferociously American film," wrote the chief film critic for the *New York Times*. "Sheen and Miss Spacek are splendid as the self-absorbed, cruel, possibly psychotic children of our time."

The psychologists who study criminal couples have discovered that the partnerships are rarely equal ones. The crimes are usually spurred on by one dominant partner: one half of the couple has the fantasy, and he or she works to bring their paramour into that fantasy world. "There's radar, gaydar, and maybe, mur-dar," criminal psychologist Gregg McCrary told a reporter in *Psychology Today*, in a story about how otherwise law-abiding individuals can together become criminals. "It resembles the phenomenon wherein normal people meet and decide that they're going to get along," he continued. "But with these couples, it takes a dark turn. They vector in on each other, sensing the excitement of a kindred spirit. It becomes electric."

Bonnie Parker was reportedly a sweet-tempered waitress before she met Clyde. She'd married another local boy before she even turned sixteen, but the relationship was abusive and ended after a few years. By the time she met Clyde, she was thirsty for love and excitement. "I never did want to love you and I didn't even try," she wrote in a letter to him during one of the stints he was in prison during their courtship. "You just made me. Now I don't know what to do."

Their love was dysfunctional, and ill-advised, and a hundred other bad things—but it was also passionate and abiding. Long before she and Clyde were ambushed in Louisiana by police who had been tipped off to their location, Bonnie had decided that she would never leave Clyde, she would never turn on him, and that she didn't even want to live in a world without him. "Someday they'll go down together," she wrote in another poem. "And they'll bury them side by side. / To a few it'll be grief, to the law a relief—but it's death for Bonnie and Clyde." And it was indeed death. The Louisianans who lived near the scene of the shoot-out were allegedly so enamored by the end of the Bonnie and Clyde love story that they sneaked over to the bodies when the police were otherwise occupied and cut off locks of Bonnie's hair.

Not all criminal romances end so poetically. When Karla Homolka and Paul Bernardo were arrested in 1993—forensic evidence linked Paul to the scene of one of the murders—Karla immediately turned on her husband. She told police officers that she had been Paul's victim as well, battered and abused throughout their marriage, and that she'd only gone along with the rapes and killings because she feared for her own life. Paul, on the other hand, told law enforcement that while the rapes had been his idea (he'd assaulted more than a dozen women before ever meeting Karla, earning the moniker, "The Scarborough Rapist"), he'd never murdered any of the previous women he'd raped, and he wouldn't have killed the three he and Karla attacked, either. Killing those girls was Karla's idea; she was afraid the victims would later be able to identify them. Ultimately, prosecutors decided that Karla's testimony was more important than his and they wouldn't be able to get a conviction without her serving as a witness. While Paul received a life sentence in prison, Karla received only twelve years and was released in 2005, remarrying and having three children. Her biographer, Stephen Williams, later called this plea agreement "The pact with the devil."

It's amazing how fast love can change. When crime-committing couples are caught, when they are separated and placed in different holding cells and questioned by different detectives, whatever delusional bonds had drawn them together can quickly dissolve. As self-preservation begins to kick in, the interrogations turn into a real-life example of a prisoner's dilemma. In that game theory scenario, two suspects in separate cells must each decide whether or not to confess. There is no other evidence aside from their theoretical confessions. Thus, the best possible outcome for the prisoners would be if both of them decided to stay silent. Another scenario is for both to confess. And then there's the murky land in the middle—the scenario where one party confesses, hoping that their cooperation will result in a lighter sentence, or using the opportunity to enhance their partner's role in the crime while diminishing their own. A prisoner's dilemma is a test of how much you trust your partner, and how much you value your own life over theirs.

Leopold and Loeb—they both admitted to luring Bobby Franks into the car on the day of his death. But until their own deaths, each blamed the other for being the one who wielded the chisel and did the actual bludgeoning.

Shortly after his capture, Charles Starkweather—the teenager who had murdered Caril Ann Fugate's entire family because her parents disapproved of their relationship—began telling police that his girlfriend was "the most trigger-happy person" he had ever encountered, and responsible for some of the deaths. Meanwhile, Caril Ann told officers that Charles had kidnapped her and she'd had nothing to do with any of the shootings. He was sentenced to death; she was sent to prison and eventually was paroled in 1976.

It turns out that Bonnie and Clyde were the exception to the criminal love story. For most, love rarely transcends the bright lights of interrogation and confession.

CHAPTER 18

"EVERYBODY HAS A REASON FOR WHY THEY DO THINGS IN LIFE"

As Charlie was transported to the drug task force in Melfa—the closest law enforcement building—for questioning, Sheriff Todd Godwin raced to find Ron Tunkel. Godwin hadn't been in the room for the profiler's earlier presentation on interrogation techniques, but now the arsonist turned out to be someone he knew, and Charlie had specifically requested Godwin's presence in the interview room. Godwin couldn't get Tunkel on the phone, so he asked another officer who had been there for the presentation for a CliffsNotes version. Be gentle and reassuring, the officer told him. Don't be combative. Be respectful.

These instructions came as a relief to Godwin; they were in line with how he liked to conduct suspect interviews anyway. It was certainly how he would have approached an interview with Charlie, who had played a cameo role in the criminal justice system on the offender side for nearly as long as Godwin had on the law enforcement side. They knew each other well enough to say hello on the street. They'd known each other well enough to sit and have coffee at the Royal Farms gas station on Christmas Day at a time when, Godwin was now realizing, Charlie had already lit more than thirty fires.

This is how he decided to begin the interview, once Charlie was sitting kitty-corner from him at a work desk at the drug task force center—by reminding Charlie that they knew each other, they had something in common. They were both from here, they both understood Accomack.

"Oh, Charles," Godwin said, crossing his ankle over his knee as Charlie sat kitty-corner from him.

"You know, I apologize," Charlie started to say, but Godwin cut him off. He hadn't been read his Miranda rights on camera and Rob Barnes, who was planning to do so, wasn't in the room yet.

"You're all right, Bubba, you're all right," Godwin said. "We go way back, don't we? Many years, Buddy. *Many* years."

"Trust me, Todd, I'm embarrassed," Charlie said, letting out one of his peculiar high-pitched giggles.

"You know, you could have called me. I've known you how many years? A long time. Twenty years, at least twenty years, Charles. If you needed anything, you could have called me, you know?"

"It was a problem that made me do this. I mean, you want to know the bad thing? I wish I was back on drugs."

"Don't *say* that."

"That way, I'd have an excuse."

Godwin clucked and shook his head sympathetically as Barnes came in the room. Barnes slid into the third empty chair at the desk, positioning it so that the three men formed an equilateral triangle, so Charlie wouldn't feel outnumbered. The room was small, with dingy carpet, a white board on one wall, and a small red cooler stashed in the corner that looked like it could contain either evidence or someone's lunch. The drug task force office was actually a ranch house, in a neighborhood with other ranch houses. It had been office-ified a little, with regulation furniture and cameras installed in the interview rooms, but it still had a homey quality to it. The kitchen had remained mostly untouched. The stove and oven still worked. On the refrigerator were interdepartmental notices, but inside the refrigerator were drinks and meal fixings that the officers brought from home.

"Is Glenn over here?" Charlie asked, thinking of the investigator Glenn Neal.

"Rob's here," Godwin offered, nodding toward Barnes. "You know Rob, so it will make it a little easier."

Charlie nodded. "It would be more embarrassing with Glenn. I think a lot of Glenn."

"All right, Charlie," Barnes said, as he took out a few official forms. He looked tired. He was tired. Godwin was still in his brown sheriff's uniform; Barnes was in jeans and a long-sleeved T-shirt. "You know who I am, I know who you are." (They were, in fact, distant cousins in some way neither was quite sure of.) He ran through Charlie's Miranda rights and then asked if Charlie wanted to talk or not.

"Talk *some*," Charlie agreed, and Godwin nodded as if the conversation was Charlie's idea to begin with.

"Okay," Godwin said.

"You know everything that has been going on with a lot of fires and stuff like that?" Barnes asked, mirroring Godwin's position, ankle over knee, flipping through some papers. To an observer, the conversation would have looked and sounded like three friends talking about the fires while hanging out at Shuckers, which is just what Barnes wanted. Charlie hadn't asked for a lawyer, and with his current demeanor it didn't appear that he had any plans to do so.

"Yes," Charlie said.

"And you made the comment to the sheriff earlier that you apologize and whatnot?"

"Yes."

"But you did state that you didn't set all of them."

"Right."

"All right," Barnes said, pressing onward. "We're at the point where we're at eighty-six fires since the time this kicked off," he said, including some that the police believed may have been accidents or set by copycats. "So we understand you were at the scene tonight. The one on Airport Drive. Who was driving in the vehicle?"

"She was."

"And her name?"

"Tonya Bundick."

These were easy questions, which the police already knew the answers to. Answering them didn't cost Charlie anything. Barnes asked which direction the van had been driving, which direction they'd approached the fire from. "Did you ride by a couple of times or anything like that?" he asked.

"Yeah," Charlie admitted, laughing again. "I knew we were busted before we did it."

"Why?" Godwin broke in.

"Too many cars. It was a dead giveaway. I even told her that. I said, 'This place is a setup.'"

"And you still set it on fire?"

Charlie shrugged. "She's a lot smarter than me, and she said it wasn't." He giggled. "But I had never seen that many cars before."

They took him through the actual setting of the fire—what part of the house he'd lit, whether he'd used any accelerants, what color the shop rag was that he'd stuffed in the house, whether he stood there after the fire was set to watch it. Backdoor, Charlie said. No accelerants. Plain white. No watching, he'd just run.

"We appreciate you, Charles," Godwin encouraged him. "We appreciate you telling the truth, Bubba. Listen to this. Nobody was hurt."

"That makes a big difference," Barnes agreed. Nobody was hurt.

Charlie shook his head. "I never wanted to do it in the first fuck-ing place."

"What made you?" Barnes asked, at the same time Godwin asked, "What happened?'

"I'm not going to tell you what," Charlie said, and then immediately apologized: "I'm not trying to be smart."

Barnes and Godwin nodded at this. They didn't need a motive in order for Charlie to be guilty. But some kind of reason would have made the whole thing make more sense to them.

"Everybody has a reason," Barnes said, "for why they do things in life."

"Trust me, I never enjoyed it." Charlie told him.

"It's something like, somebody did something to you? Pushed you away from something? Or—"

"Naw. It was just a problem I've had, and this was my way to—"

"Deal with it?" Godwin finished the sentence for him. "Was it your mom passing?"

"That don't help," Charlie acknowledged, "but there's more to it."

"Well, listen, we'll do this interview and then we'll do whatever you want," Godwin reassured him. "We'll do whatever you need to get you straight."

"Is she here?" Charlie asked suddenly. "Tonya?"

"She's not," Barnes told him.

"Is she going to be here?"

"What do you need?" Godwin asked.

Charlie folded his hands, shoulders slumped. "I wanted to see her."

Rob couldn't let the motive go. Was the problem Charlie had mentioned having—did it have to do with the fire departments? Was he mad at the fire departments? Or at law enforcement? "In our minds, we're trying to figure out—I don't want to say the motive, but, is it something against us? The state police or the sheriff or county? Or is it an individual? Or just the way you're expressing how you're pissed off?"

"I'm not even pissed off," Charlie insisted.

"You know, we thought you were mad at us," Godwin said.

"Not at all. I have the utmost respect for you all."

"That's what I thought," Godwin said.

Barnes looked down at the stack of papers he'd set on the table, each sheet containing descriptions of the eighty-six fires that had been set. If Charlie wasn't ready to talk about why he'd done them, at least he might be willing to talk about which ones he'd done.

Did Charlie do a woods fire on Dennis Drive? Yes, Charlie said. A bungalow on Seaside Road? Yes, said Charlie. Metompkin Road in Bloxom? Yes. The Drummond fire from the night before? Yes. The two-story farmhouse on Church Road? Yes. Yes, yes, yes.

"What about Greenbush Road, just outside of Parksley on 316 at Whitesville? You know, where Coor's garage is, and Associated Farms is across the street?"

"Yes," Charlie said.

"Where did you light that one?"

"Underneath of it."

"On the back side? Front side?"

"Right in the middle."

"So how did you get—"

"Crawled underneath the house."

"Okay."

Barnes had been holding the fires in his head, the geography and details of them, and he wanted to get Charlie to remember as many of them as possible. The two men swapped their knowledge of back roads, hidden shortcuts, mossy fields, and half-drained creeks. The interview became a geography bee. "Now, back on Nocks Landing Road, basically, across from Arcadia High School," Barnes said. "You're taking the road like you're heading toward Atlantic, and then it's the house at the intersection of Page Fisher Road. If you're taking that stoplight and hang a right like you're going toward Atlantic. It's a little house down there about a quarter of a mile. It's near a little intersection?"

"Yes," Charlie said.

"The unoccupied store on the highway in Parksley?" Barnes asked.

"I ain't got no comment on that."

Godwin's and Barnes's faces didn't register anything; they didn't even look at each other. But they both noticed that this was the first fire he'd refused to comment on, and they both wondered what that was about.

"Drummond Lane right down the street from the Forestry?"

"No comment."

"Hopeton Road, a big house that was for sale?"

"No comment," Charlie said. "Can I pee real quick?"

"Yeah," Barnes said, and he and Godwin both got to their feet to show Charlie to the restroom.

Charlie stood up as well. "You can write 'No comment' for the rest of them."

^ ^ ^

THE CONFESSION was taking a strange and winding path. Often in interviews like this, the suspect would do everything he could to avoid implicating himself—making excuses, pointing fingers at his cohorts, trying to rationalize his actions by claiming extenuating circumstances. Here, they had a man who had willingly and sheepishly put up his hands and admitted wrongdoing. He had gone over, in great detail, which fires he had set, and how, and he appeared to try his best to remember all of the circumstances behind them. But at the same time, he was refusing to offer the information that might help him receive a lighter punishment. He wouldn't say why he'd done it. He wouldn't say if anyone else had helped him. Sometimes he would go on in earnest detail about a how a big fire was lit, only to answer "No comment" when Barnes asked about a fire that had been smaller and more innocuous.

While Charlie peed, Godwin and Barnes each tried to puzzle through the inconsistent behavior. *Charlie* was the one with the firefighting experience. *Charlie* was the one with the criminal past. *Charlie* was the one who had some of the traits of a serial arsonist. But when he said he hadn't lit them all, did he mean that some of them had been lit by Tonya?

The three men came back into the room after the bathroom break and sat in their original chairs.

"Can I ask you this?" Godwin said. "Is there a reason you don't want to comment on some of these first fires?"

"Was there a significant change to where you started and where you ended?" Barnes offered. "Do you know what I mean?"

"Possibly," Charlie allowed.

Godwin raised his hands, as if to frame an idea: "It sounds like to me, Charles—I'm just throwing this out there—that we originally had somebody else involved in these first fires."

"I don't know," Charlie shook his head.

"If we take *her* out of the equation," Barnes tried, "other than you commenting about her, was there anybody other than her to drop you off?"

"No comment."

Barnes proceeded delicately. "The problem we're having is you're taking the rap for most of these, but we want to make sure whoever was involved in these is not going to continue. We're basically trying to stop this."

"They're not going to continue," Charlie assured them. "I'll take the rap for them."

This went on, with Charlie swearing that the fires were over and that he'd hated lighting them to begin with. Godwin and Barnes would ask how they could be sure the fires were over if Charlie kept leaving out details and saying, "No comment." Hours passed.

It was nearly two in the morning. Godwin told Charlie he had one last chance to get everything off his chest before he was escorted back to the county jail. Charlie was bouncing his legs up and down, rolling his forehead against the heels of his handcuffed hands. He talked about Tonya: how she had saved him from cocaine on the first night they'd met, and how they were going to get married.

The fire on Savageville Road in Onancock? Yes. The one on Pungoteague Road by the pump? Yes. The one in Horntown, right as you came into the town? No comment.

Remember the chickens? Godwin and Barnes asked. He had let the chickens out of his neighbor's coop. He was trying to be a good person.

Charlie asked if there was any way he'd get bond, and Godwin said that if he were being honest, and he was trying to be, then the answer was no.

Charlie stopped fidgeting. He leaned over and put his hands on his knees. "Fuck it, man," he said, "I'm just going to tell you everything."

"Now is the time to come clean," Godwin agreed. "Get it off your chest."

Charlie inhaled. "She set all of those."

Tonya had been the one to actually hold the match for the first one, and the second one, and all of the ones up to number eleven or twelve, at which point she was almost spotted by a nearby police car, Charlie said. Worried that she could be hurt or caught, Charlie told her he would take over the actual lighting part.

The fires seemed to make her so happy. Mellow her out, open her up. And she was a good mother—"She don't hit her kids, she really don't even yell at them"—and she was so stressed out, and Charlie loved her, and if it came down to it, he would take the rap for all of the fires because he didn't want her to have to go to prison. "I'll go in the fucking courtroom and agree to every one of them."

But why? Godwin and Barnes wanted to know. If he didn't want to light the fires to begin with, why would he ever agree to do it?

Charlie leaned his elbows on the desk, covered his face with his hands, and talked through muffled fingers as he said the rest of what he needed to say. "The reason I could never say no—and I will not say this in court, news, any of it."

"What is that, Charles?" Godwin asked, in a low whisper.

"We had this problem in our relationship," he started, "and I love this girl to death." He trailed off.

"Tell us the truth."

"I am going to tell you the truth. But it's hard for me."

"Tell us."

"I really fell in love with this girl. And most people that I been with in the past, they were just *there*. I settled for all of them, even the ones I was with for years, and I never was happy with them. And I was happy with this one," he said. "And the moment I fell in love with her, my dick stopped working."

There it was. The Thing. Said aloud in the conference room of the Eastern Shore drug task force office in Melfa was the mess that had defined all of the other messes in Charlie's life. They were broke, they were isolated from their families, they didn't know what to do about Tonya's son, they were low on work, and they were going to the Food Lion and they were eating garbage. But all of this could have been dealt with if it weren't for the fact that as soon as he'd fallen in love with Tonya Bundick, he couldn't perform in bed and this was the worst thing he could have possibly imagined.

Charlie paused and struggled. "Up until a few nights ago, we hadn't had sex in almost eighteen months. That was the only problem in our relationship. And I was doing whatever the fuck I could to keep her."

"I got you," Godwin said as Barnes nodded, both giving the impression that this was a normal sort of thing for them to hear in the course of an investigation. "I got you."

Doctors hadn't been able to help; he'd seen them and they told him the problem was all in his head. Ministers hadn't been able to help either; he'd brought the problem up with John Burr from Onley Baptist. The pastor suggested that talking to a therapist might be beneficial, though Charlie hadn't yet. And since none of it had helped, Charlie had done the one thing that seemed like it could make any difference at all to saving his relationship. He had lit the fires for Tonya.

Later on, the residents of Accomack would confuse this story a little bit. They would believe, and they would tell one another, that the fires had fixed Charlie's impotence: that he and Tonya would light a house on fire and then go home and have wild sex. The fires never fixed the problem, though. In the true version, the fires were not lit for sex, but for love.

"Honestly, if we hadn't caught you, it probably would have continued on," Barnes told Charlie when the story was done. "Just from what you're telling me, I don't know if from that point you could have stopped."

"I could have stopped," Charlie promised. It wasn't clear whether he believed it.

^ ^ ^

NOW THAT THE FINAL PIECE was in place, the piece that had to do with love, some of the other fires began to make a strange sort of sense.

J. D. Shreaves—the single dad who had returned to his house on Valentine's day to see it burning—was an ex-boyfriend of Tonya's. Tonya had been angry with the way they had broken up. Another man—who had woken up one morning to find a corner of his house inexplicably singed—was a friend who had a thing for Tonya, Charlie said. The man had flirted with her on Facebook, which Tonya said made her feel disrespected.

He did it for love. He tried to stop.

He didn't, during the interview, go into how much they had tried. He didn't, during that interview, talk about the times that Tonya had worried about what would happen to the boys if they were ever caught. Charlie would think they were done with the fires—but then a few days later something else would stress her out and they would be back to burning.

The one thing Charlie did go into, again and again, is that there had been no grand master plan with the fires. There had been no elaborate strategy for which house they would burn down. There had been no advanced surveillance or vision. Every night, they had merely gone out and burned down whatever house they happened to feel like burning. And that they really did try to stop.

The interview had lasted several hours, but mostly because it took that long just to list all the addresses of all the fires and ask if Charlie did them. Some of them he said he didn't remember. He swore it wasn't because he was trying to be evasive, but just that there were a lot of fires and it was hard to remember each one in particular. He suggested that he might recognize the houses if he saw them in person, and it was decided that the next step would be to pile into a patrol car and ride around to some of the sites in question.

"We'll let you go to the sites," Godwin said. "It's going to be an all-day thing, Charles. It's going to be a long day, just so you know."

One last thing Charlie wanted to get off his chest, he told them: the graffiti. The graffiti that had been all over town, disparaging the couple, Jay Floyd and Danielle. He and Tonya had done that. They were mad because their friends had said they thought Charlie and Tonya shouldn't be together.

The graffiti, which had until the arsons been the biggest crime in Accomack County, which had bothered Godwin for months—if law enforcement had just caught the graffiti artists, the arsons never would have happened.

Both Godwin and Barnes said how much they appreciated Charlie's cooperation.

At one point, Charlie asked if he could smoke a cigarette. Barnes said he could, and called for somebody to bring in an ashtray. Then he called for someone to bring in a lighter.

"I got a lighter," Charlie said.

CHAPTER 19

"I CAN'T TELL YOU SOMETHING I DON'T KNOW"

A FEW MILES AWAY, Scott Wade and his colleague Keenon Hook were not having the same luck.

Wade had been awakened at home by the sound of a ringing phone—his supervisor, hollering that two people had been caught, and that Wade needed to get his butt down to the station ASAP to conduct an interview with one of them. Wade thought it was an April Fools' joke at first; it was just a little before midnight on April 1. But when he hung up the phone it immediately rang again with another person delivering the news. By the time he finally had his clothes on, he'd had been interrupted by at least fifteen people.

He'd been told he would be questioning Tonya Bundick. He thought he knew the name, but it wasn't until he arrived at the Exmore police station, that he was 100 percent certain his memory had been right. Tonya was the woman who he and the sheriff had talked to along with Charles Smith on Christmas Day. The same woman whose house he had visited, the one who had told him the arsonist was probably on Facebook.

And now she was here, in a small interrogation room in Exmore, and it was Wade's job to get her to talk. Beside him sat Keenon Hook, another investigator.

For suspect interviews, Wade liked to base his own demeanor on the behavior of the suspect, trying to match them in tone and body language. Sometimes it was better to be bold and hard-charging, sometimes to take things easy. He had seen Tonya when she walked through the station, and paid close attention to her behavior. She was crying. Not sobbing, but she did have tears in her eyes.

"Can you bring me my ChapStick?" she asked him.

"How about some water?" he suggested, making it clear that her comfort and happiness were important to him. "We have water. We'll get you some ChapStick, too. It's not special, is it?"

"No," she said.

"Do have your ID on you, by any chance?"

"Uh-huh."

"I know it's Tonya, but what is your full name?"

"Tonya Susan Bundick."

He asked her a few more pro forma questions, and then turned back to her well-being. "Are you all right?"

"No," she said, "I'm not all right."

"Look, we're going to get through this," he reassured her. "I know you're upset. You have to take a deep breath. It's over now. We need to talk to you to get everything straightened out. We want to know where everything is—it's not the end of the world. I deal with a lot of people over here, a lot of times, and they think it's the end of the world. It's not. Everybody makes mistakes. Let's just start over right now and move on with the rest of your life. All right?"

She nodded, Wade nodded. He'd left his description of what was going to happen open-ended. "Move on with the rest of your life" could be understood to mean that at the end of the evening, he expected Tonya to walk out a free woman.

"Are you living with Charlie?" he continued.

"He's living with me."

"We'll get through it," he said again. "We'll get through it, and we will be done with it. Do you want to go see him when we're done?"

"I guess," she said. "I have kids at home."

Wade asked if there was a friend or neighbor who could come over to be with them, and she gave him a name. He asked if she'd seen enough cop shows on TV to see people being read their Miranda rights. She said she had. He explained that that's what he was going to do now—read her those rights, have her sign some forms, and ask her some more questions.

"Where do you want to start at?" he asked, when she was done with the papers.

"I don't know what you want me to say," she said.

"How did this all get started?" he tried again.

"I really don't know," she said. "I mean, because tonight, you know, we went to go to Walmart. You know, my sons are having birthdays on Wednesday, and we were just driving around. I mean, you know, we went to Walmart. We still had that stuff in the back of the van, and I mean, Charlie asked me to drop him off, so I dropped him off, and then, you know, the rest is history. The next thing I knew, we're being surrounded. I was shocked, you know, but I know he did set that fire tonight."

The gears in Wade's brain started turning. When he'd referred to "this" getting started, he'd introduced the chance for her to explain and take responsibility for five months' worth of fires. She hadn't. Instead, she'd talked about the Airport Road fire as if it were a singular event, one committed only by Charlie, and which she'd known nothing about. Wade noticed that Tonya wasn't crying anymore. She was putting herself together with each passing moment. He thought it was like watching a lightbulb turn off in front of him.

"Where did you drop him off tonight?" he continued, going along with the idea that Charlie was the only arsonist.

"In Melfa."

"And you said you were going to Walmart?"

"No," she said. "We had gone to Walmart before this, and he wanted to ride around."

"What did he say when he said he wanted you to drop him off?"

"He told me to drop him off and turn around and come back and get him."

"How many times have you dropped him off?" Wade tried, again leaving the door open to discuss other fires.

"This is the only time I've ever dropped him off anywhere."

That had been a crucial question. Tonya had no idea that nine miles away Charlie was breaking down and telling Godwin and Barnes that Tonya had been the actual fire starter in some of the arsons, and the driver in all the rest. To corroborate that, Wade needed Tonya to admit that she had been in the car on multiple occasions in which Charlie had asked to get out. That was the lever on which he would move the case.

For now, he backed off.

"Are your parents still alive?" he asked.

"No."

"Do you have anybody other than your kids?"

"No."

"Do your kids have anybody other than you?"

"No."

"You've never been in trouble before?"

"No."

"You're not on probation or anything like that?"

"No."

"You're already ahead," he encouraged her. "Most of the people we deal with are on probation. You've got a good, clean past. You've never been in any kind of trouble. Even if it was, it was something minor. You've got your kids that you have to deal with. Your kids don't have anyone else, and you're sitting here, and you're being cooperative. Everything you've got going for you is positive. Let's keep it that way."

"Uh-huh."

But keeping it that way meant that she had to be 100 percent honest, he said. Did she understand? Right now, the two of them together had to have this conversation, and she needed to be 100 percent honest. "The same sheet of music, 100 percent. Is that a deal?"

Charlie had been under stress, she offered. "He's been under some sort of stress the whole relationship. Either between work, you know, money to pay the bills—this, that, and the other. I'm not sure if you know anything about Charlie, but he's not your typical person. I sit there all the time and pick on him because, I mean, you can tell him to do something and he'll turn around twice and forget it . . . He always has these strange ways of acting that would make you think he's on drugs, but he's not."

"I like Charlie," Wade offered. "But we have to make sure we are all on the same sheet of music."

"Right."

"What is the first fire that you were aware of?"

"Tonight," she said.

"Tonight?"

"Tonight," she said. She went to Walmart to get two plastic containers to store stuff under the bed, and then another container to put shoes in, and then she got some Easter candy that was on sale. And after that, they went out driving—or actually, Charlie was driving. Then he got out and told her to take over the wheel, saying, "Go up the road and turn around and come back and get me." So that's what she did.

"You didn't ask him why?"

"No," she said.

"How many times have you gotten in the car and dropped him off—"

"That's the first time that I've dropped him off anywhere," she interrupted. Sometimes he worked late, she explained. Sometimes he worked late, and then came home for dinner, and then went back to work. Or she always assumed he was going back to work. She couldn't say for sure what he was doing.

"What does he normally drive?" Wade asked.

"He usually drives his truck, but he's been driving the van that his granddad gave him."

"How many nights have you been out riding around with him?"

"Quite a few."

"You never dropped him off anywhere?"

"No."

What had they bought at Walmart? Just the storage containers for under the bed? And they left around 9 p.m.? And then they rode around? Okay. What about when he was driving? Did he ever stop in the middle of the road "and you stayed in the truck while he went out and did anything?"

It was just another way of asking whether she'd dropped him off.

"No," she said. No times. No times had she ever dropped Charlie off anywhere.

He could feel her stiffening every time he circled back to the idea of dropping Charlie off. She was not merely closing herself off to questions, but actively deflecting them. This put him in treacherous territory. She'd agreed to proceed with the interview without having an attorney present, but as soon as she requested one, the conversation would be over. She was obviously getting wise to the fact that they weren't questioning her merely because they wanted her to implicate Charlie.

Wade decided to back off from the conversation, hoping that another agent might have more luck. Beside him, Keenon Hook had been listening in on the entire interview. Wade leaned back to let Hook take over, effectively disappearing himself from the conversation.

"Tonya, I don't think I've properly introduced myself," Hook began. "I'm not from around here, so I might need you to help me a little more to understand some of the things he knows"—he gestured toward Wade—"that I don't. Wade knows Charlie, and has told me a little bit. Obviously, I don't know either one of you. Help me to understand."

He asked her to tell him about her house, her neighborhood, her kids—the fight that put the older one out of school, and how the homeschooling was going—"Pretty good," she said. "The teacher comes out once a week." The conversation was pleasant, chatty, and he didn't touch on anything related to the fires.

"You must have been working before?" he asked. "What were you doing?"

"Taking care of mentally retarded people," she said.

"Is it like a residential care place?" he asked. "So it's residential, like the mentally retarded people live there?"

"Yes, fourteen people. I would work shifts there."

They talked more about her work and whether she liked it. He was exceedingly polite and solicitous. When he wanted clarification on something, he preceded the question by saying, "Forgive me," as if any holdups in the interview were the fault of his weak memory. If he caught a small discrepancy in any of her life stories, he would blame them on his own confusion: "I thought you stopped because of your son, though?" he inquired after Tonya told him she'd left her job in 2011—she'd previously said her son hadn't left school until 2012.

"It sounds like you and Charlie have really created a stable environment for your children," he told her. "Sometimes we have to make sacrifices in our lives to deal with their problems and issues that come up, and it sounds like you've done that, and that is, you know, commendable. I mean, I really admire and respect you for doing that."

His solicitousness continued when, several minutes later, he finally pivoted to the fires. Forgive him—but did he understand that

Charlie had been involved with the fire companies, but wasn't any longer? Hadn't he enjoyed it? Had he ever thought about going back? What about Tonya—had she ever thought about volunteering with a fire company?

"No."

What size shoe did she wear?

"Eight and a half."

"I only say one thing to you right now, and that is me and Scott Wade and everybody else in this county are truly thankful to you. Because you clearly exercised self-restraint, and you were careful. Not a single person got hurt, and I cannot tell you how happy I am to hear that. This really was a victimless situation, and these buildings were unattended, and they don't matter much anymore, and you guys were just being very careful about what you chose and where you chose it."

As Hook was describing them, the fires were a minor blip, something everyone would easily get over. He didn't mention police overtime, late night meetings, tedious roadblocks, exhausted firemen, insurance claims, men in tents, burning landmarks, and a whole county white-knuckling it through five months and dozens of fires.

Tonya stopped responding to Hook's statements, but he kept talking—offering explanations for what could have happened and what might have gone wrong. Hell, he said, she and Charlie probably hadn't even set them all. There were probably copycats who set some of them. Maybe she and Charlie were, themselves, copycats. But if she didn't talk about the ones they were responsible for, they might end up getting blamed for more than their fair share.

"Hey, I'm *not* the Eastern Shore Arsonist," he offered, suggesting an "out"—a way Tonya could confess to some of the fires without necessarily taking blame for all of them. "I'm somebody out here just relieving stress. You don't know what we have going on in our lives. I had to quit my job to take care of my son—and believe me, I know what it's like to reorganize your life around a child—and maybe things aren't going the way I wish they would, and I'm frustrated. That's an explanation that people can understand."

He waited.

"I can't tell you something I don't know," she said.

Wade, who had been sitting silently for several minutes, now broke in again.

"You need to start looking out for Tonya," he told her. "What would you say if I were to tell you that Charlie told us—just listen to me—what would you say if I told you that Charlie told us that you dropped him off for, like, twenty-five fires?"

"I don't know why he would say that," Tonya said.

Wade didn't know either. Though he'd stopped by the task force where Charlie was being questioned earlier, at this point he didn't know the extent of what Charlie had said; he'd spent the rest of the night sitting in a room with Tonya.

The two men had tried appealing to both her vanity and her humanity—providing her with "outs" that would present her in a flattering light. They had walked her up to the same questions again and again, hoping that her story might change or elaborate. They both had tried to present themselves as full of admiration and understanding. In response, she'd barely spoken more than a sentence at a time. Wade decided it was time to up the ante.

"I'm a very patient person, but I've got some other things to do," he said, feigning irritation. In fact, he was accustomed to spending hours on end with suspects, letting stories unspool and then unravel. Sometimes confessions took time. He wasn't being impatient now, he was being strategic. His presence seemed to be shutting her down, and they were running out of things to try. "If he"—meaning Hook—"wants to sit here and talk to you, he's more than welcome." As a final tactic, he would leave.

As Hook's final tactic, he would invite in the profiler Jon Cromer, who was currently waiting outside the interview room door, and who, just a few hours earlier had been wondering, along with the other psychological profilers, whether they would ever catch the arsonist at all.

Like Scott Wade, Cromer had assumed that the arrest of the arsonists was an April Fools' joke. He had been in his room at the Holiday Inn when he got the call from one of the investigators. "Nice try, I'm not buying it," he'd said. It was only when he saw the blue lights of a marked vehicle pull up in the parking lot that he believed it wasn't a prank and grabbed his wallet and keys. Nobody had planned on him interjecting into Tonya's interview, but at this point it couldn't hurt.

He entered the room and addressed Hook first. "The guys that are meeting with Charlie called, and I'm waiting on the situation," he said, before turning to Tonya.

"I'm Jon Cromer. I'm with the state police," he told her.

A few times during the interview, Wade and Hook had alluded to the fact that Charlie was being questioned at another station. Cromer was the first person who had been in steady contact with the police interrogating Charlie, and who could attest to what Charlie had said or not said. And he'd made that clear to Tonya, with his first statement to Hook upon entering the room.

Cromer knew it was a common technique for officers to tell suspects that their accomplices were tattling on them, whether or not that was true. He sensed Tonya would be smart enough to know this, too. He wanted her to understand that this conversation wasn't just a ploy. He decided to put all of his cards on the table.

"I've been in with Charlie," he told her. "He's been going through them one by one. I want you to understand. You are going to stand in front of a judge regarding these fires, in one of two ways. Number one, you are going to deny it. Or you are going to say, 'I made a mistake.' Listen to me. Charlie told us at 2:34 a.m., he told us that you lit the church fire. He also said you lit twelve of the first fifteen. He said he never got out of the car, because you did it.

"Now I wouldn't lie to you, but what has me worried is that you are going to be standing there in front of that judge, the only one in the mix who is denying that they were there. And I'm thinking, I would not want to stand there. We don't need a confession from anybody to take them to court. We need evidence, and trust me, there's plenty of evidence. Ma'am, I am going to tell you, when the evidence is brought through the Commonwealth's Attorney's Office to court, it is going to be overwhelming."

He told her about the photograph from Church Road, the one in which there was a figure that everyone had suspected was a woman. He talked about her cell phone, and how technicians would be able to see whether it had really been at home all those nights she said Charlie was at work and she was at home.

He knew he must be using the right tone, because her eyes were locked on his, she was leaning in and fully engaged. Cromer felt like he was watching her balance on a precipice, and it wasn't clear yet which way she would fall. He'd been in plenty of interviews before where, as a strategy, he'd feigned a certain position or set of emotions in order to elicit a particular response. This time he found it wasn't necessary. He genuinely believed it would be better for Tonya if she confessed. He could see her future stretching in front of her, two possible paths depending on what she said now. He found himself talking to Tonya like he talked to his own daughter, as calmly and matter-of-factly as he could, worried that she did not understand what her silence was costing her.

"Everywhere your phone has gone, whether it's been in the on position, it has been pinging towers logging your location," he told her. "That is the truth. You will not see your phone. You will not see the routes the phones were drawing on a map. You will not see that man until you testify, and he is honest, and he's a good man. He's the only one that is going to admit to the fires. He's going to come clean with me. I do not want you to admit to something you did not do, but I want you to understand this clearly. I want you to tell the truth about what you did do, because if you don't, you will stand in front of the judge. There will be Charlie. And he will say,

'I'm sorry. I made a mistake. These things in life set these things into motion, and it went crazy. For two days of it, we had fun. Then it went crazy, but that's the truth of it, judge.' And when Charlie gives details that no one but the person who was there would possibly know, then the judge will know he's telling the truth. And where will you be? I would not want to—"

"You give me a paper and I'll sign it," she broke in, "because I haven't done anything. So write it up and let me put my signature on it, and you can take me to a cell and do what you need to do."

"Help us—" he began again.

"I don't know what to tell you all. Write it up and let me sign it and let me go. Put me in a cell."

"Tell me—" he stared again.

"That's all I know."

"Here's what I want to tell you. They said—"

"What don't you get? I didn't do it, and I don't know. What don't you all understand?" she asked.

"I don't believe you."

"Well, then I don't know what you believe."

"I believe Charlie," he said.

"I don't care. I didn't do it. So believe it. I'm over it. I'm done talking. I'm pleading the Fifth. I want a lawyer, because I'm done."

Cromer felt his chest constrict. It was over. He'd barely been in there for five minutes before she had ended the interview by asking for an attorney. He didn't know whether he'd read her mood completely wrong, or whether he'd hit such a nerve that he'd made Tonya scared. Either way, his chance was over. He left the room and Wade reappeared, preparing to handcuff Tonya so she could be left alone while they figured out how to proceed next.

"Put your hands up for me," he instructed, when it was just the two of them in the room. "Is that too tight?"

"No," she said.

He knew they hadn't gotten much of anything that would be useful in court. Two years later, after everything was all over, he would still feel like he hadn't understood her at all. Later, Todd Godwin would wish he had been in the room with Tonya. He would wonder if, because he'd once asked about her sons at the Royal Farms and because she seemed to like him, he could have gotten her to talk. But Wade knew he was good at his job. He knew Keenon Hook was good at his job. He knew that Jon Cromer was one of the most skilled interviewers he'd ever encountered in his life, and none of them had been able to get her to talk. He didn't know if anyone would ever be able to get her to say anything at all.

"We'll be with you in just a minute," he said now, and left the room.

CHAPTER 20

"MIDNIGHT WITHOUT MAKEUP"

T HE NEWS TRAVELED THROUGHOUT THE COUNTY in messy, unpredictable ways. The idea that the suspected arsonists had been a couple was shocking. Bonnie and Clyde of the Eastern Shore.

The Facebook groups dedicated to speculating over the identity of the arsonists now dedicated themselves just as fully to analyzing Charlie and Tonya. It took seven hours, postarrest, for someone to post Tonya's bedraggled mug shot on the site, and a few minutes after that for someone else to comment, "Midnight without makeup is not how you want to make your close-up with the mug-shot camera."

Then someone posted a different picture, from Tonya's personal Facebook page and with better lighting, and the narratives began to change. People recognized her from out at Shuckers, or from way back when in high school. Another person wondered if this was the same Tonya Bundick whose mother used to submit recipes to the church cookbooks.

People remembered Charlie as a volunteer firefighter, the kid their brother sat next to on the bus, the guy who fixed cars and had those drug troubles. During the course of these postings, the moderators periodically removed information that they felt held too many personal details, or too many unverified rumors. Periodically, someone interrupted the discussion to offer thoughts and prayers, prayers and thoughts, to all of the victims of all of the fires.

Off-line, a man who lived down the street from Tonya and happened to share the same last name was bombarded at work by friends wanting to know if they were related. "Yeah," he lied, practicing a shake of the head that seemed appropriately mournful. "She was my first wife." One coworker replied that Tonya, in her mug shot, was looking pretty rough. "Yeah," the neighbor said again. "She took the breakup pretty hard." Another Bundick, no relation, found himself subject to similar speculation—faraway media members who didn't know anything about the shore had gotten their hands on a couple of phone directories and started dialing everyone with the name. This Bundick spent the morning fielding phone calls from harried junior producers of radio and TV news shows. He didn't bother to hand the phone to his cubicle mate at work, who really was related to Tonya, a cousin, but had a different last name.

On Matthews Road, Lois Gomez woke up to see a police car parked in the driveway of her neighbor's house, but she assumed it was nothing, maybe a domestic dispute, or maybe there had been another fire and the police were again making the rounds.

Phil Kelley, the chief of the Parksley fire station, who lived less than a mile from Charlie and Tonya, drove past their house on his way to work the next morning and assumed the same thing.

Tasley chief Jeff Beall was still sleeping, the morning after being turned back from the fire on Airport Road. His wife, Renee, saw the 6 a.m. news, ran into their bedroom, and shook him awake. "Jeff," she said. "It's Charlie! It's *Charlie*."

"Where?" he asked, assuming that Charlie had come to the house for a visit. "What does he want?"

"No," Renee said. "Charlie is the *arsonist*. He's the arsonist."

That morning for Beall was a fog. He wasn't scheduled to work, and he didn't have any plans. He drove to Charlie's step-dad's auto shop to tell him how sorry he was, and to make sure George knew that nobody would blame him for what had happened. He watched as his voice mailbox filled with numbers he didn't recognize—acquaintances who wanted to know if Beall had suspected anything, reporters who had learned Charlie was still on the Tasley roster and wanted a comment. Beall didn't know how to comment. He didn't know why Charlie was still on the roster; he hadn't run fires in a year. An aging hippie from NPR came to his front door, wearing corduroys and Crocs and carrying a giant boom mike, and Beall, still feeling raw, told the producer, "You have ten seconds to get the fuck off my lawn." He then spent the rest of the hour thinking about how strange that was, that of all the news outlets scrambling for the story, only one had the gumption to come to his personal place of residence, and it was wimpy National Public Radio.

As the day unfolded, one thing that became clear was that profiler Ron Tunkel had been right all along. There had been unknowing witnesses. The whole county had been unknowing witnesses.

Shannon Bridges, the Tasley firefighter, remembered one night that the Tasley department had left on a call. When the engine drove past Charlie's shop, she saw Charlie parked inside his truck out front, watching them all drive by. When they got back from the fire a little later, he was there again. It seemed explainable to Shannon—maybe he had a big job and was working late. But something about the situation made her turn to Richie and joke, "Richie—what if Charlie was the arsonist?"

Sheriff Todd Godwin had seen Charlie and Tonya out at the Royal Farms gas station on Christmas Day.

One of Godwin's deputies had pulled them over for a routine traffic stop. The deputy asked what they were doing out so late and they told him they were trying to catch the arsonist. He'd laughed and said that's what he was doing, too.

Scott Wade had gone to Charlie and Tonya's house on the advice of the geographic profile created by Isaac Van Patten.

Glenn Neal had gone there to ask about a burning truck.

And hundreds of people had read Tonya Bundick's comments on Facebook, speculating over the identity of the mastermind who was burning up the Eastern Shore.

Later, Bobby Bailey, the Fire Marshal's Office instructor whose pride had been so wounded during the investigation that he left in the middle of it without even bothering to fully pack up his hotel room, would nurse his hurt by telling himself that they had been dealing with geniuses, in a way. "They were so freaking stupid about their fires," he decided, "that they were smart."

Beall, when his grief about the situation turned to anger, would express the same frustration in a different way. "The greatest arsonist in the history of all of Virginia—the one who kept us up night after night after night—and it was fucking Charlie Smith in a fucking gold minivan."

CHAPTER 21

THE BROKEN THINGS

BY APRIL 2, THE MORNING AFTER THE ARRESTS, 2013 was shaping up to be an odd year for Gary Agar. First, the Commonwealth's attorney had to figure out how to prosecute a Navy SEAL war veteran who randomly stole a giant boat belonging to the Virginia Marine Resources Commission, hitched it to the back of his vehicle, and lugged it across the Bay Bridge-Tunnel, where he was captured on camera. Next, a young police officer got in a car accident, dialed 911, and then proceeded to pull out a knife and stab the two firefighters who showed up to help him. He claimed that demons told him to do it because the firefighters' helmets depicted the evil number four. Later it was discovered that the officer was having a psychotic reaction to the drug Biaxin, which he had been prescribed for an upper respiratory infection. Agar prosecuted the first crime, withdrew charges for the second. And now came the arsons, the biggest crime spree in the history of Accomack County.

Agar knew who Tonya Bundick was. His ex-wife had owned a home health care business that had years ago employed Tonya.

The Agars held annual company picnics at their house and it was likely Tonya would have attended them. Long before that, he'd gone to high school with Tonya's mother. One day he'd run into Susan at the Rite Aid and she'd introduced Agar to her daughter. It was unavoidable that one would get to know everybody, after being an elected official as long as Agar had. He'd been the Commonwealth's attorney for several terms. Agar, sixty, was short and sturdy without much neck to speak of, a fire hydrant of a man. But when he spoke in front of juries, he moved his arms in the graceful patterns of an orchestra conductor during a legato movement. This, combined with a deep, rumbling voice—constituents compared it with James Earl Jones—made him a hypnotic performer in courtrooms.

Agar learned there had been an arrest for the arsons on the night of April 1. He knew that the police and sheriff's deputies had caught Charlie in the act of lighting the fire on Airport Road.

But he lacked the forensic evidence and witness statements for the other eighty-odd arsons. Without Charlie's confession, he would never be able to convict. So early on the morning of April 2, Agar closed the door to his office and watched the whole six-hour taped interview to see what he had.

What he had, he decided, was good. Charlie seemed believable. There were times that Charlie had said, "No comment," before he admitted Tonya's involvement, but he had never asked for a deal or tried to shift the blame away from himself. And he came across, Agar thought, as a person who lacked the creativity necessary to come up with such an odd excuse—the impotence, which attacked his own manhood and revealed deeply personal information—on the spot. Charlie would be a good asset.

Tonya's interview was all but useless. Just as she hadn't revealed much factually, she hadn't revealed much legally. One never knew what might end up being useful in the future, though. Agar found himself latching on to the phrase "riding around." Tonya had admitted that she and Charlie spent several nights "riding around"—she'd just never admitted to any particular destinations, or to letting Charlie out of the car. Agar kept the phrase in his pocket, figuring that trying to pin down her location would be necessary in cross-examination.

While Agar was reviewing the videos, another attorney named Carl H. Bundick (no relation, just another Bundick), was walking into his own offices less than a block away. Bundick, fifty-four, with a white buzz cut and a mustache, thought of himself as a "country lawyer," a Swiss army knife of an attorney who handled a broad manner of petty thefts, drug possessions, land disputes, and bar brawls on behalf of the citizens who walked into his law offices on any given day. He or his assistant would typically begin the morning by checking the voice mail for new cases, and on the morning of April 2, the voice on the recording belonged to a family member of Charlie's. She knew Carl Bundick socially and wondered if Carl would again be available to help her relative out of a patch of trouble. It wasn't the first time. Carl had been Charlie's attorney on record for more than a decade, scrape after scrape, relapse after relapse. He also knew Tonya a little bit, and had helped the couple navigate a lien on her house.

Carl figured out that Charlie was being held at the Accomack County Jail, and immediately placed a call to his client. "Are you okay?" he remembered asking. "Did they do a Miranda warning? What evidence do they have against you?"

Charlie remembered the interaction a little differently. He remembered reaching Carl the night before, when Carl was at his house—the sheriff's deputies had brought Charlie to the jail and given him the number to dial. In Charlie's version, Carl had already heard from the family member by the time Charlie called, and Charlie remembered only one part of the conversation. He remembered Carl saying, "Don't say another word."

He didn't know if Carl understood that, by that point, he'd already given a confession that would fill four DVDs and print out at several hundred pages.

^ ^ ^

STATE POLICE INVESTIGATOR SCOTT WADE had come home from his interview with Tonya frustrated and exhausted and wishing he understood Tonya better. But now he would get one more chance. While Gary Agar was reviewing the confession footage, and the residents of Accomack were gossiping and crying and thinking about what they should have known, Wade was putting himself to bed for a few hours and then getting on a plane to New Jersey.

He was going to see Tonya's sister, Anjanette. She lived about two hundred miles up the Atlantic Coast, and was Tonya's only living immediate relative. When Wade first telephoned, Anjanette, who went by Anjee, was at the grocery store. She said it would be fine if he came to interview her, but she assumed he meant later in the week. Instead, he telephoned again a few hours later and said he was already there. He asked her to meet him at the local police precinct.

"Do you think your sister did these?" he asked her, when they sat down together.

"I don't know," she said. She still had friends in Accomack and had followed the arsons along with them. All that time, she had never suspected her sister—not of burning down so many strangers' houses.

But then she started to tell him a story. A different night. A different fire.

In the middle of the night about a year ago, she'd woken up to a text message on her phone from a number she didn't recognize. No words, just one picture of a burning house. The image was small but she thought it looked like her grandmother's house down in

Accomack. "Who is this?" she wrote to the sender, who wrote back a little later: "It's your sister."

Tonya and Anjee didn't talk much and had been in only sporadic contact since their grandmother died a few years before. The estrangement was complicated, but it had to do partly with the house, which is why some murky intuition prompted Anjee to write back the way she did: "Why are you sending me a picture of the house burning? I know you burned it."

"No," Tonya replied, "*you* were the one who said you were going to come here and burn it."

The reply had baffled Anjee. She'd never threatened anything like that—*Why would she drive four hours in the middle of the night just to burn down the family homestead?*—but it scared her to see the accusation in writing. Unsettled, she made a quick decision. "Don't e-mail me," she wrote to her sister. "Don't call me, don't message me, don't contact me."

She kept the photo, because it was the last picture she would ever have of her grandmother's house, but she otherwise tried to forget about the incident and move on. She told herself she couldn't really know what had happened. And also that it was just one house. One little house that nobody lived in anymore.

It was the last time she and her sister had spoken. She didn't even know Tonya was engaged, she told Wade. She couldn't remember if she'd ever met Charlie. She didn't know anything about the other fires in Accomack, but if she were being honest with herself, she thought Tonya had lit the fire at their grandmother's. It had never been solved.

Wade had asked Anjee the questions he'd come for, but found he wasn't ready to leave. He asked whether she could add anything else. Not anything related to the investigation. Not anything that would be used in court—not anything that would help prosecute Tonya. But was there anything Anjee could tell him that might help them to understand her?

Anjee wasn't sure how much to say. Their house had been full of secrets, the kind that Tonya had never wanted to tell Charlie. But now two of the secret keepers were dead, and one was arrested, and she alone was the person who could explain how her sister wasn't the evil person that the rest of the county might soon claim she was.

She told Wade that they hadn't just been Accomack poor growing up, but cripplingly poor. There was no money in the house. Not for toys, not for clothes, sometimes not even for food. After holidays, they would dread going back to school, because the other kids would all be talking about their presents and would want to know what they got. Anjee learned to tell stories, inventing dollhouses and other presents that she would say were too big to be carried into school. Occasionally, their mother would be able to secret away a quarter from the grocery money so they could each buy an ice cream at school. She would quietly slip it in their hands as they were leaving for school in the mornings. This was the happiest memory that Anjee could conjure when she thought of her childhood, and it was tinted with sadness because she also remembered her mother saying, "Don't tell your father."

She told Wade that their father had been more than mean. He wasn't an ornery coot, like some of the other townspeople thought. He was scary, she said. Beatings were daily, sometimes with his hands, more often with the buckle end of a belt when the girls failed to follow an arbitrary order, like picking up a piece of lint from the floor. Anjee would look and look for the piece of lint but not be able to find anything. Their mother's best advice was to try not to make their father mad, but she didn't know how to stop it; he hit her, too. Tonya wasn't targeted as much, partly because Anjee set to taking the blame for some of the things her father perceived as infractions. "Who did this?" he would ask about something he'd decided was unacceptable that day, and Anjee would say, "I did," even though she knew it had been Tonya. She thought it was her duty; Tonya was so much tinier than she was.

They weren't allowed to sit at the table during dinner; they had to eat in their room. Sometimes they weren't allowed to eat at all, and Anjee never knew whether it was because there was no money for food that night or if it was because she and Tonya were being punished for something else they had done wrong. He would eat. They could hear their father eating at the table.

People didn't know that when Tonya was fighting with bullies on the bus, half of the time they weren't her bullies. They were Anjee's. Anjee got picked on for her clothes and shoes, too, but she was too meek to defend herself. Tonya, who was three years younger and half Anjee's size, would do it for her, not hesitating for a moment before flying on them and yelling, "Leave my sister alone." Maybe it was repayment for how Anjee covered for Tonya at home.

As an adult, Anjee realized their father must have been troubled himself. He had gone through the family albums at one point and cut his own face out of the family pictures, leaving photo after photo of a man whose head was replaced with jagged little holes. He must have carried a lot of self-hatred to do something like that. As an adult, she realized that her father must have been a miserable person.

Anjee had run away from home before she was eighteen and didn't keep in contact with the family. She had made a life on her own, away from the Eastern Shore. She had children she was devoted to, and started a business refinishing antiques. She'd sent letters to her mother for a while but they came back marked "Addressee no longer lives here," even though Anjee knew they hadn't moved and the return-to-sender message was in her mother's handwriting. She was sure her father had made her mother write those messages. It's how he'd always dealt with any mail from people he didn't want to talk to.

After running away, the first time that she came back home was because she heard that their father had died and—she knew it sounded crazy—she wanted to know if he really was dead. On the way down the Delmarva peninsula for the funeral, she stopped and picked up Tonya, who at that time was living in Pocomoke City, Maryland. At the funeral home, she learned that her father had had cancer of the liver and lungs and that it spread to his brain. She was sure it was the chemicals in all the fields that the farmers of Accomack County inhaled so they could eke out livings and bring food to the rest of the world. She hadn't seen Tonya in more than four years, and her sister had become so beautiful.

The two of them tried, after that. Sporadic contact, introducing the cousins, and trying to learn sisterly behavior. Tonya and Anjee had two properties promised to them—the one they had grown up in, which belonged to their mother, and the one that belonged to their grandmother, which their father had been raised in. After Tonya found their mother dead in the backyard of her home, Anjee came down to help her deal with the estate.

When they were done cleaning out the house, they came up with the agreement that deeded that property to Tonya, with the idea that their grandmother's house would go to Anjee. And their grandmother did die, and Anjee did move back to Accomack, at least for a little while. She came down with her boyfriend at the time, a guy she retroactively realized was no prize. One night at Tonya's house, the boyfriend hit on Tonya, leaning in to kiss her when he didn't know Anjee was in eyesight. She didn't know if Tonya had encouraged it, but it didn't look to her like Tonya had discouraged it, either. Shortly after, it happened again, and they got in a big fight. Anjee said things. About how she thought Tonya disgraced herself looking like she did when she left the house. About how Tonya thought people were jealous, but really they were just horrified that a mother would be wearing the kinds of clothes that she did. "You're not in a photo shoot, you're in a bar!" she remembered shouting, or something like that. And Tonya shouted back. And one of the things she shouted was that their deal was off. Anjee couldn't have their grandmother's house. "I'll burn it down before I sign over those papers," she remembered Tonya saying.

A year or so later it burned down.

But all of their history, all of their past—maybe that's why Tonya dressed the way that she did. Because after a childhood of never having anything pretty, she longed for people to notice her as something beyond ugly and poor. And maybe that's why Tonya loved her boys so furiously, because she had never felt that kind of protective love at home.

And maybe that's why it had been so hard for the two sisters to have a relationship, for all those years. Because they had both been through something scary and sad, the kind of thing that could bring two people closer together, or it could make it impossible for them to be in the same room with each other because of their shared memories. Anjee had gotten out, and after therapy, had gotten better. Maybe some people were affected more than others, in ways nobody ever could have predicted.

When Anjee considered Tonya and their strained relationship, she thought about the oddest things. Like about how, when they were younger, Anjee didn't like chicken and only wanted to eat her vegetables. But food was scarce, and she was hungry, and she knew she would be punished if she left food on her plate. So Tonya would offer to trade. She would tell Anjee she could have all the vegetables, saying she wanted more chicken for herself. It was only after a while that Anjee realized Tonya didn't like the chicken, either. Sometimes Tonya wouldn't eat it, instead hiding it under the bed and throwing it away at school the next day. Which meant sometimes Tonya didn't have dinner at all.

Anjee would think about those small, delicate acts of kindness from her sister, and she would cry.

She didn't know whether Tonya had lit those fires. But either way, she was afraid the county would see her as a monster, and she wanted Wade to know her sister wasn't that.

∧ ∧ ∧

LATER, IT WOULD TURN OUT THAT ANJEE wasn't the only person whose heart would pang when she thought about Tonya.

A woman who had known Tonya during the time she lived in Chincoteague remembered how Tonya had offered to help her with her hair and makeup, and how, when the woman thanked her, Tonya said that she knew how important it was to be made to feel pretty. Her own family, the woman remembered her saying, never made her feel anything but bad.

Another friend remembered Tonya saying that her father had been mean, but not as mean as he'd been to her sister.

Another acquaintance, a man named Dale, heard about Tonya's arrest when his father called him. Dale hadn't thought of Tonya in years. They had dated during her last year of high school; he was a year or two older and they'd been introduced through friends.

Their relationship worked this way: the Bundick family didn't have a telephone in the house, at least not one that Tonya seemed allowed to use. On Thursdays, her mother would drive her to a pay phone so she could call Dale and arrange a date. If she didn't call, he would know that meant he wasn't going to see her that weekend. If they did arrange a date, sometimes he got to her house and nobody would come to the door. The cars would be out front; he would know they were home. He would knock and call out that if Tonya didn't want to see him, she only had to come to the door and say that herself. She wouldn't come to the door. When he'd see her again a week or two later she never wanted him to mention those times.

Something in the house felt odd to Dale. He was young, and he couldn't put his finger on what it was, mostly just a bad feeling. It seemed off when Carroll would scream at him for his tires taking up too much space on the skinny driveway. Or when Tonya would sneak a phone call from the burger place where she worked, and tell Dale to never mention it to her parents or they would make her quit the job.

On the first occasion he invited her to dinner at his father's house, he got back from driving her home and his father pulled him aside and told him, "Something's not right. Something's not right there."

One night during her senior year of high school, Dale got a call and it was Tonya. She told him she'd gotten in a fight with her parents and one of them had thrown boiling water on her. She didn't say what the fight was about. She just asked him to come and get her. His father pointed out that it might be better for an adult to be the one to go to the house, so Dale called his grandparents, who lived near Tonya. It was the first time, as he remembers, that Tonya ever acknowledged something was wrong in her house.

She lived with his grandparents for a few months, he remembered, before going to live with one of her distant relatives, an aunt or uncle who lived a few towns over. Before, Tonya had been merely quiet. Now she seemed completely closed off, even to him. They couldn't connect the way they used to. She seemed resentful, or maybe she was just embarrassed that he knew about her private life. The relationship didn't last much longer. The experience had changed Tonya, but it had changed Dale, too, opening him up to a world of adult complexities. A few years older than Tonya, he'd already graduated high school and had his eye on joining the military. There had been things holding him to Accomack, though, and one of those things was Tonya. Now the biggest thing that had been keeping him there felt like a reason to leave. It wasn't about Tonya, it was about the situation and how powerless it had made him feel.

No one else in Tonya's life appeared to know that she wasn't living at home anymore. In the "senior will and testament" section of her twelfth-grade yearbook, which was published after all of this happened, she left a note thanking Dale for a wonderful relationship, and giving "lots of love" to her mom and dad.

When Dale heard about Tonya and the arsons, it was because his father called him on the telephone and said, "Well. It looks like your ex-girlfriend's been setting the world on fire. Didn't you hear? Tonya's the one they arrested."

Dale let the news settle in and then told his dad, "It sounds horrible to say, but for some reason or another I'm not really surprised." If someone had told him that one of his acquaintances had become an arsonist and asked him to guess which one, Tonya is who he would have picked. "By the time I had a chance to think about her childhood and family life," Dale told his father, "I think she'd garnered a lot of anger. No doubt in my mind about that."

It made him sad to think about the things in her that were probably broken a long time ago.

CHAPTER 22

"TIME TO WAKE UP"

T HE COUNTY SEAT OF ACCOMACK was Accomac, which had come to be the center of government but lost a *k* along the way. It had little in the way of commerce but bail bondsmen and lawyers, clustered in small offices around the redbrick courthouse, and a small café that catered to the bail bondsmen and lawyers. The sheriff's office and jail were directly across the street from the courthouse. The office of the Commonwealth's attorney was kitty-corner from the courthouse, and in the middle of the triangle formed by the courthouse, jail, and Commonwealth's attorney were the offices of Charlie's defense attorney, Carl Bundick. It was within this small parcel of land that the preparations for the arsonists' trial would begin to unfold.

Charlie didn't need a trial. Charlie had already pleaded guilty; Charlie needed only to be sentenced. But the amount for which Charlie would be sentenced would depend on what happened with Tonya, who had pleaded not guilty. Tonya needed a trial. Because she'd been caught at the site of only one fire, and because there was no physical evidence linking either of them to the other crimes, she'd been charged with only one count of arson and one count of conspiracy. For the prosecution to charge her on anything else, or to get a guilty conviction on the charge they already had, what they needed was Charlie.

But first there was the matter of love.

The matter of love was proving difficult for Carl Bundick, who wanted to get the best situation possible for his client. Carl was, as his last name suggested, a Born Here, who had left the shore only to get a bachelor's and a law degree. He'd once run for Commonwealth's attorney against Gary Agar, but after being defeated, set up his private practice in a converted colonial house filled with ramshackle antiques and dusty candy bowls. Now, the issue at hand was this: While Charlie had eventually implicated Tonya in his confession, he hadn't fully grasped what that would mean. In his mind, he'd done it as a means of explaining the fires. The police wanted to know if they'd caught all of the perpetrators, or if the arsons would keep going. Charlie wanted them to know that if they had caught him, and if they had caught Tonya, then there wouldn't be any more fires.

Now Charlie was realizing the implications of that confession. The police and lawyers wouldn't let him just volunteer to take the blame and have it be over. The lawyers wanted her put away, too, and they wanted him to help them do that. They wanted him to testify against her. Carl was pushing it hard, telling Charlie it would be good for him. How good, he couldn't say. Gary Agar hadn't approached Charlie's attorney with any specific kind of deal, for two reasons: one, he knew that sentencing would ultimately be up to a judge, not him. And two, he knew that if Tonya did go to trial, juries tended not to trust witnesses whose testimonies they felt had been bought and paid for. It was better for Charlie to be able to testify and say, truthfully, that he hadn't been offered anything specific in return.

So all that Charlie knew was that the maximum sentence for his crimes was up to 584 years—lifetimes of incarceration. And that he still loved Tonya.

Loving Tonya was more easily navigable than one might have imagined in the Accomack County Jail. The building was a small structure attached to the sheriff's office. It had only a hundred beds and a kitchen that seemed, to inmates, incapable of producing anything but bologna sandwiches. Occasionally, inmates wrote letters to the local newspaper to complain about other issues with the jail: the paint was peeling, they said. It was small and crowded. There weren't any activities or programs, such as Alcoholics Anonymous, to keep the inmates (who ranged from shoplifters to drunk drivers to murderers) minimally occupied. Before Charlie and Tonya arrived, the jail's most famous inhabitant had been a man named Richard Godwin—no relation to the sheriff—an insurance and real estate mini-tycoon who preferred going by "Wrendo Johnson Periless Godwin" and was the Eastern Shore's only presidential candidate to date, in the 2008 election. Wrendo Johnson Periless Godwin's seventy thousand-dollar Mercedes-Benz had accrued multiple overdue speeding tickets, but the candidate decided that it was more important for him to keep on the campaign trail than to make his court date. Eventually, he was sentenced to ten days in the jail, and afterward told the *Salisbury Daily Times* that the place was in "severe" trouble. "You could hardly get to the bathroom," he said, explaining that one night there were five inmates in his holding cell. (He eventually withdrew from the presidential campaign.)

Charlie knew the jail—it was where he'd spent time while awaiting sentencing for his previous crimes. The men and women were housed separately. But since the jail was small, and because there were windows that abutted the recreation yard where inmates walked around a weather-beaten flagpole, there were ways of getting in touch with other prisoners of the opposite sex.

After Charlie had been there several weeks, he heard someone outside of his cell window. The voice belonged to Tonya, he says.

She was out for her fresh-air break, and the guard didn't seem to be paying any attention.

It was the first time they'd spoken to each other since the night of the arrest.

In a whispered conversation in a miserable prison yard, she told him he knew what he had to do: he had to take responsibility for the fires—all of them. He had to explain to the police that he'd been on drugs when he gave his confession, and that's why he had implicated Tonya, right? Because he knew she didn't have anything to do with it, right? And that's what he needed to tell the police. The right story, the true story.

He believed he understood what she was doing—communicating to him what she wanted him to do in a way that would be unimpeachable to anyone listening. He didn't blame her for it. She had two kids who needed her: the younger was currently living with the boys' father but the older was in foster care. The only person who needed Charlie right now was Tonya, and what she needed was for him to tell everyone that she had nothing to do with the fires.

Mostly, as they talked through the prison wall, he just told her how much he loved her.

After that first time in the prison yard, there were ways of staying in contact. There were cell mates to be whispered to who could pass messages. There was a small library shelf, and there were ways of sharing which book to look in for a letter, and there was the flagpole at one end of the miserable exercise yard. Inmates in some generation past had figured out that this pole made a serviceable landmark to bury notes near. This information had trickled down as general knowledge for the rest of the population. The preferred method was to write tiny notes in tiny handwriting, and then fold the paper up between two pieces of the plastic cutlery that was passed out with the bologna sandwiches, and then plunge the cutlery into the ground.

There was a different method that Charlie liked to use, which seemed appropriate given Tonya's propensity for lip balm: he took a

ChapStick container, sliced off a thin circle from the top of the balm, and discarded the rest. Into the mostly hollowed-out container, he rolled notes, some written in numeric code. Charlie wrote to Tonya this way, and Tonya wrote back. They passed messages about what their lawyers had said, and what they thought might happen and about how, despite everything, they were still deeply in love.

"You're my Tiny Toot and I love you and I never want to lose you," Charlie wrote. "I'm already scared if I get too much time, I'll lose you. Sometimes I don't think you really know just how much I love you. I'd rather die than lose you. I can't picture life without you."

Shortly after that, toward the end of September 2013, with money Charlie was never quite sure how she or anyone she knew had scraped together, Tonya was released on bond. She continued to write him letters from the outside. "Do they know that we didn't do this?" she wrote. "Did you tell them about your drug use since your mom died?"

She was a good pen pal. He called her collect once a week. How could he agree to testify against her, when it was his fault they were trying to prosecute her to begin with? If he had just kept his mouth shut, everything would be fine. His lawyer didn't know Tonya like he did. Gary Agar didn't know Tonya like he did. They didn't know how sweet and loving she could be.

But it was all confusing. One day a deputy came to his cell and told him that the sheriff wanted to see him. Charlie was escorted from the rear part of the building, where the cells were, up to the front, where Godwin's office was just off the lobby and overlooked a parking lot. Charlie sat down on the visitor side of Godwin's big wooden desk, and Godwin got straight to the point.

"If she really loved you, why is she out on bond seeing another guy?" Godwin asked him. He had it on good authority that Tonya had been spotted going on dates since being released from the jail.

Charlie had no earthly idea what Godwin was talking about. He told himself it was a ploy, just them trying to get him to turn against Tonya. He told Godwin that the whole jail system and the whole county was probably corrupt.

Tonya did love him. If she didn't, why had she recently agreed to marry him, even now, while she was free and he was in jail? Marriage seemed the prudent thing to do—they both had heard of the rule that prevented married couples from having to testify against each other in court—but also, Charlie wanted to. So now they were trying to plan a wedding, even if it wasn't quite the wedding they'd originally had in mind. Charlie's job had been to ask his youngest sister to procure a wedding ring and get it to Tonya.

"Make sure you get up with Sarah," Tonya wrote him in a letter one day. "Hopefully she will do as promised."

"So have you gotten up with Sarah yet?" she asked in another letter. "Hope she does it before my court date. If not, it will be too late."

"I never got vows. When did you send them?" she wrote another day. Eventually, she mailed him the vows she'd written that she planned to use in a theoretical ceremony. She told him, as he remembered, that she was going to ask her lawyer whether it was possible to bring a preacher into the jail's visitor space, to do their ceremony right there.

Would she have done any of that if she wasn't in love with him?

The friends and family who still talked to Charlie told him he was being a fool. The whole business about marriage being for their mutual benefit didn't make any sense. What did it matter if Tonya testified against Charlie? He'd already confessed to the crimes. The only person who would benefit from this arrangement was Tonya, who had continued to say she was innocent. That's why she wanted the ring before her court date, people told Charlie. She didn't want Charlie testifying against her.

"Have you asked Sarah about the ring?" she wrote again. "Don't say I know about it," she instructed him. His sister, she would later explain, was not Tonya's biggest fan. She wasn't sure if Sarah would buy the ring for her if she thought Tonya was orchestrating it.

Eventually, she would decide that the importance of getting married outweighed any fear of her future sister-in-law's negative feelings. "Does he still want to?" she wrote in a letter directly to Charlie's sister, trying to move the process along. "Can we get married here? What is the law on this? Because I want to, soon."

Through all of this, Charlie sat, and he thought, and he wrote, and he called Tonya, once or twice a week as she would allow. The Accomack jail was boring, even as jails went, but he had Tonya's letters, and she was a faithful correspondent and they were going to be married. There was so little that was certain in this world and that was certain.

One afternoon a guard came to him again and said someone wanted to talk to him. Charlie thought it might be his lawyer. But instead of leading him to the visitor's room, the guard took him back to Todd Godwin's office. Charlie sat again at the big desk with the front window across from the sheriff who, despite what Charlie had said in anger the last time, he actually believed to be a fair and trustworthy person. In front of him on the big desk were a pile of papers.

"Charlie, we've known each other a really long time," Charlie remembered Godwin saying. "I just can't believe you're going to spend the rest of your life here for a girl who didn't really love you."

"You need to know what's going on," Godwin remembered telling Charlie. "She might be telling you something, but she's got another boyfriend."

Charlie was ready to protest again, but this time there was evidence. There was a stack of papers on Godwin's desk, and he now slid them over to Charlie. The papers were photocopies, and the photocopies were of letters, and the letters appeared to be from Tonya. Charlie recognized her handwriting. When he read the words, he recognized her in those, too. In these letters, she talked about her favorite sexual positions and other intimate things. "Suckin' and fuckin'," he would later describe the content. "One asked how big the guy's dick was." After a few paragraphs of a few letters, he couldn't read any more. They were love letters that Tonya had written back while she had been a prisoner in Godwin's jail, where all correspondence could be monitored. They weren't to Charlie. They looked to be to another inmate at another jail, someone she'd met through a prisoner pen-pal service.

"I need a cigarette," Charlie said.

The sheriff arranged for a pack to be brought in, opening the front window so Charlie could blow smoke outside. Neither of them talked much. Charlie felt dazed.

A little while after that, Carl Bundick came to visit again, sat in front of his client and said in grave seriousness that testifying against Tonya was Charlie's only shot. It was a possibility or even a probability that if Charlie did not cooperate, he would never be a free man again.

"It's time to wake up," Carl said.

For the first time, Charlie forced himself to think of what was at stake. If he didn't cooperate with the prosecution, there was a good chance he wouldn't see his daughter again. He wouldn't have a chance to rebuild a new life. He wouldn't have the chance to make amends for his old one. He would be sentenced and sent to a prison on the mainland. It would be too far and too expensive for anyone to come and visit him, and that was assuming anyone even wanted to. And while he was there, the whole time, as he turned forty, fifty, seventy, he wouldn't have Tonya because Tonya didn't really love him anymore. When he eventually got out, if he eventually got out, he would be alone.

So this time, when his attorney laid out the situation in the same matter-of-fact way that he had done several times before, Charlie still didn't say anything, because saying something made it feel a little too final. But he nodded.

The love story, the one Charlie had thought was too good for him from the beginning, was now breaking into pieces. In the coming days, he would call her again, and they would talk again, and he would cry on the phone again, telling her how much he loved her again and wondering if he should tell her about the way that he'd just agreed to betray her, or that he knew about the way she'd betrayed him.

But there wouldn't be too many of those conversations. On December 2, 2013, Tonya Bundick was arrested again and indicted on sixty-one additional counts of arson. This time she would be taken to the Eastern Shore Regional Jail down in Northampton County where they couldn't pass any more notes. "I know you love her," Charlie remembered his attorney saying, on the afternoon that he finally agreed to testify. "But she don't no more give a damn about you than she does the Man in the Moon."

CHAPTER 23

BURNED

O R MAYBE SHE DIDN'T DO IT.

So far, Tonya Bundick hadn't announced any alibis for any of the nights of any of the fires, but what did that mean, anyway? The fires had happened over the course of several months. Memories could get foggy; she couldn't be expected to know what she was doing those nights. And maybe there wouldn't have been alibis anyway. Wouldn't most people be at home, alone, during those times?

Maybe she was the provocatively dressed mom who bragged too much on Facebook, and Charlie was the aw-shucks good old boy who was friendly with the cops and the fire department. Maybe it was easier for people to like him than her, for the abstract ways it's sometimes easier for people to wrap their heads around difficult men than complicated women. All of the conversations that Charlie claimed they'd had, about burning houses and broken dreams—all of those were, she would continue to steadfastly maintain, a lie.

A while after this was all over, a self-published book appeared on Amazon.com, printed by one of those companies that will print any book whose author is willing to pay for the copies. The title was *Burned*, and it was about a woman named "Sonya Booneswick" who lived in "Accolake County" and was framed for a bunch of arsons that her boyfriend "Harley" committed. The author went by the pseudonym Z. Jasmine BelFord, and claimed to "have the unique ability to see the story from inside the heart and mind of Sonya." The story, which is told in the first person, opens with the couple's arrest, and follows Sonya as she is pitted against a system that is out to get her: the sheriff, the police, the media, the Commonwealth's attorney, her own attorneys. She begins an affair with her bail bondsman, she begins an affair with another man, and all throughout, she protests her innocence, sometimes in verse:

> *Who set those fires in the county, everyone's hoping to collect*
> *the bounty*
> *It wasn't me, was it you? Does anyone have a clue?*

Some of the poems read like Sonya-isms.

In the book version, the character Harley ultimately kills himself at the end, riddled with grief over ruining Sonya's life. "May his soul rise to Heaven before the Devil finds out he's dead," the author wrote.

Maybe the book reflected what happened in real life to Charlie and Tonya. Maybe Charlie was orchestrating a massive plot, while playing completely dumb. It was a possibility.

Maybe nobody knew Tonya Bundick at all.

CHAPTER 24

"WE'D DONE IT BEFORE"

THE TRIALS OF TONYA BUNDICK were turning into the biggest spectacle the Eastern Shore had ever seen. Media from outlets all over Virginia had sent in requests to place cameras in the courtroom. The local news was printing updates on every incremental court procedure related to the trial.

As it turned out, the trial wouldn't even be on the shore. The judge, Glen Tyler, had granted the defense team's request for the trials to be moved to Virginia Beach, a ninety-minute trip down the peninsula, through Northampton County, and across the Bay Bridge-Tunnel to the mainland. The publicity was one thing—more pressing was the fact that it might be impossible to seat a jury where one or more members didn't own something that had burned.

Allan Zaleski, Tonya's court-appointed defense attorney, had been relieved for the venue change but disappointed in the ultimate location. The Norfolk-Virginia Beach area was heavily populated by military personnel, who tended to be conservative and trusting of law enforcement, and perhaps, Zaleski feared, more inclined to believe the prosecutor's account over Tonya's. Zaleski tried but failed to have it moved again to a county even farther away.

Zaleski was tall, white haired, and wore a pair of glasses that he used to gesture, with grandfatherly effect, in the courtroom. He had a lot of courtroom experience, and the arsons did not represent his strangest case. That honor went to a man he'd defended for rape and murder more than a decade ago. The victim was a sailor's wife, discovered by her husband when he came home from sea. As a suspect, police latched on to her neighbor, also a sailor. The neighbor first proclaimed his innocence, but after an eleven-hour interrogation, he not only confessed but also implicated a second assailant, his roommate and fellow seaman. The roommate initially said he was innocent, but eventually also confessed, and additionally implicated a third suspect, who in turn implicated still another. Zaleski's client was the third suspect, a man named Derek Tice, arrested in what was originally believed to be a shocking example of mass depravity and sadism within the U.S. Navy. Their confessions were disturbing: "Dan started to strangle her to keep her from talking," Zaleski's client told investigators after nine hours of interrogations, "so I made a statement that, 'Just get a knife and stab her.' Then Dan stabbed her, then I stabbed her, then Eric stabbed her, Joe stabbed her."

But there was one problem. Every time a new assailant was introduced—the group eventually became known as the Norfolk Four—the man's DNA would be tested. And none of the DNA collected from any of the alleged perpetrators ever matched what had been found at the crime scene. Their confessions didn't match up with the evidence either: one man said they had beaten the woman to death; in fact, she had not been beaten at all. All of them went to prison anyway. Some of them protested their innocence, saying they'd only confessed out of exhaustion and fear: the interrogating detective said unless they confessed they'd get the death penalty. One of them grew to believe he must have been involved, even though he'd had an alibi. It was the only way he could make sense of how he'd ended up in jail. And then, after all that, there was another stunning twist in the case: the real killer, a man none of the Norfolk Four had ever even met before, confessed unprompted in a letter to a friend, which the friend brought to law enforcement.

It would still take several years, and multiple complicated legal machinations, for the wrongly convicted men to be released. What had been thought of as a gang rape instead became a case study in false confessions.

Now Zaleski was seventy-two years old and made his own hours out of a Norfolk law firm that also employed his son, Christopher. Allan also kept a small office for his occasional work on the Eastern Shore. The court system was a tricky thing over there, because so many attorneys had conflicts of interest due to prior cases. For high-profile matters, a judge would occasionally recruit a defense attorney from the mainland. Over the years, Zaleski had become one of these attorneys. He'd defended, for example, the drunk driver who killed an off-duty state trooper and his young son as they drove together to a Harry Potter book release party. No lawyer on the shore wanted that case. Zaleski took it, and the driver went to jail for ten years and then got out and crashed another car in another DUI.

Zaleski wasn't a true believer, not the type to think all his clients were innocent. What mattered was what could be proved in a court of law. And that's what he asked clients. Not "Did you do it?" but "Can they prove you did it?" He hadn't been Tonya's original assigned attorney, but the original lawyer had recused herself due to a conflict of interest. Judge Tyler called Zaleski to ask if he would take over.

The duration between Tonya's initial arrest and her first trial was eight months. Commonwealth's attorney Gary Agar had used every day of it strategizing how to build his case. The fact that Charlie had agreed to testify was important; what Agar didn't know is whether Charlie's testimony would be sufficient. He was, after all, a convicted felon. The jury might hold that against him, just like they might hold against him the fact that he was Tonya's spurned lover and not exactly an unbiased party. Agar needed corroboration. But he didn't have any fingerprints or DNA evidence. He didn't have any other witnesses. What he had besides Charlie was a lot of "riding around."

And, he had phone calls. State troopers Johnson and Burke, who caught Charlie, thought they had seen him communicating on the phone as he ran away from the fire. Charlie himself had said that Tonya would typically drop him off to light a fire, and that he would call her cell phone when he was ready to be picked up. If that was true, there should be records of those calls. Agar had never employed cell-phone tower evidence before, but he was familiar with the general concept: When a cell phone was used, it connected to the nearest available tower. Each tower's coverage was divided into three sectors, facing in three different directions. Placing a cell phone within a certain sector gave the information even more specificity.

Agar decided three things were necessary in order for the cell records to be useful. First, he needed to look for nights in which the cell phones had called each other around the same time that a fire had been reported. Second, during the times of the calls, the two phones both had to be located in the same sector of the same cell phone tower, near the fire, which would aid in supporting the idea that Tonya was idling in the car nearby, waiting for a pickup call. And third, the calls couldn't take place within the same sector as Tonya and Charlie's house on Matthews Road—if it did, the defense could argue that Tonya had been talking to Charlie while she was at home and while he was, unbeknownst to her, out lighting a fire.

Agar found several calls that fit those criteria, including on the night Charlie and Tonya were caught. To his list of potential witnesses, Agar added a Verizon Wireless expert.

While Agar's office combed through phone records looking for the best evidence against Tonya, the Zaleski team—Allan and son Christopher, who would be joining his father for Tonya's defense—focused on negotiating how the charges against their client would be tried. If all sixty-two counts were packed into one trial, Allan worried the jury would get exhausted. They would stop paying attention to the evidence, or lack thereof, and just assume that anyone brought forth on that many charges must be guilty. So he wanted lots of trials. "Each case, fresh and new," he explained to the *Virginian Pilot* newspaper in an interview. The prosecution wanted the opposite. Multiple trials would stretch county resources and further anger an already agitated community. Besides, the fires were part of a "common plan," Agar had argued to Judge Tyler at a hearing on the subject, which meant they should be part of a common trial. "All were at night," he said. "All buildings were unoccupied, no accelerant was used, all were on secondary roadways." The judge had sided with the Zaleskis, ruling that the trials could be split up, one per count if necessary.

Sixty-two trials. Even if they moved along at three per year, a quick clip, there was a good chance that by the time the legal proceedings were over, many of the main players would be dead.

Given the judge's ruling, Agar's next best hope was that Tonya would be found guilty in her early trials. In that situation, the defense might decide to plead guilty for all the other charges, in exchange for a packaged sentence. Zaleski, on the other hand, hoped Tonya would be found not guilty and the other charges might eventually be dropped. For a felony count of arson of an abandoned structure, the minimum penalty sentencing was two years per count, and the maximum was ten years. If the trials didn't end soon, Tonya could live out the rest of her days in prison.

^ ^ ^

THE FIRST TRIAL took place on January 13, 2014. It was the first trial but the final fire, the one that got Tonya and Charlie arrested on Airport Road.

In contrast to Accomack's old brick courthouse, the Virginia

Beach court complex was modern, with escalators and glass walls, and bland courtrooms that looked like they'd been outfitted with an Office Depot catalog. In the spectator pews, the handful of Accomack residents who'd gotten the day off of work and come to the trial out of curiosity were clustered behind the desk reserved for the Commonwealth's attorney. The journalists, mostly local media and television affiliates who set up cameras in the back, clustered on the side of the defense, eager for a glimpse at Tonya.

When the court was called into session at 9 a.m. on the thirteenth, prospective jurors also peered curiously at her as she strolled in slowly, chin high, to her seat between Allan and Christopher Zaleski. She had lost weight in prison and appeared fine boned and fragile. She was wearing a blue button-down shirt and black slacks, brought for her by a friend, but funds hadn't been deposited into her temporary Virginia Beach commissary account in time for her to buy makeup and hair products. She looked unkempt, stripped of the armor she normally applied so carefully. A few in the panel recognized her anyway, from following the news, but to most of them she was nobody. Her face was expressionless. Some of the jury panel didn't know what to make of her: at least one, a retired nurse, looked at the small woman surrounded by the hordes of uniformed men—deputies from both Accomack and Virginia Beach, members of the Virginia State Police—and immediately felt sorry for her.

Once court had been called to order, Judge Tyler began to explain why there were both blue Virginia Beach law enforcement uniforms and brown Accomack uniforms present in the court. "This is a case that arose in Accomack County, on the Eastern Shore," he said. "I know from having been raised in the western part of Roanoke County as a child and then moving to the shore after I started practicing law that 50 percent of the people in the Commonwealth of Virginia don't know where the Eastern Shore is. Now, I presume that people in Virginia Beach know that if you go across the Bay Bridge-Tunnel for seventeen miles, when you fall on the land over there, you're in Northampton County, Virginia, and if you go seventy miles from the Bridge-Tunnel, you'll come into Maryland. I apologize to all of you who know where the Eastern Shore is; I just have run into so many people who don't."

Tyler was a retired judge, who occasionally came back to serve on rotations. He'd been on the bench eighteen years and had, over time, developed an excruciatingly patient way of explaining things that assumed jurors did not know anything, but did not make them feel guilty about it.

"I am going to tell you a story," he continued, still perfecting his description of the uniqueness of the county. "A friend of mine was a great Virginia Tech advocate. He went to all of their football games. They solicited him to give a donation to Virginia Tech. When the band formed up on the field, the football field in the shape of the Commonwealth of Virginia, they never added the Eastern Shore. So he made them add a little strip of the Eastern Shore of Virginia before he would give them $50,000. So that will give you some idea. The location of this event—Mr. Agar, state the location of this event, please?"

"The town of Melfa," Gary Agar said, rising halfway from his seat to supply the judge with an answer.

Only after Tyler felt that the atmospherics had been properly and thoroughly set did he pivot again to talking about the case at hand and how he would be selecting jurors for it. From time to time, he remarked on a name that seemed familiar. "Killmon is an Eastern Shore name—do you have any relatives over there?" the judge interrupted one prospective juror's questioning.

"It is—my grandfather is from there. He met my grandmother on Tangier Island and he carried her off," the prospective juror said.

"Well, he had to carry her off," the judge said, "because those people won't go unless you take them."

The selection lasted all morning. In the end, the jury consisted of, among others, a nurse, a federal safety compliance officer, a homemaker, a counterintelligence counsel agent, a college student. When it was lunchtime, Tyler remarked that he planned to obey Virginia Beach custom on some court-related things, such as breaking for lunch at 1 p.m. instead of noon the way he usually did. However, there were some things he preferred to do his way. "It's going to be the Accomack rule on clothing, bailiffs," he said. "Nobody's coming in with torn jeans, flip-flops, T-shirts, field clothes, et cetera."

And it was time for the trial to begin.

^ ^ ^

"We have all heard of arson."

Gary Agar stood before the newly assembled panel with his graceful hands, and introduced the jury to the charge they would be asked to evaluate. "This arson is one dealing with the burning of a structure, the structure having a value of over $200. It's not that difficult a statute, and the proof is just this: The Commonwealth has to show that the structure was burned in whole or in part. And that the defendant did that with malice. Malice is just the doing of a wrongful act intentionally, without any cause or excuse.

"The second charge faced by this defendant is that of conspiracy. Conspiracy is where—and let me just read it from the statement of the law: 'The defendant entered into an agreement with another, and that agreement was to commit arson, and they both intended to commit arson upon their entering into that agreement.' So it is not a complicated law, but it is exacting. The Commonwealth needs to show this beyond a reasonable doubt. That's what we have to show—now let me tell you how we're going to prove it."

The Commonwealth would begin, Agar continued, by calling as a witness the owner of the property in question. He would then call the troopers who witnessed the fire being lit by a man—a man who ran, "lickety-split" back to a van driven by the defendant, Tonya Bundick. He would call the sheriff's deputy and the police officer who stopped the van, and the firemen, and the officials who had performed the search of the van, and Scott Wade, the investigator who questioned Bundick, and a man from Verizon Wireless who would tell them technical things about an important call made at 11:35 p.m. on the night the defendant was arrested.

"There will be a lot of evidence here," he finished. "But I think at the end of this it will be very clear the defendant cannot sit back here in this position of 'Gee, I just didn't know what was going on.' The evidence will show she's just not in that situation at all."

Agar returned to his seat, and without a transition, Allan Zaleski rose from his. He moved slowly, almost creakily; there was a vague Columbo quality to him—a man who feigned simplicity while retaining everything. After a brief introduction, he got to the facts: "Charles Smith and Tonya Bundick were lovers. They were not married, but they lived together in the town of Parksley. It was a two-year relationship. My client had two—has two—children, is the single mother of a thirteen-year-old and an eleven-year-old. She met Charles Smith. He was a self-employed man, and he later moved in with Ms. Bundick." One night the couple was running a few errands, Zaleski said, and this was the night that Charlie got out to light a fire. But Tonya didn't know anything about it.

"It's interesting," Zaleski continued, philosophically. He was in the habit of taking off his eyeglasses, and gesturing with them. "You'll find that the fire was set with a cigarette lighter, something you can stick in your pocket. Not a can of gasoline anybody could carry, or turpentine or anything like that. You can stick it in your pocket, run out, do what you intend to do. It's obviously what Charles Smith intended to do. He's confessed to it."

In order for Tonya, the purported getaway driver, to be found guilty on arson and conspiracy to commit arson, the Commonwealth would have to prove that Tonya was a driving force in the plot. It wasn't even enough for her to be aware of the fires—not that he was saying she was—but she had to have "encouraged" Charlie in the crimes. "I think you'll all conclude that Mr. Agar has failed in the duty of requiring that level of proof," he said, finishing his opening argument. "Thank you very much."

^ ^ ^

IT'S AMAZING how boring trials can be. How even the most salacious of crimes committed under the most colorful of circumstances can result in testimony that is tedious and snoozy.

Claude Henry, the owner of the house on Airport Road, was brought in and questioned for several minutes about the material comprising the driveway (packed grass) and the existence of a water heater (there wasn't one; he'd had it removed because he was afraid vandals would steal it), and whether or not the house had working electricity. Troopers Willie Burke and Troy Johnson were each brought on the stand to discuss the placement of their tent, and the use of their night-vision goggles, and approximately how long it appeared to take Charles Smith to light the house on fire.

Trooper Martin Kriz took the stand and explained that Tonya, when he searched her, had told him about a ChapStick in her bra. Because of the trooper's Eastern European accent, the word "ChapStick" ended up with an "ah" sound in it. "Chahpstick."

"Did you find any weapons?" Allan Zaleski asked Kriz.

"No, sir."

"Any lighters on her? Cigarette lighters?"

"No, sir."

Gary Agar, on redirect with Trooper Kriz, unintentionally revealed that he had been flummoxed by the young trooper's accent when the trooper talked about discovering Tonya's lip balm. "You stated she had a *chopstick*?" he asked incredulously. He had a habit of slowly repeating back the witness's final phrases in his rumbling, singsong voice. "Did she indicate where she had the chopstick?"

"She told me it was in her bra," said Kriz, who didn't understand that Agar misheard him.

"In her *bra*?" Agar repeated. "What, if anything, did you do at that point?"

"I removed it," Kriz said. The accent confusion was never cleared up, and approximately half of the courtroom was left with the impression that the accused arsonist must have a proclivity for Chinese food.

The cell phone expert that Agar had found was a custodian of records from Verizon Wireless, a man named Avram Polinsky, who took the stand holding a sheaf of papers and explained what they represented: calls and text messages occurring between two particular cell phone numbers on the evening of April 1. Agar explained that the fire in question took place at 11:35. Did Mr. Polinsky have any calls that were placed at that time between Charlie and Tonya? Polinsky shuffled his papers and said he did—three of them, all placed at 11:35. One lasted five seconds, one lasted six, and the final one lasted a full three minutes. Those were the only calls between the phones that evening.

The last witness of the day was Charlie. The only witness anyone cared about was Charlie. The ten or so reporters in the courtroom had half expected him not to show up; Charlie himself had reconsidered his decision more than once, up until the last minute.

His hair was close shaven and his hands were shackled, which made him hunch even further into himself as he entered from the right, through doors that led to a small holding cell. The path to the witness stand took him directly in front of the defense table where Tonya sat between her two attorneys. Behind her, the journalists sent to cover the trial picked up their notebooks, ready to write down anything the former lovers said or mouthed as Charlie walked past. The two hadn't seen each other in months, since Tonya was released from the Accomack jail on bail. But they didn't look at each other, not even once. Tonya kept her eyes straight ahead and

Charlie kept his on the floor until he settled into the witness stand and hunched forward into the microphone.

"Mr. Smith, I think if you just sit back, I think that thing picks up pretty good," said Judge Tyler, motioning that Charlie didn't have to bend quite so close to the microphone. "You don't need to lean up."

Charlie nodded and backed away, but only by a few inches, as Agar approached him.

"Have you come to tell the truth today?" Agar asked.

"Yes, sir."

"Is this difficult testimony for you?"

"Yes." Charlie's voice was barely more than a whisper, and despite the judge's promise that the microphone would pick up his voice, the attendees in the gallery had to strain to hear him.

"Judge, I would object to that," Allan Zaleski said. "It's leading."

"Sustained."

Agar continued, barely missing a beat. "Mr. Smith, do you know Tonya Bundick?"

"Yes, sir."

"*How* do you know her?"

"She was my fiancée."

"Would you point her out to the jury, please?"

Charlie raised his eyes the barest minimum in order to accomplish the task of looking, for the first time, at the love of his life. "She's right there," he said.

"Your feelings for her?" Agar asked.

"I still love her," he said, and his throat caught.

Agar knew that the defense, during cross-examination, would light upon Charlie's previous criminal record, so he decided to get there first, pivoting to the check forgeries that landed him in prison the first time. He asked Charlie how many felonies, exactly, did he currently have under his belt? Charlie shook his head as if the number was near unfathomable. "Thirtysome?" he guessed. Agar affirmed the number and pointed out that the number was so high because all of the forgeries had happened at once—Charlie had burned through an entire book of checks. But he admitted to those forgeries. And he'd admitted to the breaking and entering.

And he'd admitted, more recently, to setting the arsons. "Yes, sir," Charlie agreed. He had done those fires.

Periodically, Agar would stop roaming the room to glance back down at the prosecution's desk. On it, he had laid out a legal pad, with the questions he planned to ask Charlie written in neat print.

15) Riding around?
16) Who driving?
17) Purpose in driving around?

The questions stretched all the way down to number thirty-five, by which point he planned to have guided Charlie up to the night of his arrest.

"Now, were you living with Tonya Bundick when these arsons began?" he asked.

"Yes, sir."

"And *how* did they begin?"

On the stand, Charlie shrugged, as if the thing was just as much a mystery to him as anyone else. "It just kind of happened one night. Having a bad night and rode by an abandoned house and decided to set it on fire."

"*Who* set it on fire?"

"I went into the house first, and I didn't set it on fire, and then she went in and set it on fire."

"Did you do any more arsons other than that?"

"Yes, sir," Charlie said. They had done them until they finally got caught.

"Did you develop a particular scheme or manner of doing those fires?" Agar asked.

Again, Charlie shrugged. "It was just what we always did. A phone call. Get dropped off, then pick up the phone and tell them where to come pick each other up. I couldn't tell you word for word because it I don't remember, but it basically stayed the same . . . She would drive most of the time except for in the beginning."

"Why was it different in the beginning, Charlie?" Agar asked—question number twenty-one on the list.

"Because I really didn't want no part of it. But then, she almost got caught, and I couldn't stand it. She got all cut up, and I couldn't stand seeing her that way, and I told her if we had to keep doing it, then I'd do the arsons."

"Did you change your mode of arson at that point?" Agar tried asking. Charlie hadn't explicitly said that Tonya had lit the first fires, and Agar wanted that clarification.

Charlie shook his head in confusion at the word "mode." "I don't know what you mean by that," he said.

Agar tried again: "*Who* lit the fires in the beginning?"

"Tonya did."

"And after that, were there other fires?" Agar asked.

"Yes."

"And *who* lit the next fire?"

"She did."

"And *who* lit the next fire?"

"She did."

Agar asked Charlie a few questions about how they would select properties, and then consulted his notes again. "Now, on April 1, did you and Tonya Bundick leave the house in Hopeton that evening?"

They had, Charlie said. On the evening of April 1, they had been out as usual, riding around. They had eventually ended up at The Wine Rack to get gas. After The Wine Rack, he said, "I went to go burn down a house."

"You went to go burn down a *house*?" Agar repeated.

At first they had driven down Texaco Road to burn a house

there, Charlie said, but it was too close to the state police barracks, and they decided it wasn't safe, so they headed toward Melfa instead, and while they drove they made plans for the evening.

"What, if anything, were you talking about?" Agar asked.

"I was going to burn down a house."

"What did you say?"

"That I was going to burn down a house."

"And what, if anything, did Tonya Bundick say?"

Charlie shrugged. "Nothing, really. Just that she didn't think it was smart to burn that one in front of the road that came out in front of the state police barracks."

She had suggested they go farther into Melfa, at which point they selected the house on Airport Road, at which point Charlie told Tonya he worried it was a setup, at which point she said it wasn't, so he got out to burn down the house, calling Tonya once to tell her he was about to do it, and again while it was being done.

"Did you do a whole lot of planning for that operation?" Agar asked.

"No."

"Why is that?"

"Because," he said, "we'd done it before."

Agar had finished his direct examination. Judge Tyler called a recess then, until the next morning. It was after 5 p.m., he never liked to go beyond 5:30, and he assumed the Zaleskis would take longer in their cross-examination of Charlie Smith than half an hour. The reporters, who had been required to leave their cell phones and laptops outside of the courthouse, ran to their cars so they could Tweet and file updates from the trial. "Eastern Shore arson suspect's fiancé testifies," they wrote. "At arson trial, all eyes on Tonya Bundick's former lover."

The next day the cross-examination started. Christopher Zaleski would be handling it. He had a more fiery questioning style than either Agar or his father, and a slight smirk that implied he didn't believe any of Charlie's answers, even before they were given.

"You're pretty comfortable up there today?" he began.

"I guess as good as I can be?" Charlie said, appearing confused by the question.

"Well, you've done this before. This isn't the first time you've testified in a courtroom, is it?"

"Testified?"

"Been sworn in."

"Oh."

"Gave statements under oath."

"No, it's not."

Agar had been right in his assumption that the Zaleskis would gravitate toward Charlie's criminal past; it was the surest way to set him up as an unreliable witness. The younger Zaleski pointed out that Charlie had testified before, because he'd been in trouble before, and when he'd been in trouble, he'd cried, just as he had on the stand the day before.

"No," Charlie said, he hadn't cried.

"You didn't?"

"No."

"*Okay*," Christopher scoffed. "You blamed it on the drugs, though, didn't you?"

The Zaleskis's plan, it became clear, was to paint Charlie as unreliable from multiple angles. He was unreliable because he was a repeated convicted felon. He was unreliable because he was a drug user, who had relapsed multiple times. He was unreliable—this whole trial, by de facto, was unreliable—because Charlie was on a first-name basis with the sheriff, because Godwin had told him, "We're going to help you out, Charles," on the night that he was arrested. Charlie, the drug-addicted repeat offender who was personally acquainted with the police, knew that the only way to help himself out was to throw someone else under the bus and hope for a good deal in exchange. "Your plan was to implicate her, wasn't it?"

"No."

"*Okay.* But you did."

"I know I did."

"You're doing this to get some assistance, aren't you?"

"Not that I know of."

"To get your time cut?"

"Ain't nobody offered me nothing."

Eventually, Christopher came around to the real reason that Charlie's testimony should not be considered reliable by the jury: because he loved Tonya. Too much, unhealthily. He wanted to own her.

"Own her?" Charlie repeated.

"You wanted people to know she was taken. Didn't you write, 'I want you to wear a ring so people know you're taken'?"

"Well, yeah. That was after she wrote me a letter saying to buy her a ring."

"You would do whatever it takes to be with her, right?"

"Yeah," Charlie said.

"And you know if you're in here and she's out there, she's not going to wait around, don't you?"

"Well, yes, I'm concerned about that."

"Because you know you've got thirty-one felony convictions plus these new ones, right?"

"Yes."

"It would kill you if you found out that she was dating somebody else, wouldn't it?"

"Yeah, it would."

"You love her so much it isn't funny?"

"Yeah."

Christopher moved on to his next point: that Charlie had been the one to volunteer in the fire department—the one to excel there, to learn how to move around in the dark, to learn how to set fires without accelerants. What about the fact that Charlie wasn't on good terms with the fire department, and must certainly have wanted revenge on the members there? Wasn't that a sign that he must have been in a pretty desperate place, the kind of place that might lead someone to light fires? And finally, what about the bedroom issues he was having with Tonya?

"There were problems with your relationship," Christopher said. "I mean, she was your girlfriend. You were supposed to be doing things."

"Yeah."

"You couldn't perform physically with her, could you?"

"No, I couldn't."

"In fact, for eighteen months leading up to this, and these are your words"—he paused for effect—"'My dick stopped working.'"

In the press gallery, journalists collectively picked up their pens, ready to capture the outburst that seemed sure to follow from Charlie. They'd read the transcripts of his confession and knew how mortified he seemed to be by the idea of other people knowing his bedroom problems.

But an explosion didn't come. "Yeah," Charlie said.

"And you were concerned about that, weren't you?" said the younger Zaleski. "Because you knew if you couldn't satisfy her she was going to look elsewhere?"

"Yes, sir," Charlie said sadly.

Christopher let that hang in the air before moving on. When Charlie had confessed to the sheriff, he'd talked about a broad manner of things, Zaleski prompted, pacing the floor. "Talked about your demons. Your drugs. Your relapse, your history, your work in the fire department, getting kicked out of the fire department."

"I never talked about getting kicked out of the fire department," Charlie answered, which was true.

Charlie offering this sort of specific correction wasn't good for Tonya, because it made Charlie look like a man who not only told the truth but told it exactingly. In the grand scheme of things, it didn't matter whether Charlie had talked about being kicked out of the fire department. He was a readily admitted forger and drug user and arsonist with erectile dysfunction. But when he bothered to correct Christopher Zaleski about whether he'd specifically talked about being kicked out of the fire department, he came across as a person who wanted to be helpful and make sure the story was told right.

Christopher was getting visibly agitated. It seemed, he pointed out, that Charlie was really good at blaming other people for things. He was now blaming Tonya for his lighting the fires. But hadn't Charlie, in fact, enjoyed those fires? "You set some of them for revenge, didn't you?"

"What do you mean?" Charlie asked, and Christopher brought up the fire that Charlie had lit because an acquaintance was hitting on Tonya on Facebook.

"*Those* weren't instances where you guys were having a bad day and riding around and decided to set the place on fire. You did those on your own, right?"

"What do you mean?" Charlie asked again. "By myself?"

"Yes."

"No sir, I didn't."

"You told the sheriff you did those by yourself."

"I mean I lit them by myself," Charlie explained. He had held the lighter; Tonya was waiting in the van.

Gary Agar kept his redirect brief. Christopher Zaleski had touched on Charlie's sense of inadequacy in the relationship, specifically the problems of his impotence. Agar was looking for a little clarification.

"How, if at all, did that relate to these fires?" he asked.

"I didn't have no clue. Just, I did whatever it took to make her happy. Because they kept telling me at the [doctors' offices] that it was all in my head, that I thought she was too good for me that that's why I couldn't perform, and I didn't want to lose her."

"Why would a fire improve a situation where you had no sex?" Agar asked.

Allan Zaleski rose. "I object to that, judge. Calls for speculation."

"Sustained," the judge said.

CHAPTER 25

"THEY CAME OUT OF EVERYWHERE"

I T WAS ALLAN ZALESKI'S BELIEF that when you had a client whose defense was that they were innocent, then you had nothing to lose by putting them on the stand. Tonya wanted to testify. She wanted to tell her story. On the second day of the trial, she got her chance.

The courtroom was quiet as she was called to the stand. Even her walk was divisive: some of the watchers in the gallery thought that her languid stroll was a sign that she considered herself to be above the proceedings, that she was treating the affair like a red carpet walk instead of a felony trial. Others saw not defiance, but dignity, an admirable refusal to be dehumanized by the seediness of the situation. She reached the stand and slowly took a seat, a cat settling itself. Her voice in the courtroom was soft and lilting as she repeated her name to the bailiff; there was an air of gentility that people who hadn't heard her speak before weren't expecting.

She was forty years old, she told the elder Zaleski, Allan, as he began her questioning with basic biographical details. She was the mother of two children. She had lived with Charlie in a three-bedroom, one-bathroom house, and he had done auto-body work, and she had been a certified nursing assistant until she left that job to take care of her son. She had been in jail from April to September of the previous year, and then she had made bail, and then she had been arrested again in December. Charlie always had bad self-esteem when they were together. "It was like I constantly had to reassure him why I was with him, why I loved him, what I saw in him," she said. She'd known he had drug problems. That's why she'd asked him to take a drug test after they'd been dating a little while; she wanted to make sure he hadn't relapsed, because sometimes his actions were "sporadic." She might call him and ask him to pick up a loaf of bread on the way home, and he'd get home and there would be no bread. That's what she meant by sporadic. He was forgetful. He acted funny.

Allan nodded thoughtfully to all of her responses, and then said he wanted to steer her attention to April 1. Did she remember that night?

"I do," she said. It was the night she was arrested while driving Charlie's van, and Zaleski was careful to underscore that point—that Tonya owned two vehicles, but on the night of April 1 they weren't even in her car. They were in Charlie's van as they drove north to Maryland for a shopping trip.

"We had left my house, I guess it was probably around 6 o'clock because I was going to go birthday shopping for my boys," she explained. "Their birthdays were going to be April 3 and April 9. So I wanted to get their birthday gifts, so we had gone to the Walmart in Pocomoke." Her sons wanted smartphones for their birthdays. The ones in the Walmart electronics department were more expensive than the $300 she'd allotted, so they tried a nearby GameStop, and Family Dollar, and then they went back to Walmart, which had turned out to have the best deal after all. Before they checked out, she and Charlie decided they needed a few groceries. "So when we got into the grocery section—mind you, I was the one, I was buying the items that night, I was the one who had the money—and Charlie wanted a box of Steak-umms. And to make a long story short, when we would use his money to go to the grocery store, everything had to be bought as a meal. You know, everything had to be a meal. And he picked up these Steak-umms and he said he wanted to get those and he was going to take them home and fix them. And, of course, I'm like, but you can't do that because everything has to be a meal. You know, we're planning our money out. We have to get enough to make meals that will last. So we got in an argument over a box of Steak-umms."

Tonya kept talking, and what she was talking about suddenly wasn't a story about the night that the fires stopped and her life changed in Accomack County. It had become a story about relationships, and those nights when the person you love is suddenly the person who irritates you most, and when Steak-umms grow to represent not a dinner choice, but the symbol of financial independence, and finally getting it together to move up in the world.

Tonya's story was about a waning love affair, and the relentless struggle of being alive and working class in 2013.

She made him put the Steak-umms back. She was touchy. He was touchy. They left the Walmart, Charlie driving, and they were supposed to stop to make a car payment at a nearby auto center but Charlie didn't even stop the car. They got closer to their house, but then before they could turn onto their street, Charlie turned to her and asked if she wanted to go down to Onley, to a different Walmart. She thought maybe he wanted to get his own presents for her sons. He hadn't gotten anything for them at the other stores.

"So we went—we got back to my house because I wanted to check on the boys and make sure they were okay, put the groceries away, and we proceeded to go down to the Onley Walmart. And when we got there, things still weren't right," Tonya said. She went to look in the underwear section and he was right there, glued to her elbow, the way he used to be glued to her in her own clothing store, only this time it wasn't cute and it wasn't endearing. "And I mean I won't lie. I was a little irate with him. So I was like, 'Do you have to be up my ass while I'm looking—excuse me—while I'm looking at underwear?'"

They left the second Walmart. They drove a while, stopped at The Wine Rack to get gas. Tonya told Charlie that he seemed like he was in a bad mood that night and that he didn't want to be there with her. It had been a hard stretch of time for them, she said, with his mom passing away and business being rough. She offered him an out. She said, "You know, if things are too hard for you to deal with with my sons—if things are too hard for you to deal with, just tell me. You know, all you got to do is walk."

After they got gas, Charlie said he wanted to ride around for a while. A bit later, he stopped and peed and then asked Tonya if she could drive. She drove a little more, through the back roads of Melfa, and then he asked to stop and be let out again. She didn't bother to ask why; she was already pissed at him. She eventually doubled back and tried calling his cell, but he didn't pick up.

"And did he call you then?" Allan asked.

"He called me a little while later."

"All right. And what did he say?"

"Well, at first when he picked up the phone, I didn't hear anything. It was just a lot of muffling," she said. "It sounded like somebody was holding the phone in their pocket or something."

"But then what happened?"

"And then he just told me—he said, 'Come back and get me.'"

"When he first got out of the van, did he have anything in his hands?" Allan asked, angling at whether Tonya would have seen him carrying a lighter or anything that indicated what he was about to go do.

"No."

"When he got back in the van, did he have anything in his hands?"

"No."

"And so then did he ever mention to you anything about, 'We've been caught,' or anything like that?"

"No."

"Did you see any other traffic on the road?"

"I did not," Tonya said.

"Okay. So after he got back in the van, what happened?"

"I got to the Melfa light, and a car came up behind me and I had to stop because the light was red; and when I proceeded to make my left-hand turn when the light turned green, there was the cops. I mean, they came out of everywhere."

She didn't know Charlie was going to light the fire. She didn't know he had lit any fires. She didn't know anything about the fires, she said. What she knew is that Charlie was the type of guy who acted "sporadic," who would leave the house to pick up bread and then get to the grocery store and forget why he was there. She thought he might be back on drugs. Everybody knew Charlie had a drug problem. Those nights when Charlie was out lighting fires, she assumed he was working late, trying to bring in extra cash for a business that didn't seem to be going well since he'd moved out of his stepdad's shop. That's what she knew.

Gary Agar approached his cross-examination with an air of disbelief.

"Now, you're very articulate," he said. "You speak very well. How much education do you have?"

"I graduated high school," she said.

"And then Charles had low esteem, he always needed assurances, and you were his girlfriend."

"Yes."

"And did you give him those assurances?"

"Well, of course. I loved him."

For the jury who had just seen Charlie bumble through his testimony and not understand some of the terminology, Agar was trying to illustrate one of his central theses: Tonya was the dominant partner in the relationship. Charlie depended on her, for everything from a place to live to the building of his own self-esteem.

He might have been the one caught with a lighter, but if there was an orchestrated plot behind the actions, it would have been orchestrated by Tonya.

Agar tried to bring her to the concept of "riding around" that he had noted in her interrogation with Scott Wade. Hadn't she told Wade that she and Charlie went out riding around a few times a week? How was it possible that she wouldn't have been aware of Charlie's fire-starting proclivities, if she was in the car with him so much? He brought up the prison phone calls, the fact that when she and Charlie talked on the phone while she was out on bond and he was in the county jail, she had made a point to say, "They're recording this." (She hadn't wanted to discuss the case, she explained.) He brought up their prison letters, and the fact that Tonya sounded like she was pretty good at tracking down legal information online. ("I wouldn't say that. I know how to go online and Google something.")

He wasn't expecting to get a sudden courtroom confession, and he didn't. Tonya was poised and collected, never displaying a negative emotion stronger than slight irritation. She had good comedic timing. When Agar asked what she'd made of the fact that Charlie—who by her account had already asked to pee once—asked to be let out again, she sighed in a way that anyone familiar with the daily exasperations of a relationship could relate to: "You know what? I really didn't ask him anything because we were already not getting along."

And then she did let him out, and she did pick him up, and the police arrested them, she explained again to Agar. And then she went to jail and was put in solitary confinement and for several weeks she had no idea what Charlie was saying about her or anything else.

"Had you been trying to train him?" Agar asked one final time.

"No. I have not been trying to train him."

"Well, you had been trying to assure him. That was the nature of your relationship, wasn't it?"

"If I could have trained him," she said, "I would have trained him two years ago and we wouldn't even be sitting here."

She confirmed that they hadn't been sexually intimate for a year and a half prior to their arrest.

"Wasn't it normal that in difficult times in your relationship, perhaps something would occur that would improve things—relieve stress, so to speak?" Agar asked.

"What are you saying?" she asked.

"Like lighting a fire?"

"Not that I'm aware of."

One last, desperate attempt: "Wasn't lighting a fire a means for you and he to enrich your relationship?"

She looked flabbergasted. "On my part, that's news to me."

^ ^ ^

THE DEFENSE HAD CITED several potential witnesses they planned to call, but Tonya turned out to be the only one.

At noon on the second day, Judge Tyler told the jury that all of the evidence was finished. But even so, it was important that they not discuss the case among themselves until they had heard final arguments and received specific instructions, which would happen after lunch, at 2 p.m. "That's the protocol here in Virginia Beach. While we are rather more flexible on the Eastern Shore, there are different reasons why the protocol is different here, and they're very good reasons." It was 12:20, and he called a recess for lunch.

On the one hand, the Zaleskis thought they had put up a compelling case for Tonya's innocence. Why would the jury believe Charlie? He had been on drugs, and he had been in prison, and he was a firefighter with fire know-how, and he did have the most to gain from testifying against Tonya. On the other hand, there were the phone records, which affirmed that he and Tonya had exchanged calls exactly at the time of the fire, at a location near the fire. And there was the fact that the van, driven by Tonya, had been spotted letting him out, and spotted picking him back up.

Tonya had pleaded not guilty at the beginning of the trial the morning before. Now, the jury had sat through her testimony, Charlie's, and the findings of a cell phone expert and a raft of law enforcement and fire officials, and it was time for the defense to decide whether that plea had been wise. In the Commonwealth of Virginia, juries were responsible for not only determining guilt or innocence but also for offering sentencing recommendations, which, in Allan Zaleski's experience, judges tended to ratify. But the sentences of juries were often harsher than what a judge would have determined—lacking judicial experience, juries might think that if someone was guilty, they also deserved the maximum punishment.

As soon as the jury left for deliberation, it would be too late for the defense team to do anything for Tonya except hope. But at the moment, it was still possible for Tonya to change her plea to guilty, which would put her sentencing back in the hands of Judge Tyler. Now, in a small meeting room in the Virginia Beach Courthouse, that's what the attorneys began suggesting she should do. The defense team had misgivings about the trial's outcome. It wasn't that Tonya had done badly on the stand; she hadn't done badly at all. The trouble was that Charlie had done particularly well. Tonya's defense team worried that the jury had believed him for the same reason that Gary Agar had believed him, way back when he'd watched the confession tapes in his office the night after their arrest: Charlie must be telling the truth because he came across as a person lacking the creative faculties with which to lie. It was the intangible Charlie-ness of Charlie. (Zaleski's gut feeling wasn't wrong. In the gallery, among the journalists and the other spectators, there was a prevailing sense that mostly Charlie seemed honest because Charlie seemed dumb.)

If Tonya could bring herself to change her plea, she wouldn't even have to admit guilt in order to do so. Virginia allowed an Alford plea—a plea that maintains factual innocence, but which acknowledges that the state has enough evidence to result in a likely conviction. In the plea's most famous pop culture moment, the men known

as the West Memphis Three—a trio of teenagers who were convicted of killing three small boys based on evidence that amounted to
Satanic panic and a coerced confession—agreed to submit an Alford
plea upon their prison releases. Historically, the plea was rooted in the
case of a man named Henry Alford who, though he wanted to plead
not guilty of murder, feared that a jury trial would find him guilty
and result in his execution (the death penalty was the usual penalty for
murder in his state, and there was considerable evidence against him).
The have-it-both-ways plea allowed him to maintain his innocence
and get a life sentence instead of execution, and it allowed the state to
spare the expense of a trial. Three states didn't allow the Alford plea
at all, and some judges looked on it with disdain, preferring criminals
who were contrite rather than those who tried to maneuver the legal
system but keep their own innocence. So it wasn't without risk. But
with the damning cell phone evidence and Charlie's confession, it
seemed like the best option.

At about 12:45, just twenty minutes after the judge had recessed
and while some of the spectators were still across the street picking
up lunch at the smoothie bar, Tyler called the court back to order.
"The defendant is present with her counsel," he said to a half-empty
room. "The Commonwealth's attorney is present. The jury is not in
the courtroom." He nodded toward the defense table, where Allan
and Christopher Zaleski flanked Tonya as they had from the beginning of the trial. "Mr. Zaleski."

Allan Zaleski rose. "Yes, Your Honor. The defendant would ask
for the court's leave to change her plea at this point."

"All right, sir. She will be given leave to change her plea," the
judge said.

"If the clerk would read the charges, she's ready to plead."

The clerk stood and read the first charge, the one for conspiracy to commit arson. "On or about April 1st, 2013, in the County
of Accomack, Tonya Susan Bundick did unlawfully and feloniously
conspire, confederate or combine with another to maliciously burn

or destroy by the use of explosive, in whole or in part, a building or structure having a value of over $200. For this offense, you're now to be tried. Are you guilty or not guilty?"

"Guilty," Tonya said.

The clerk read the second charge, the one for the actual burning. "Guilty," Tonya said. Pleading guilty, even an Alford plea, meant that Tonya could be sentenced for up to ten years in prison for each count, twenty years total. It meant that she waived her rights against self-incrimination and the right to defend herself, and that eventually she might be deprived "of her privilege to drive or operate a motor vehicle as a result of conviction."

She agreed to all of it.

"Ms. Bundick, if you'll please stand," he instructed, and she did. "On your pleas and on the evidence I've heard in the courtroom in the last two days, the court finds you guilty as charged."

Judge Tyler told the bailiff that he wanted to bring the jury back in to explain to them what had happened, but that Tonya didn't have to be in the room for that. The jury filed back in, looking confused as Tyler explained: Their services would no longer be needed, which he expected they would receive with "mixed emotions." It was a little unusual, he conceded in his teacherly way, but not so unusual as to be cause for alarm, and the jury should certainly feel confident that the legal system had unspooled in a proper manner. He asked if any of the jurors had any questions.

"Why did she change her plea?" one wanted to know. Tyler responded that it wasn't for him to say.

"What sentence will she get?" asked another juror, and Tyler said that, while he would eventually be the one to make that decision, he wouldn't be making it for some time.

"And how will we know what happens?" the same juror followed up.

"You will probably read about it in the newspaper," Tyler told her. "I'm almost certain you will."

CHAPTER 26

"MORAL TURPITUDE"

THE SECOND TRIAL, SPECTATORS BELIEVED, would be a bellwether for all of the other trials. The first one had been the Commonwealth's strongest case against Tonya: They had Charlie's testimony and the phone records, but most importantly, they had eyewitnesses watching Tonya drop off and pick up the confessed arsonist. The count at the second trial, "count fifty-two" as it came to be known, was more nebulous. Count fifty-two, at an abandoned migrant camp, had happened several weeks before Charlie and Tonya were caught, so there were no eyewitness accounts of her presence. If Tonya was found not guilty here, she would likely press on and keep trying her luck with the jury. If she was found guilty, on the other hand, then she might think about pleading out to the other charges. Gary Agar and Allan Zaleski were in a game of legal chicken.

The second trial looked much the same as the first. More cell phone experts, testifying that there had been calls placed between the two phones at the time of the fire. More Charlie, looking melancholy on the stand. More Accomack sheriff's deputies, hanging out in the hallway, complaining about Virginia Beach traffic.

Tonya's defense produced a new witness, a man named William Ashbrook, who had been Charlie's cell mate in jail. Ashbrook testified that Charlie'd told him about setting the fires, all by himself and without Tonya's help, by riding to and from the sites on his stepson's bicycle. Gary Agar responded by putting a giant county map on an easel and pointing out that the fire in question, set at an old labor camp, was seventeen miles from Charlie and Tonya's house. Charlie, he scoffed, had pedaled there and back, thirty-four miles total, at night, down unlit roads, on a child's bicycle?

Tonya was inscrutable, again. It was tedious, again.

It was notable only for the following reason: in addition to William Ashbrook, Tonya's defense called one additional witness who had not been at the first trial.

His name was Frank Dickerson. Allan Zaleski asked him to the stand as a character witness, for Tonya. He was identified as a minister. Dickerson was in his early fifties with a sandy goatee and a peacefulness to him associated with a man of the cloth, although Dickerson today was wearing a denim shirt. He had been ordained by the United Christian Church of America out of Tennessee, he testified. He'd lived on the Eastern Shore for twenty-nine years, and he knew a number of people who lived there including Tonya Bundick. The defense did not ask how he knew her; people in the gallery assumed she must have been a member of his congregation. Dickerson told the jury that Tonya's reputation in the community was that she "was brutally honest." As for whether she was the kind of person who could commit arson: "She's not that kind of person. [It's] not in her nature," he said.

Gary Agar said that he had only a few questions for this witness. First, he wondered, was it possible that Frank Dickerson had ever gone by "Frasure Francis Dickerson Jr."? It was, Dickerson acknowledged, although it was rare for anyone to call him Frasure these days.

Next, Agar wondered whether Dickerson had ever been convicted of a crime "of moral turpitude? Of lying, cheating, or stealing?" Dickerson said he had not, but Agar pressed him. What about a time in 1998 that a Frasure Francis Dickerson had been convicted of a misdemeanor larceny?

"I thought that was changed to something else," Dickerson responded. "Thrown out." He went on to explain: "Before I was a minister, I had a bad drug problem and I had a charge against me for taking a clock off of the wall in our home where my wife and I lived and selling it to an antique dealer." That was more than a decade ago, though. He didn't think it would still be on his record.

"How often do you visit [Tonya] in jail?" Agar asked.

"Almost every week."

"Almost every week," Agar repeated. "Do you call her?"

"We talk on the phone."

"How many times a week do you talk to her on the phone?"

"Three or four times a week."

"You pay for the calls that she makes to you?"

"Yes, sir."

"And have you given presents to her children?"

"Yes, sir."

"You're basically her—like her boyfriend then, aren't you?"

The spectators in the courtroom rustled in their seats at the phrase, but if Dickerson was thrown off by the question, he didn't show it. "Yes, sir," he said. He was basically like her boyfriend, as a matter-of-fact.

"And you've come here today as her character witness?" Agar asked theatrically. "But you didn't tell the jury you were her boyfriend when you came here to tell them what the community thought of her, did you?"

"Nobody asked me until now," Dickerson said.

The cross-examination of the Reverend didn't last much longer than that. It had accomplished two things. It had stipulated that the character witness had previously undisclosed emotional involvement. It didn't look good for Tonya that of all the people in the county, the only one they'd brought in to testify that she was a good person was one who was in love with her. The other thing it accomplished, of course, was publicly ending the love story between Charlie Smith and Tonya Bundick.

"Bundick Has a New Boyfriend," read the headline the next morning on the news site Delmarvanow.com. "Bundick Trial Begins, Has New Relationship," read another headline.

Charlie and Tonya wouldn't be getting married in a "November Rain"-themed ceremony, the reception at Shuckers with a guest list in the hundreds and hired security to keep out the riffraff. They wouldn't be getting married in a jailhouse, using rings procured by Charlie's sister, vowing to never testify against each other. Tonya was in love with somebody else.

^ ^ ^

AFTER BREAKING FOR LUNCH and deliberating for less than an hour, the jury returned with a verdict: Tonya was guilty. For that single charge, they recommended a sentence of three-and-a-half years.

CHAPTER 27

WHAT HAPPENED NEXT

S HUCKERS—the site of Charlie and Tonya's meeting and romance and engagement—it closed. I couldn't ever figure out exactly why. A couple of folks on Facebook referenced an undesirable element, like maybe there had been one too many fights, and management thought the bar needed a fresh start. The owner announced he'd be renovating and reopening the restaurant under a different name. New ceiling, new signs, new bar, new menu. As it turned out, the last big hurrah that Shuckers would ever have under its original name happened on Halloween 2012, twelve days before the arsons began. Charlie had put on a long black wig, and Tonya had worn plastic vampire fangs, and they came to the bar to dance to classic rock played by a Virginia Beach cover band, along with all the other people dressed as vampires, pimps, geisha girls, and sexy witches at the Eastern Shore's Studio 54.

When the remodeling was finished, the new place was called Salty Dog Country Bar and Grill. It was less booty-poppin' and more boots-and-sawdust: the logo was a Labrador retriever wearing a cowboy hat and a red bandana. Then, while Tonya's court proceedings dragged on, Salty Dog closed down, too. It reopened as The Fair Grounds, a family-friendly, Chuck E. Cheese-y restaurant with corn hole tournaments and arcade games in the back. By the time I first visited the address, the building was in that phase; I ordered a plate of fettucine Alfredo in the booth that, someone told me, used to be the location of the stage that women like Tonya danced on. Even though the building had been renovated and the roof had been repainted a bright blue instead of gray, there were still auras of Salty Dog under The Fair Grounds, and Shuckers underneath everything. A palimpsest of Eastern Shore history, on a slab of a parking lot with weeds sprouting through fractures in the concrete.

∧ ∧ ∧

LOVE IS A WEIRD ACT. An optimistic delusion. A leap of faith and foolishness. Sometimes when it is tested, imperfections that were there from the beginning, lurking deep, can begin to work their way to the surface. Even two people who love each other deeply will always be two people, two souls. You can't ever completely get in someone else's head, or in someone else's heart. It is the greatest tragedy and the greatest beauty of a relationship: that at some level, the person you are closest to will always be a total friggin' mystery. Maybe the real mystery is why we ever do it at all. It must be something incredible.

Charlie and Tonya together had felt, to Charlie at least, like an epic love story. But by the end it was a mess, and maybe it always had been. Did lighting fires save a struggling relationship, at least for a time? Or did those fires crush a relationship that might have otherwise had a chance, by sweeping two people up in something that was crazy and that neither one of them would have done alone?

The trouble with being the type of person who would do anything for love was that you would do anything for love. If Tonya had wanted to rob banks, Charlie might have bought a ski mask and a handgun; if Tonya had wanted to pickpocket strangers, he might have worked on his light-fingers techniques. Tonya, according to Charlie's version of things, wanted to spray paint a bunch of buildings, and later she wanted to light a bunch more on fire, so that's what they did.

And that's assuming Charlie was the one telling the truth. This was a love that had resulted in one of two scenarios: Either Charlie loved Tonya so much that he was willing to light a string of fires just to make her happy, or he loved her too much to allow her to go free while he went to prison. Either Tonya had trusted Charlie enough that she never suspected Charlie was lighting the fires while she was innocently at home, or she trusted him enough to believe he wouldn't tattle on her—and now he'd talked and she hadn't, and she'd lost.

Here was a county that had almost burned down. Here was that county moving on. All of these fires could have happened only in Accomack, a place with empty, abandoned buildings, prominently signaling a fall from prosperity. Where else was there so much emptiness, so many places for someone to sneak around undetected? Except that maybe it could have happened in Iowa, heart of the heartland, where rural citizenry has been decreasing for the past century. Maybe in southern Ohio, where emptying factories led to emptying towns. Maybe in eastern Oregon, where rural counties had aged themselves almost out of existence. Maybe it could have happened anywhere.

By the numbers, Accomack could look like a desolate place to live. The Opportunity Index, a nonprofit measurement of sixteen different indicators of success in every county in America, gives it a forty-three out of one hundred. But numbers can be misleading. To residents, statistics could not account for the deep feeling of belonging that came from being able to find your surname in three hundred-year-old county records. They couldn't account for how clean the air felt and how orange the sun was setting over the Chesapeake Bay.

How do you calculate fish fries in the backyard, kiddie pools in the front yard, and unfettered views of a thousand stars in the night sky? So much of life is intangible, and places don't feel like they're disappearing to the people who are living there.

I went to Accomack County and I found endless metaphors for a dying county in a changing landscape. There were endless metaphors that went the opposite way, too: rural life as a fairy tale, better than the rest of the country.

The reality is probably somewhere in between. The people who lived in Accomack were happy to live in Accomack. It wasn't small, it was close-knit. It wasn't backward, it was simple. There weren't a hundred things to do every night, but if you went to the one available thing, you were pretty much guaranteed to run into someone you knew.

As economies change, as landscapes change, nostalgia is the only good America will never stop producing. We gorge on it ourselves and we pass it down to generations. One afternoon in Accomack, I drove to the Barrier Islands Center, an old house (an "almshouse," actually, a place where the poor and the mentally ill used to be sent to live and labor) that has been converted to a museum exploring life on the old Eastern Shore. I watched a short documentary about Hog Island, a community off the coast that once had its own culture and its own traditions, but then was forced to disband when the waters got too high. The documentary was full of people nostalgically talking about how it no longer exists. The island had been unpopulated for eighty years by the time of the documentary's making, but the tone was still wistful, even though all of the living interviewees were people who had left the island as babies.

But maybe rural America isn't dying so much as it's Shucker-ing: adjusting, adapting, becoming something new, getting a new outdoor sign and adding jalapeno hush puppies to the menu. I'd like to think that.

In the end, the grandest sweeping statement I can make about Accomack is this: There were buildings that burned down. Some of the buildings that burned down had meant something to people, and their burning was a tragedy. Some of the buildings that burned down were ugly and old. Nobody knew who they even belonged to and why they were still there. Those buildings weren't missed. A normal person wouldn't have burned them down, but the fact that Charlie and Tonya did—well, that wasn't the worst thing in the world, either. And the people who really made the county, the firefighters and teachers and librarians and police officers, they were all still there. That mattered.

^ ^ ^

TWO TRIALS WERE OVER and there were as many as sixty left to go. It seemed almost incredible to the residents of Accomack County that they could still be so far from completion. The houses that had burned down began to be reclaimed by the land, with grass and vines growing over the broken structures.

Tonya hadn't broken. She hadn't asked for a plea deal, despite the guilty verdict with the second case. What she did do was fire Allan Zaleski. "To Whom It May Concern," she wrote in neat cursive on a page of notebook paper addressed to the courthouse. "I am writing to find out the proper procedure for having your public defender removed from your case. I don't find the legal advice I am given to be in my best interest." While Judge Tyler was considering her request, there was also the matter of her sentencing. Charlie still hadn't been sentenced. Tonya had received a sentencing recommendation from jurors in her second trial, in which she had been found guilty, but the judge needed to affirm those recommendations. He also had to sentence her for the first trial, in which she had submitted a last-minute Alford plea.

On the morning of her sentencing, a brisk day in April 2014— over a year since her first arrest—Judge Tyler explained what he'd been thinking as he'd mulled over Tonya's punishment. It was true, the judge said, that sometimes the court gave more leniency to felons who had pleaded guilty. That was because a guilty plea, submitted ahead of time, relieved the Commonwealth of the burden and expense of a trial. Criminals were rewarded for that. But this is not what had happened on this occasion, he said. Tonya had pleaded guilty only at the end of a costly and inconvenient trial.

Because of this, he planned on following the method he'd established for sentencing over a long career on the bench. If he had a repeat offender in his court, "I just simply look at what their jail time was last time and double it," he explained. Therefore, because the previous jury had recommended a sentence of three-and-a-half years for the charge in which Tonya was found guilty, he would impose a sentence of seven years for the one in which she'd submitted an Alford plea. He wanted the sentences to run consecutively.

That meant the total time she would spend in prison, for just two out of her sixty-odd charges, would be more than a decade.

While Tonya stood impassively, not reacting at all to the judgment that had just been placed, Tyler said that there was one more piece of business to deal with. Tonya had written a letter requesting a new attorney. Did she still want that?

"Yes," she said.

Okay, then, he said. He would have a new attorney appointed for her, and that new attorney could take her through the rest of her trials.

^ ^ ^

ELSEWHERE, as the court proceedings continued:

A proposal to build eighty-four new chicken houses was brought forth to the county, and Accomack began debating its past and its future. Were big, modern farms the pathway to rebuilding the shore's financial success? Were they a temporary solution that would ruin the land? The county began planning town halls, to which hundreds of neighbors would come and listen to environmentalists and chicken executives, and argue, and watch slide show presentations debating the merits and downfalls of chicken poop.

The Tasley Volunteer Fire Department, which had long ago come to the conclusion that it was time to upgrade from their old, out-of-date space, began searching for a plot of land on which to build a new station. Ultimately, they chose a lot right across from the now burned-down Whispering Pines resort, big enough to hold a three-bay, modern station with modern equipment. Jeff Beall decided not to run for chief of the Tasley department the following year. He knew people didn't blame him for the fires, but he was the guy whose roster Charlie had been on, and that knowledge weighed on him. There was some infighting in the station about which direction the department should go, and several members ended up leaving. One of those members was Bryan Applegate. It didn't have anything to do with his brother, he told people. He was just looking for a change of scenery so he started running with the company in Onancock.

Of the Virginia State Police investigators who had worked the case, Scott Wade and Rob Barnes stayed in their same jobs with their same titles. Glenn Neal, who was deeply affected by the knowledge that the arsonist had been his friend, ended up leaving the investigative branch of the police. He went back to being a highway trooper. He was happier that way.

After the arsonists were caught, nobody had much need for an Eastern Shore Arsonist Hunters T-shirt anymore. The ones that had already been purchased—sometimes people would still wear them while doing yard work or washing the car, but it wasn't with the same sense of civic pride as during the arsons. It was more of a memento of a weird time in everyone's lives, or a talisman from a shared experience. ESAH founder Matt Hart ended up donating the leftovers to a nonprofit and heard that those somehow ended up at a homeless shelter in north Philadelphia.

Jon Cromer, the police profiler who had questioned Tonya on the night of her arrest, would silently add her to the mental list of prisoners he hoped would one day talk to him about what they'd done and why they'd done it. He thought that he would learn a lot from her.

CHAPTER 28

"IT'S OVER"

I T ENDED. OF COURSE IT DID, it finally did, and like a lot of things, by the time it actually ended, people were starting to become a little less aware of the fact that it was still going on at all. As the third trial approached, there was a sense of exhaustion, of gearing up all over again for another trial where Tonya would say she didn't remember anything and Charlie would say that in spite of the fact that he was testifying against this woman, he still loved her.

Tonya's new attorney, a short-haired, no-nonsense woman from Virginia Beach named Janee' Joslin, was not going down without a fight. At a motion hearing she argued that the venue of the third trial should be changed yet again. "It's my opinion, Your Honor, that Virginia Beach is no longer an appropriate forum for any further trials of Miss Bundick in this matter," she said. The saturation of the crimes had now traveled miles across the Bay Bridge-Tunnel; the arsons were just too famous.

The judge denied that request, and so everyone suited up again, and on a Monday morning in early April of 2015—now two years after Tonya's arrest—everyone traveled to Virginia Beach again, at an expense rate that one local news outlet reported was costing the Commonwealth $3,000 a day just in motel and meal costs for all of the personnel required.

Gary Agar checked into his hotel room at the midpriced chain that all of the Commonwealth staff was staying in. Later when interviewed about this, he couldn't remember exactly the order of what happened next. It was either late that Sunday or early the next morning, when he'd already put on a dark suit and a blue striped tie and was about to drive to the courthouse, that he got a phone call.

Tonya's new attorney. She was willing to arrange a deal.

The trial was scheduled to begin at 9 a.m. For all of the previous trials and hearings, Judge Tyler had started exactly on time, with the courtroom open fifteen or twenty minutes early for spectators to get seats. That Monday, the doors remained shut. Spectators arrived and tugged on the door a few times, just to be sure. There were a diminished number of reporters compared with the previous trials, as news organizations decided they couldn't afford to keep sending staff to cover trials in which the pattern had become predictable. There were other crimes to follow. Other weirdos. Accomack had its moment, but after a while, the whole thing went from exciting to just tiresome.

Maybe Tonya had an even newer new boyfriend than the minister, people joked. Maybe he was getting ready to testify. Maybe he and Charlie had somehow run into each other and gotten into a fight.

Finally, the doors were opened. Inside, the jury panel had not been seated. The air-conditioning was working overtime. Tonya wore an orange prison jumpsuit and by her side, instead of Allan Zaleski, was Joslin, a middle-aged woman in a navy pantsuit.

Judge Tyler explained what had just happened. Tonya had submitted another Alford plea, the same guilty plea she had submitted for the previous trial, the one in which she had said she wasn't actually guilty at all. This time it was not for just one count, but for all of them, all sixty-one remaining counts of arsons.

"I think," Judge Tyler said from the bench, once he had ascertained that the plea had been entered into willingly by both parties, "This concludes the matter."

The trials were over.

In the end, nobody knew what made Tonya change her mind. Was she spooked by the previous verdict? Did she begin to see her situation as hopeless? Was she simply exhausted? Would she ever say?

The journalists who had expected to have at least two hours of jury selection before they needed to begin taking notes in earnest or file web updates for their stories now realized that something big had happened; there was the sound of pens clicking as they tried to keep up.

The plea deal arranged by Gary Agar and Tonya Bundick's attorney called for seven additional years. Added to the sentencings from her previous two trials, the amount of time she would spend in prison would be seventeen and a half years. By the time she got out, she would have spent nearly a third of her own life in prison. Too old for short skirts and tube tops, too old to turn heads in the same way she had before this whole mess started. The bars she had gone to already didn't exist anymore. The sentencing worked out to around three and a half months per fire.

Joslin left the courtroom without commenting, walking briskly to her car and waving off the reporters who followed her with microphones and notepads. Gary Agar emerged from the courtroom and, in his deep, slow, rumbling voice, gave interview after interview to the reporters who had lined up for comment.

"It's a long time in prison for her," he said to the first local news station, which put a microphone in his face and caught him in the hallway. "This was a horrendous crime that they committed over a long period of time, and now they need to spend a long period of time in the penitentiary because of what she did, and to prevent others from doing the same thing."

The last part of his statement was, perhaps, superfluous. The chance of there being another person managing to do the same thing Tonya had just been convicted of, burning down a county, building by building over half a year's time, was very, very small.

Two days after Tonya's sentence, Charlie would be sentenced, too, to fifteen years—a shorter sentence than hers, presumably because of his original confession and his cooperation throughout Tonya's trials. He'd already served two of the fifteen years in the Accomack jail. By the time the sentencing came along, he was mostly just relieved that he would now get to be moved to a bigger facility, someplace with a better exercise yard and maybe a woodworking class and a cafeteria with more variety. He'd spent a lot of time practicing drawing tattoo art with a pen and paper and he knew how to use a pen and a wire to ink prison tattoos. This, he knew, could be a lucrative business in prison, and he wondered if he might be able to get into it himself. Eventually, Charlie was moved from Accomack to a facility in Central Virginia.

The day after the trial that wasn't, Carol Vaughn, the *Eastern Shore News* reporter who had been covering the trial, began her story with an opening paragraph that was only two words long: "It's over." Unlike the early articles and Facebook posts, which gathered dozens and dozens of comments and reactions in the early days after the arrests, these got one, or two, plus a handful of weary "Likes" from people who couldn't be bothered with any more of a reaction. "Good," wrote one commenter on an article published by the local public radio station. "Now lock the stupid c--- up and throw away the key; let's not have to see her fugly face again." The only other comment was a cheeky two-word response: "Bonfire Bundick."

Immediately after the trial that wasn't, the court clerk, along with Sheriff Todd Godwin and a handful of deputies, decided to go for an early lunch at a nearby hoagie chain. The mood was celebratory, the clerk bought everyone a cookie, the deputies talked and joked and speculated about how bad the traffic would be on the ride home. Bad in Virginia Beach, at least, which was why none of them lived in

Virginia Beach. Once they crossed the Bay Bridge-Tunnel and were back safe on the Eastern Shore, all of the cars would fall away. It was the off-season. Only locals would be driving through.

The hoagie place was a little bit out of the way, but it was reasonably priced and everyone liked the sandwiches. Also, it wasn't a chain that existed on the Eastern Shore, which made going there seem even more like a special occasion. Appropriately, though nobody commented on it at the time, the name of the place was Firehouse Subs.

A little after noon, they got back in their cars. The lunchtime traffic was bad but not too bad, and they hit the Accomack border some ninety minutes later, and everything was quiet and whatever passions had caused the fires had ended, and nothing was burning anymore.

ACKNOWLEDGMENTS

When I talked about moving to Accomack for several months to research this book, people issued all kinds of warnings about small-town life: how closed-off it could be and how it would be difficult to find anyone who would talk. I have never found a warning to be further from the truth. People in Accomack invited me to barbecues, met me at the movie theater, sat with me at church potlucks, rescued me when I ran out of gas, and helped fix broken taillights on my car. Most importantly, they gave me their time, lots of it, helping me to understand as best I could what it was like to live in Accomack County during the deeply bizarre five and a half months of the arsons. They dug through old meeting notes, Facebook updates, and phone records to check their memories, which greatly aided me; the book would have been impossible without their help.

I didn't keep track of how many people I interviewed for this book. But the number well exceeds a hundred, including Accomack County government employees; Virginia State Police investigators and patrolmen; investigators with the Bureau of Alcohol, Tobacco, Firearms and Explosives; members of the Accomack County sheriff's department; town historians; property owners whose buildings were burned; defense attorneys; employees of the office of the Commonwealth's attorney; employees of the courthouse; staff at the Eastern Shore 911 Center; friends and family of Charles Smith and Tonya

Bundick; and many, many volunteers with the Accomack County volunteer fire departments. In particular, the firefighters in Tasley let me come to their meetings, play pool with them, eat pizza with them. They let me sleep in the firehouse and ride in the fire truck with the sirens blaring. At the end of my stay, they voted me in as a support member for the station, and I can honestly say there are few honors I have ever been more proud of.

I also interviewed Charlie Smith, on multiple occasions, in person and on the phone, in conversations totaling more than a dozen hours. I am sure he had his own motivations for wanting to talk to a reporter. He obviously had his side of the story to tell, but among other reasons, by the time I contacted him he had been in jail for a year already, and he was lonely and bored.

Prior to deciding to write this book, I had interviewed Tonya Bundick for a feature article about the fires. Tonya subsequently declined to participate in any further interviews, which I requested on multiple occasions in writing and via intermediaries. I do not blame her—she had trials under appeal, and maybe she thought that talking with me would impact her chances for those appeals, and maybe she was just done with it all. I do wish she had agreed, because I always think it's better for people to be the narrators of their own stories, but I tried to tell hers with as much honesty and nuance as I could based on information gleaned from trial transcripts, court documents, and interviews with people who knew her or had known her. She has never wavered from protesting her own innocence.

This book began as a six-thousand-word article in the *Washington Post*, which was carefully and lovingly edited by Rachel Dry and Ann Gerhart, who comprise one half of my work family. I am grateful for their attention, and grateful to Martin Baron, Tracy Grant and Liz Seymour for allowing me the leave time to turn the article into a book. And once it became one—or most of one—Hank Stuever and Dan Zak, the other half of my work family, were the clear-eyed readers I needed, to tell me what was and wasn't working. I once had a dream that Hank whipped a pair of scissors out of his jacket and fixed my bad haircut; naturally, this was a metaphor for the story beautification he performs so skillfully. In less metaphorical hair news, Jade-Snow Joachim signed on to gather and secure permissions for all of the images used in this book; I would have ripped my own hair out without her help.

Katie Adams at Liveright saw the article version of this story when it was printed and became convinced, long before I was, that the story could be a book. She is a brilliant editor, and she—along with my equally brilliant agent, Ginger Clark, put up with many e-mails' worth of me sharing tidbits of life in Accomack, which they at least pretended to find as interesting as I did.

The last person I need to thank is my husband, Robert Cox. He watched me head off to Accomack with the dog and the car, to go live in a county where my cell phone worked only sporadically. And when I returned several months later he was, as he often is, my most eagle-eyed reader, resulting in my most dogged editing sessions. He was almost always right, and his thoughts challenged me to become a more thorough and humane reporter. I would never want to be married to a writer, but I'm glad he doesn't feel the same way.

NOTES

Below are a few research notes meant to supplement references in the body of the book, or to explain the sourcing of information if I feared it would not otherwise be clear. Unless otherwise stated, all information and memories attributed to individuals in the book came from personal interviews with those people. When two people recalled the same interaction differently, I tried to reflect that in the text. Memories can be faulty; by the time I interviewed some folks, the fires were a few years past, although many of them remarked it felt like yesterday.

1: "CHARGE THAT LINE!"

Jeff Fluornoy, the exceedingly smart director of the Eastern Shore Regional 911 Center, sat with me for the equivalent of several work days, helping me retrieve the 911 calls and dispatch recordings that formed the spine of this and many other chapters. All radioed communications, here and elsewhere in the book, are a direct transcription of the dialogue that occurred at the scenes of the fires. I'd previously interviewed Deborah Clark, the first 911 caller, for the *Washington Post*, and I referred to those interview notes for this book.

Interviews with the firefighters who were called to that fire formed most of the rest of the chapter, along with reviews of the fire companies' incident reports from the night, and visiting the fire location itself.

2: "THE SOUTH STARTS HERE"

The Eastern Shore Public Library's greatest treasure isn't a book but a man, Brooks Miles Barnes, the historian who runs the library's local history room and weighted me down with books from the very old (*Ye Kingdom of Accawmack: Or the Eastern Shore of Virginia in the Seventeenth Century*) to newer tourist books. His scholarly article, "The Countryside Transformed," about the impact of the railway on the Eastern Shore, is one of the loveliest and most elegiac academic works I've read and I referred to his research liberally. The Eastern Shore Railway Museum was similarly useful in giving me a sense of what the railway had meant to the county.

Two additional historians also provided guidance: Kirk Mariner, who has written several guidebooks and histories of the shore (my favorite is *Revival's Children: A Religious History of Virginia's Eastern Shore*), and Don Amadeo, an amateur history buff whose day job is in the Accomack sheriff's department. Don has an extensive collection of Accomack ephemera, including old county maps, photos, and fliers and menus from Whispering Pines.

Information about the Eastern Shore's chicken industry came from the Delmarva Poultry Industry, a local trade organization, and from meetings about chicken waste runoff, which I attended, and from *Delmarva's Chicken Industry: 75 Years of Progress*, by William H. Williams, a book that is more interesting than any book about chicken farming has the right to be. Data from the Virginia Employment Commission's annual reports confirmed that Tyson and Perdue are Accomack County's largest employers.

3: "ORANGE IN THE SKY"

Glenn Neal and Rob Barnes walked me through their fire investigation techniques, and for greater understanding I sat in on a day of classes taught by Bobby Bailey at the Virginia Fire Marshal Academy in Richmond, in which he discussed evidence collection and introduced students to the burn trailer. There were several law enforcement officials whose names didn't make the book, but whose recollections helped reconstruct the early weeks of the fires. In the sheriff's office, Todd Wessells, Billy Murphy, and David Mullins were particularly helpful.

Here and throughout, I also took advantage of the local news coverage of the fires, both the *Eastern Shore News* and the *Eastern Shore Post*. Reporters from those papers were doggedly covering the fires long before the national news arrived.

4: CHARLIE

Charles Smith's criminal past is well documented in files in the Accomack Courthouse, the criminal division of which is helmed by the relentlessly competent and kind deputy court clerk, Theresa Handy.

Friends and acquaintances ranging from Charlie's former parole officer to the woman who made the breakfast egg sandwiches at Charlie's favorite diner to old classmates and colleagues provided additional information.

The mother of Charlie's daughter agreed to speak with me, but asked that her name not be used. The largest source of information in this chapter was Charlie himself, but there was very little he told me that I was not able to corroborate through additional sources.

5: *MONOMANIE INCENDIAIRE*

Dian Williams's *Understanding the Arsonist: From Assessment to Confession* is intended for practitioners—Williams is a psychologist—but it was extremely helpful in laying out a general framework of an arsonist's mind. Several scientific articles by Dr. Jeffrey Geller provided a historical context for the way arson has been studied: "Pathological Firesetting in Adults" and "Pyromania: What Does It Mean?" by Geller, McDermeit, and Brown were particularly helpful. For information about arson and women, I referred to "Female Arsonists: A Clinical Study" by Dominique Bourget and John M. W. Bradford, and for general statistics I referred to "Firesetting, Arson, Pyromania, and the Forensic Mental Health Expert" by Paul R. S. Burton, Dale E. McNiel, and Renée L. Binder. Descriptions of impulse control disorders came from *The Oxford Handbook of Personality Disorders*; descriptions of pyromania came from the *Diagnostic and Statistical Manual of Mental Disorders*.

6: TONYA

Unlike Charlie, Tonya's prior criminal record was virtually nonexistent. She did have two shoplifting charges from her late teens—she stole a box of Junior Mints from a grocery store—but otherwise had remained under the radar, with very few public records. Old yearbooks at Arcadia High School helped me trace her teenage life and connected me with people who had known her in earlier years. Two family members, a former work colleague, two former boyfriends, and multiple friends who knew her from Shuckers helped provide additional context for her life before she met Charlie.

7: "LIKE A GHOST"

In addition to the firefighters already mentioned elsewhere, I am indebted to the following for helping me understand the firefighting experience on the shore during the time of the arsons: Tom Schwartz; Jody Bagwell in Bloxom; Adam James in Onancock; Chris Davis in Onley; and Frank Ulrich, Cindy Ulrich, Myles Belote, and Bob Harvey in Tasley.

This chapter is the only location in the book in which I interrupted the timeline of any of the events: reporter Chip Reid did not conduct his interview with Phil Kelley until March; for the sake of thematic cohesion I included it with events that happened earlier in the year. That interview is still available online, as is the video of the "Tasley Shake," which I highly recommend.

Statistics about the changing rural population come from the U.S. Department of Agriculture's Economic Research Service—mostly from the *Atlas of Rural and Small-Town America*, but also from the "How Is Rural America Changing?" report. Numbers regarding the 502 Direct Loan program came from "Rural America's Silent Housing Crisis," a 2015 *Atlantic* magazine article, and a different *Atlantic* article titled "The Graying of Rural America" provided information about aging rural demographics. The calculation for Accomack's farm subsidy payouts came from data collected by the nonprofit Environmental Working Group.

Statistics about the decline in volunteer firefighters nationwide come from a 2014 *New York Times* article, "The Disappearing Volunteer Firefighter." The U.S. Fire Administration study mentioned was "Retention and Recruitment for the Volunteer Emergency Services," published in 2007.

8: "TELL US WHAT YOU KNOW ABOUT THAT"

Ron Tunkel, the profiler with the Bureau of Alcohol, Tobacco, Firearms and Explosives, is the only ATF staff member I ended up mentioning by name in the manuscript, but Darrell Logwood, Michael Scott, and Dan Wozlocsynowski were all members of the ATF's Washington, D.C., field division who were dispatched to the shore, and they discussed the investigation with me as well.

To better understand geographic profiling, Isaac Van Patten recommended I read the book *Geographic Profiling* by D. Kim Rossmo, the father of the field. It's a bit academic, but deeply fascinating.

9: CHARLIE AND TONYA

By the time I began working on this book, Charlie and Tonya were both in jail and awaiting trial. Tonya had, according to multiple sources, deleted much of the couple's Facebook page during the time she was out on bail. The portions that I quoted from were what remained on the page's public view—both her personal page and the page she created for her store, A Tiny Taste of Toot. Online, she posted pictures of their Halloween costumes and recollections of their domestic life together.

Jay Floyd and Danielle did not talk to me for this book, though I made requests multiple times, in person, via text, and over phone messages. Their dialogue in this chapter is as Charlie remembers it; other parties corroborate that the couples were close friends and that Jay and Danielle introduced Tonya and Charlie.

10: "SCHRÖDINGER'S EVIDENCE"

The technician who processed many of the arson materials submitted to the Virginia Department of Forensic Science is Brenda Christy. She could not discuss specific pieces of evidence from the fires, but she went into great detail about general scientific procedures and techniques, and assured me they would be the same for any piece of evidence.

In this chapter, again, sheriff's deputies David Mullins and Billy Murphy were helpful in reconstructing the investigation. Mullins was the man in the plane, who spent the arson months in the passenger seat of a Cessna scanning the ground below. Murphy was one of the deputies in charge of orienting the out-of-town officers, taking them to their assigned posts and then spending the night in his car nearby, ready to be called upon for a fire.

11: THE EASTERN SHORE ARSONIST HUNTERS

After Tonya's arrest, it was discovered that she had earlier posted on several of the arson-related Facebook pages. *Eastern Shore News* reporter Carol Vaughn wrote a story about that. When Tonya was out on bail she deleted those posts; the ones I quoted came either from Carol's article, or from screenshots that others had captured before the deletion. Incidentally, the food truck that Tonya speculated wasn't burned by the real arsonist but by an owner for insurance reasons—Charlie never confessed to that one, and it might, in fact, have been an insurance-related plot.

13: "LIKE HELL WAS COMING UP THROUGH THE GROUND"

I owe several paragraphs of this chapter to the reporting of Carol Vaughn, who wrote about Whispering Pines history in her story about the resort's burning.

Information about the Whispering Pines damage costs, and similar information for other properties, all came from a "joint stipulation of facts" submitted by the Commonwealth's attorney and Charlie's defense attorney as part of his plea bargain. The documents included descriptions and photographs of all of the fires, plus information on the structure's history, insurance status, and damage costs, and they allowed me to track down property owners who otherwise would have been difficult to find.

14: TONYA AND CHARLIE

Both Charlie and Tonya discussed problems they'd been having with Tonya's oldest son in their police interrogations and later in Tonya's trial. As Tonya's sons are minors, I did not include either of their names in this book, though they were used at the trial. Charlie and Tonya also separately addressed the fact that money and the death of Charlie's mom were stressors in their lives.

Charlie's story of how they came to burn down the first house is what he told me; it's also what he told police during his confession. Tonya continues to deny this interaction ever took place.

15 AND 16: "THEY'RE NOT HUNTERS AT ALL" AND "I DIDN'T LIGHT THEM ALL"

Troy Johnson's and Willie Burke's recollections of the night of the arrest were gleaned from the transcript of Tonya's first trial, which I also attended. I separately interviewed Troy Johnson for additional backstory on the night and on the pair's experiences in Accomack. Dialogue from Martin Kriz, Tonya's arresting officer, came from his trial testimony. Details about the house and it location came from personal visits to it, and from the trial testimony of the home's owner, Claude Henry.

17: "SOMEDAY THEY'LL GO DOWN TOGETHER"

I never envisioned acknowledging a website called Murderpedia.org—but the writers there are meticulous in their cataloging of humanity's more depraved acts, and I thank and blame them for sending me down a rabbit hole of research-related crime-committing couples.

Most information on Bonnie and Clyde, including the quotes from Bonnie Parker's letters and poems, came from *Bonnie and Clyde: The Lives behind the Legend* by Paul Schneider and from *War on Crime: Bandits, G-men and the Politics of Mass Culture* by Claire Bond Potter. The primary reference for information on Charles Starkweather and Caril Ann Fugate was a project sponsored by the Wyoming State Historical Society entitled "The Killing Spree That Transfixed a Nation." In the book *Invisible Darkness*, Stephen Williams chronicled the bizarre and horrifying love story of Paul Bernardo and Karla Homolka; I referred to that book as well as to online transcripts of the home movies the couple shot together recounting their exploits.

Hal Higdon's *Leopold and Loeb: The Crime of the Century* is one of the best narratives of the true crime genre—apologies to Mr. Capote; I like it better than *In Cold Blood*—and I used it both for factual information on the Leopold and Loeb case as well as structural inspiration.

18 AND 19: "EVERYBODY HAS A REASON FOR WHY THEY DO THINGS IN LIFE" AND "I CAN'T TELL YOU SOMETHING I DON'T KNOW"

Charlie's confession was recorded and spanned four DVDs. I watched them all, and also interviewed Todd Godwin, Robert Barnes, and Charlie himself about what was going through their minds as the interrogation progressed. I couldn't obtain a DVD of Tonya's interview, but I did get a transcript, which I walked through with Scott Wade and Jon Cromer, who told me how they recalled Tonya behaving through the course of the interrogation.

21: THE BROKEN THINGS

Gary Agar was the first person to tell me about the other crimes Accomack had been dealing with in 2012 and 2013; I gathered additional details from articles in the *Virginian Pilot*.

Recollections of Anjee Ritchie's conversation with Scott Wade were gleaned mostly from their memories, though I verified some details—the arrangement of Anjee deeding Tonya their parents' house, for example—through court records and property deeds in the Accomack County Courthouse. Scott had promised Anjee to keep portions of their conversation confidential. He did not divulge them to me until Anjee gave him written permission to do so, and he asked me to make that clear. Tonya has not ever confirmed abuse in her childhood—at least not in detail and at least not to me or anyone else I interviewed.

22: "TIME TO WAKE UP"

Charlie waived his rights to attorney-client privilege in order to allow me to speak to his attorney, Carl Bundick, and to look though his client case file, which comprised two large crates in Carl's office.

I visited Charlie at the Accomack jail multiple times. Descriptions of the visitors room—in which visitors and inmates must stand and communicate through thick-paned windows—and of the sheriff's personal office are gleaned through observation. Information about the cell and prison menu came from Charlie and two other inmates who were all housed there at the same time. The strange tale of Wrendo Johnson Periless Godwin—who wanted to become president but instead ended up in jail—ran in the *Salisbury Times* newspaper.

Some of Charlie's and Tonya's letters were read out loud during their trial, which allowed me to quote from them here. I was not able to quote from the letters that Tonya wrote to other men while at the Accomack jail, as they weren't entered into the official record. I confirmed their existence and the general tone of their content with Sheriff Todd Godwin and Gary Agar, the Commonwealth's attorney.

23: *BURNED*

I have no way of knowing whether Tonya Bundick is the real author of *Burned*. The publishing company, citing client confidentiality, couldn't tell me. They did agree to pass on a message to the author requesting an interview, but the author never wrote back. I do believe it was either Tonya or someone very close to her: some of the information about "Sonya's" relationship with "Harley" mirrors very closely things about Tonya and Charlie's relationship that I'd previously heard only from Charlie himself.

24 AND 25: "WE'D DONE IT BEFORE" AND "THEY CAME OUT OF EVERYWHERE"

I attended both of Tonya Bundick's trials, as well as the almost-trial that was truncated with her plea agreement. The dialogue in these chapters comes from official court transcripts. Gary Agar also shared with me some of his handwritten notes so I could get a sense of how he prepared for trial.

The truly bizarre case of the "Norfolk Four" was chronicled in great detail on an episode of *Frontline*. Dialogue from the sailors' confessions was taken from this documentary. Allan Zaleski agreed to meet with me for this book. He wouldn't discuss the specifics of the case, but he spoke generally about it and about his career as a whole. Explanations of an Alford plea came from the original Alford case *North Carolina v. Henry C. Alford* and from Crimefeed.com, and from the trio of fascinating Errol Morris documentaries that explore the case of the West Memphis Three.

28: "IT'S OVER"

I know the sheriff and his deputies went to a Firehouse Subs restaurant because I went with them. After the third trial didn't come to be, all of the law enforcement who'd anticipated spending the day in a Virginia Beach courtroom instead had the whole afternoon free. Todd Godwin had been politely ducking my interview requests for months, but now that the trials were over, he said he guessed it would be okay if I came along to lunch. He told me he couldn't imagine anyone could write an interesting book about his county. I hope I proved him wrong.